Voices
from the Edge
of Eternity

Voices
from the Edge
of Eternity

Compiled by John Myers

A BARBOUR BOOK

ISBN 1-55748-548-8

Published by   Barbour and Company, Inc.
                 P.O. Box 719
                 Uhrichsville, OH 44683

Printed in the USA.

Contents

Index To Famous Persons

Preface

Death is a subject no one can treat lightly. It is too *final* for that. Beauty, honor, wealth, earthly power, hopes, and dreams — all are swallowed up in that finality. Man was born with his hands clenched; he dies with them wide open. Entering life he desires to grasp everything; leaving the world, all that he possessed has slipped away.

But it is not so much death itself, as the mystery of what lies beyond that closed door, that has haunted mankind since time immemorial. Seemingly there is no tangible answer to this mystery — *or is there?*

Several years ago I was impressed with the striking glimpses into eternity afforded by several accounts I read here and there of deathbed testimonies. Then one day I stumbled across an old book, published in 1898, which contained scores of such testimonies. I was amazed and deeply shaken. Here was a cross-section of people from every walk of life — young and old, saint and sinner — who, just before leaving this life, saw quite clearly beyond the grave. Their testimonies were sharp and clear, and each bore witness to the same essential facts.

From that hour I knew I would compile this book, though it has taken nearly ten years to at last finish it. The final result is far from exhaustive, but I believe it constitutes convincing evidence that God has again and again answered man's fateful question concerning eternity.

The testimony of this book is that thousands of men and women — unbelievers as well as believers — standing on the very edge of eternity, caught up in life's most dramatic experience, have quite clearly seen beyond the grave. What they saw and sensed not only bears evidence as to the *fact* of man's immortality, but also answers many very pertinent questions that perplex the minds of thinking people today. I refer to such questions as the accuracy of the Biblical account of life after death, the truth or fallacy of reincarnation, etc.

But far more important than a mere collection of scientific evidence, to many the reading of this book will constitute the dawn of what the prophets of old called "hope" — that glorious sense of goal and destiny which alone can defy the death grip of materialism which threatens to plunge our generation into the madness of purposeless life.

It is to that word "hope", and all its treasures for the human heart, that I dedicate these pages.

John Myers

Introduction

A book of this nature is essentially history and as such is dependent upon the records of the past. Aside from the contemporary, and some older testimonies gleaned from here and there, I am indebted primarily to three books published in the nineteenth century. The first of these works, entitled *Dying Hours* by D. P. Kidder, was published in 1848 by Carlton and Phillips, New York; the second, *Dying Words* by A. H. Gottschall, was published in England in about 1888; while the third, *Dying Testimonies* by S. B. Shaw, was published by the author in 1898 in the United States. It is this last book to which I refer in the preface as being the original inspiration and basis for the compilation of this present volume.

In my search for choice subject matter I have deleted more than I have retained, especially with regard to the testimonies found in the above mentioned books. Also, in many cases I have condensed and adapted the text in order to get to the essential message meant to be conveyed. In such editing, however, I have endeavored to retain not only the original last words, in no way tampering with their meaning or import, but also the colloquial expressions current to that time in history and the author's doctrinal outlook.

In view of future editions, I shall be grateful to receive additional testimonials or any information which will enable me to further enhance the material already included.

—*The Editor*

Voices
from
the Edge
of Eternity

"O death, where is thy sting—
O grave, where is thy victory?"
                                    Paul

"I Want To Be Aware Of Every Sensation"

A dying girl's amazing triumph over death

This story is told by Natalie Kalmus, who helped found and organize the Technicolor Motion Picture Corporation. At the time of this writing she was in complete charge of color for all pictures here and abroad made by Technicolor.

"Don't worry, but come to me as soon as you can," my sister, Eleanor Smith, wired. At the time I was in London working out Technicolor problems with one of the British motion picture companies.

I felt a deep, numbing pang. I knew Eleanor had been ill some time. Surely this was her gentle way of telling me the end was coming.

I could not picture — or accept it. Always radiating charm, friendliness and an inner happiness, my sister had been a wonderful inspiration to those close to her. She had that rare trait of always giving others a pat on the back, lifting their spirits and sending them off with a fresh outlook on life.

When first stricken by the most fearsome of medical enemies, the doctors told her that her days were numbered. Knowing this had not made the slightest difference in her warm interest in people — nor in her deep abiding faith in the wonder of God.

But now she needed me. I returned to the States and hurried to Eleanor, expecting to find her in bed in great pain. Instead she was in the living room perched jauntily on the sofa, looking more like a school girl of seventeen than an incurably ill woman.

"Natalie," she held out her arms joyously, "I'm so happy now that you're here. We have so much to talk over." To anyone listening I might have dropped in for a casual call.

After Eleanor had later retired for the night, the doctor drew me aside. "Mrs. Kalmus," he said, "I think that it will be a most trying experience for you if you stay here through to the end. I'm afraid that your sister's last hours will be an agony of pain."

Medically I knew he was right. Yet the exquisite radiance I noticed in my sister's face seemed somehow to refute his statement. The strange feeling swept over me that the strength of my sister's spirit could well triumph over her pain.

During the next few days I discovered that Eleanor was doing many things to baffle the doctors. They were preparing her for some very grim final moments. She was ignoring their solemn suggestions and remedies. One night she had me sit down on the side of her bed.

"Natalie, promise me that you won't let them give me any drugs. I realize that they are trying to help relieve my pain, but I want to be fully aware of every sensation. *I am convinced that death will be a beautiful experience.*"

I promised. Alone later, I wept, thinking of her courage. Then as I tossed in bed on through the night, I realized that what I looked to be a calamity, my sister intended to be a triumph.

One afternoon Eleanor, in the most airy and lighthearted manner, asked several friends to a dinner party which she, on the spur of the moment, decided to hold. I was stunned. But Eleanor grinned at me impishly in high spirits. The sight of the happiness in her face checked my objections.

On the night of the party Eleanor dressed meticulously, concealing the pain I knew she felt. We helped her downstairs before the guests were to arrive. Sitting in a turquoise chair in her yellow evening gown, she sparkled with life and gaiety. Again I noticed the school girl look on her face.

The party was a grand success; the guests were never once aware of the illness which my sister concealed so expertly. That night, however, when she was carried to bed, her deep physical weariness appeared on the surface. Then I realized that my sister knew this was her final social fling. She had planned it that way.

Ten days later the final hour drew near. I had been at her bedside for hours. We had talked about many things, and always I marveled at her quiet, sincere confidence in eternal life. Not once did the physical torture inside overcome her spiritual strength. This was something that the doctors simply hadn't taken into account.

"Dear kind God, keep my mind clear and give me peace," she had murmured over and over again during those last days.

We had talked so long that I noticed she was drifting off to sleep. I left her quietly with the nurse and retired to get some rest. A few minutes later I heard my sister's voice calling for me. Quickly I returned to her room. She was dying.

I sat on her bed and took her hand. It was on fire. Then she seemed to rise up in bed almost to a sitting position.

"Natalie," she said, "There are so many of them. There's Fred . . . and Ruth — what's she doing here? Oh, I know!"

An electric shock went through me. She had said Ruth!

18

Ruth was her cousin who had died suddenly the week before. *But Eleanor had not been told of Ruth's sudden death.* Chill after chill shot up and down my spine. I felt on the verge of some powerful, almost frightening knowledge. She *had* murmured Ruth's name.

Her voice was surprisingly clear. "It's so confusing. So many of them!" Suddenly her arms stretched out as happily as when she had welcomed me! "I'm going up," she murmured. Then she dropped her arms around my neck — and relaxed in my arms. *The will of her spirit had turned final agony into rapture.*

As I lay her head back on the pillow, there was a warm, peaceful smile on her face. Her golden brown hair lay carelessly on the pillow. I took a white flower from the vase and placed it in her hair. With her petite, trim figure, her wavy hair, the white flower and the soft smile, she looked once more — and permanently — just like a school girl.

Never again will death frighten me in any way. This was my sister's inheritance to me — her final, beautiful gift. I had seen for myself how thin was the curtain between life and death. I had glimpsed part of the wonderful truth about everlasting life.

—Reprinted from *Guideposts* Magazine
Copyright 1947 *Guideposts Associates, Inc.,* Carmel, N.Y.

* The mention of her cousin Ruth by the dying girl and the evident fact that she saw her clearly is a phenomenon that recurs again and again in the incidents which have come to my attention. So repetitive is this phenomenon and so similar are the characteristics of this experience as described by many that it amounts to a substantial evidence that the people whose names are called, whose faces are seen, are actually present.—Norman Vincent Peale

—Power of Positive Thinking by Norman Vincent Peale
Prentice-Hall Inc.

David Appleby
Young Husband Of Veteran Missionary
Rosalee Appleby

If I lived a thousand years, I would not forget that September morning of 1924 when we took the ship in the New York harbor for Brazil as Christ's messengers. Our wedding was just seven weeks in the background, and life was radiant with promise. The image in our hearts of the Homeland was the America of Woodrow Wilson. From the deck we watched the Liberty Girl vanish into the blue distance.

After eleven days of blue above and blue beneath, we came into the bay of the world's most beautiful city, Rio de Janeiro. During the next ten months we studied the Portuguese language in this charming place.

Our place of service was to be in the interior of the giant state of Minas. We were invited to remain in the Minas capital, Belo Horizonte, until after the birth of our baby. Plans were to go immediately after this anticipated event to the interior.

During the days of waiting, David had a check up, which revealed the necessity of an operation for stomach ulcer. Our physician marked the first anniversary of our arrival in Brazil as the time for surgery in the local hospital.

A beloved missionary couple, Mr. and Mrs. J. R. Allen, stayed with David. She had taken nurses' training, and they were tireless in their loving care through the six days he survived the operation. A copy of a letter that Mrs. Allen wrote my family will describe David's witness.

"About two-thirty a.m. he began saying, *'They are calling, calling, calling — there in Heaven!'* Then for an hour he sang and talked about Heaven. I had heard of people having a vision like this, but never witnessed it. It was the most beautiful thing I have ever seen.

"Upon one occasion he said, *'I didn't know it could be so beautiful. All is well with my soul!'* We stayed by him until he went to the place where there will be no more pain. His life and influence here have been, and will be, a blessing to all those with whom he came in contact."

It has been a source of thanksgiving to God that I could be with my husband during the last hours. His body was still in the adjoining room when our son came just at dawn. During that long, long night doubt crept in. I looked up into my Savior's face and asked Him if I had run unsent, mistaken in the call I had been so sure of before. Into my heart came the assurance that all was well, and that Jesus was at the helm of everything.

—Rosalee Mills Appleby, Canton, Mississippi

EDITOR's NOTE: As I read this account I was reminded of the verse, *"Except a corn of wheat fall into the ground and die, it abideth alone; but if it die, it bringeth forth much fruit."*

This touching scene was not the end, but rather *the beginning* of something much more glorious than could have been had it not occurred — *"Our times are in His hand."* For not only did the young husband receive a glorious entrance into his heavenly reward, but also from that desperately lonely night of child-birth, so full of sorrow, pain and doubt — with her lover's body lying in the very next room — Rosalee Appleby rose to become one of the great missionaries to Brazil, spending nearly forty years in that needy land.

Our correspondence with "Miss" Appleby during the past two years has not just revealed her to be a woman of indefatigable spirit, with keen insight into the richest truths of God's word, but also — and what is more important — a woman of prayer who has travailed for Brazil over these many years.

Who can say that the unprecedented spiritual growth recorded today in that country has not come out of the tears of Rosalee Appleby's prayers, and others like her. And who can say that these precious tears of intercession would ever have been sown if she had not *first* sown those tears of earthly sorrow and loneliness as a bright young girl giving birth to a fatherless baby and facing a difficult future alone in a strange land?

Last Hours On Earth Of The Noted French Infidel, Voltaire

When Voltaire felt the stroke which he realized must terminate in death, he was overpowered with remorse. He at once sent for the priest and wanted to be "reconciled to the church." His infidel flatterers hastened to his chamber to prevent his recantation, but it was only to witness his ignominy and their own. *He cursed them to their faces* and, since his distress was increased by their presence, repeatedly and loudly exclaimed, "*Begone!* It is you that have brought me to my present condition. Leave me, I say — begone! What a wretched glory is this which you have produced for me!"

Hoping to allay his anguish by a written recantation, he had it prepared, signed it, and saw it witnessed. But it was all unavailing. For two months he was tortured with such an agony as led him at times to gnash his teeth in impotent rage against God and man. At other times, in plaintive accents, he would plead, "O Christ! O Lord Jesus!" Then, turning his face he would cry out, "I must die — abandoned of God and of men!"

As his end drew near his condition became so frightful that his infidel associates were afraid to approach his bedside. Still they guarded the door, that others might not know how awfully an infidel was compelled to die. Even his nurse repeatedly said *that for all the wealth of Europe she would never see another infidel die.* It was a scene of horror that lies beyond all exaggeration.

Such is the well-attested end of this man who had a natural sovereignty of intellect, excellent education, great wealth and much earthly honor.

—*The Contrast Between Infidelity and Christianity*

Dwight L. Moody

To the world, December 22, was the shortest day of the year. For D. L. Moody, its dawn in 1899 ushered in that day that knows no night. For forty-four years he had been a partaker of the divine life, and the transition from the seen to the unseen, from the sphere of the temporal to the eternal, was no interruption in his life. In other realms he continued to serve the same Master whose cause he loved with devotion and served with tireless energy.

Until within a few hours of the end, Mr. Moody shared with the family the conviction that he was improving. The day before, he had seemed rather more nervous than usual, but spoke cheerfully about himself. In reply to an inquiry if he was comfortable, he said:

"Oh, yes! God is very good to me — and so is my family."

No man loved his family and work more devotedly, and frequently he had been heard to say:

"Life is very sweet to me, and there is no position of power or wealth that could tempt me from the throne God has given me." It was not being tired of life and wanting to be done with service that made him so ready to leave, for he knew the joy of Christian service as few have experienced it.

The final summons came unexpectedly. During the first half of the night his son-in-law had been on duty at his bedside. Mr. Moody slept the greater part of the time. At three in the morning his son, W. R. Moody, came to his bedside. For several hours the patient was restless and unable to sleep, but about 6 a.m. he quieted down and soon fell into a natural sleep.

He awoke in about an hour. His son suddenly heard him speaking in slow and measured words, "Earth recedes — *Heaven opens before me.*"

His son's first impulse was to try to arouse him from what he thought was a dream.

"No, this is no dream, Will," he said. "It is *beautiful!* It is like a trance! If this is death, it is sweet! There is no valley here! *God is calling me, and I must go!*"

Meanwhile the nurse was summoning the family and the physician, who had spent the night in the house. Mr. Moody continued to talk quietly on and seemed to speak from another world his last messages to the loved ones he was leaving.

"I have always been an ambitious man," he said, "ambitious not to leave wealth or possessions, but to leave lots of work for you to do. You will carry on Mount Hermon — Paul will take up the Seminary when he is older — Fitt will look after the Institute — and Ambert (*his nephew*) will help you all in the business details."

Then it seemed as though he saw beyond the veil, for he exclaimed:

"This is my triumph; this is my coronation day! *I have been looking forward to it for years.*"

Then his face lit up, and he said in a voice of joyful rapture, "*Dwight! Irene!* I see the children's faces," (referring to his two little grandchildren, whom God had taken home within the past year).

With this he became unconscious. Up to this time no drugs whatever had been administered. In half an hour, however, he revived under the effect of heart stimulants, and as he regained consciousness he feebly uttered these words:

"No pain! No valley!"

Presently, as he rallied further, he added:

"If this is death, it's not bad at all! It's *sweet!*"

A little later, suddenly raising himself on his elbow, he exclaimed:

"What does all this mean? What are you all doing here?"

His wife explained that he had not been well, and immediately it all seemed to be clear to him, and he said:

"This is a strange thing! *I've been beyond the gates of death*

23

to the very portals of Heaven, and here I am back again. It is very strange!"

A little later he again said: "*This* is my coronation day! *It's glorious!*", and talked about the work he was leaving behind, assigning to his two sons the Northfield schools and to his daughter and her husband the Chicago Bible Institute. Asked what his wife's charge would be, he said:

"Oh, mamma is like Eve, the mother of us all!"

To the urgent plea that he remain longer with his family, he said:

"I'm not going to throw my life away. I'll stay as long as God wants me to; but if my time is come, I'm ready."

Something was soon said that showed how clear his mind was, for he remarked, with deliberation, "This is the twenty-second of December, isn't it? Five months ago today Irene died . . . and in this room." It was actually but four months, but any one might make such a mistake.

To the very last he was thinking of those about him and considering them. Turning to his wife, only a little while before he left, he said, "This is terrible on you, mamma; it's such a shock. I'm sorry to distress you in this way. Brace yourself. It is hard to be kept in such anxiety."

A few minutes before noon he was evidently sinking once again, and as the doctor approached to administer another hypodermic injection of nitroglycerine, Mr. Moody looked at him in a questioning and undecided way, and said, perfectly naturally, "Doctor, I don't know about this. Do you think it wise?" The doctor said he thought it would be all right.

"Well," Mr. Moody said, "it's prolonging the agony for the family!" The doctor turned away, seeing that the patient's life could not be saved. In a few moments more another sinking turn came on, and from it Mr. Moody awoke in the presence of Him whom he loved and had served so long and faithfully.

It was not like death, for he fell asleep quietly and peacefully, and it was not hard to imagine his reception in that other world among the host of loved ones awaiting his coming. The whole occurrence was such, in the mercy of God, that the *substance* as well as the sting of death was removed.

—*Shorter Life of D. L. Moody* by A. P. Fitt (Moody Press)

Little Willie Leonard Sees Jesus

The following account of the death of Willie Leonard, only six years old, will be of added interest to some who may have read the little book written by Mrs. Anna Leonard, *One Year With Jesus*. It is taken from a letter written by Willie's mother at the time of his death in 1881.

One day, about two weeks before Willie died, he came in from his play and said, "Mamma, it seems to me I wouldn't want to die." When asked why, he said, "Oh, I wouldn't want to leave you folks here. But then, I suppose I would be very happy in Heaven, and, Mamma, I would watch over you."

His mother clasped him in her arms. She loved him — oh so much — yet somehow she felt that the angels were beckoning to him, and she talked with him of the joys that awaited him in Heaven and that they would meet him there.

He then said, "Mamma, I don't want any little lamb on my tombstone, but I want a little boy lying on the grass as you have seen me lie in the summertime when I was tired out with play." (He had never seen nor heard of anything of the kind, but such a stone now marks his grave.)

The premonition proved true, for he soon took sick with scarlet fever of a diphtherial form, and lived but two days.

He was such a patient little sufferer through it all! When asked if he was not a pretty sick little boy, he replied, "No, not very sick, but I think Jesus is going to take me to Heaven to live." As he spoke, an angelic look of holy rapture and a radiant smile came over his face. His father was called, and as he talked with him about it, that same glorious smile again illuminated his face. He then talked about the disposal of his toys, books, Sunday school cards and papers.

He then spoke of a new hat, which he said he would not need now, and his mother talked with him of the beautiful crown awaiting him in Heaven, although her heart seemed bursting with grief.

"Willie," said she, "no one can see Jesus when He comes except the one He comes after, so *when you see Him will you tell me?*"

"Yes," he replied, "if I can talk — and if not, I will point to Him."

When his little brother told him that his father had gone after the doctor, he said, "Oh, I would rather that Jesus would take me to Heaven, than for Dr. Taplin to make me well!"

In a few hours he was quite restless and delirious. I now quote from the letter verbatim:

"As we laid him back on his pillow, his eyes remained wide open and fixed. We felt his feet and found them cold. I hastened and warmed flannels and wrapped them. We chafed his hands, although his fingernails were blue. How could we believe that our Willie was dying — Willie our hope, our pride, the joy of our home. But so it was, and as we gathered round his bed, we wept as only parents can weep at such times and talked loving words to his inanimate form.

"He was lying very still, when all at once one little hand was raised and he pointed upward for a moment as his dear lips moved in an effort to speak.

"'Willie,' I cried aloud, 'do you see Jesus?'

"His hand was laid again by his side, he breathed shorter and less frequently a few times and then ceased forever. In his last moments he remembered the signal agreed upon between him and me and pointed to Jesus.

"When the body that was so beautiful and dear to us was lowered into the silent grave and the earth fell with a hollow sound upon the box below, it seemed as if I could not rise above the shock.

"Then I felt, as it were, a light breath fan my cheek and a sweet voice seemed to say, 'Mamma, I am not there; don't cry. I am happy!' My tears dried in an instant, and I cannot now think of him as anywhere but in that beautiful Heaven where he longed to go."

—Adapted from an article by Mrs. Eva Simkins, Lester, Mich.

The Advice of Ethan Allen, The Noted Infidel, To His Dying Daughter

Ethan Allen was a professed infidel and the author of a book against the divinity of Jesus Christ. His wife was a Christian, earnest, cheerful and devoted. She died an early death, leaving behind an only daughter, who soon became the idol of her father. The fragile, sensitive child entwined herself about the knotty and gnarled limbs of the oak. Before long, however,

26

tuberculosis marked this fair girl for its own, and she gradually wasted away, until the sight of her was enough to bring tears to the hardest heart.

One day her father came into her room, and sitting down by her bedside, took her wan little hand in his. She looked up into his face and said, "My dear father — I'm going to die."

"Oh no, my child. No! The spring is coming, and with the birds and breezes and the bloom, your pale cheeks will blush with health."

"The doctor was here today," she continued. "I felt I was nearing the grave, and I asked him to tell me plainly what I had to expect. I told him that it was a great thing to exchange worlds, and that I did not wish to be deceived about myself. If I was going to die I had some preparations I wanted to make. He then told me my disease is beyond human skill.

"You will bury me by the side of mother, for that was her dying request. But, father, you and mother did not agree on religion. Mother often spoke to me of the blessed Savior who died for us all. She used to pray for both you and me, that the Savior might be our friend, and that we might all see Him as our Savior when He sits enthroned in His glory."

Her eyes looked desperately into his, "I don't feel that I can go alone through the dark valley of the shadow of death. *Tell me, father, whom shall I follow, you or mother?* Shall I reject Christ, as you have taught me, or shall I accept Him? He was mother's friend in the hour of her great sorrow."

There was an honest heart beneath that rough exterior. Though tears nearly choked his utterances, the old soldier said, "My child, cling to your mother's Savior. *She was right.* I'll try to follow you to that blessed place."

A serene smile overspread the face of the dying girl, and who can doubt there is an unbroken family in Heaven?

—Adapted from an article by S. B. Shaw in *Dying Testimonies*

Anne Boleyn A.D. 1536

Anne Boleyn, the second wife of Henry VIII of England, was beheaded at the instigation of her husband, who the day after her death married Jane Seymour. The charge brought against her was adultery, but it was never proven.

27

Four others were beheaded with her, one of whom was Norris, a faithful and virtuous servant. He was promised his life if he would accuse her, but instead he declared that she was innocent and that he would die a thousand deaths rather than defame her. The three others who were executed also vindicated her to the last. So little respect was paid to her body that with brutal insolence it was put into a crude chest made to send arrows to Ireland.

To those sent to lead her to execution, she said, "Commend me to the King, and tell him he is constant in his course of advancing me. From a private gentlewoman he made me a Marchioness, and from a Marchioness a Queen. Now, having no higher degree of earthly honor left to offer, he hath made me a martyr."

Then she was heard to say, "I hear say the executioner is very good, and I have a little neck. *To Christ I commend my soul.*"

—*Dying Words* by A. H. Gottschall

Saved — Just In Time

Alice's life had always been a sad one — at least, as far as she could remember. Perhaps the first three years of babyhood had been as pleasant and happy as if she had been born in a more comfortable home, but Alice couldn't be sure about this, and no one else could speak for her.

Certainly there was misery and unhappiness from *one* day on — misery that lasted for nearly fifteen years of girlhood life. That was the day which came shortly after her third birthday, the day Alice ceased being a baby.

She couldn't remember much about it, but it seemed like a big, round, black spot, big enough to shut out all the sunlight from life. On a dark and gloomy day, some strange men Alice had never seen before came to the little house. They were all dressed in black and took away something in a long, dark box — and Alice never saw her mother again. No wonder it seemed to the child like something black and awful. Besides, after that life was bitterly hard for this, the youngest of five motherless children, no longer watched over with the care only a mother can give.

Things at home, which had been in some ways bad enough before, were worse now, and the child grew up in an atmosphere of such moral degradation that it is a wonder she did not fall sooner and sin more deeply than was the case. Two of her sisters lived an openly sinful life, and assuredly the brother for whom she went to keep house as soon as she was old enough was no better.

One day a companion of this brother came to the house. When he went away he was as light-hearted and careless as ever, but he left behind a girl of seventeen with a burden of shame and sorrow and disgrace such as she felt she could not bear.

Alice went to her two sisters with the weight of sorrow and wrong — the only people in the world who could stand in the place of a mother to her.

"Nonsense!" said Kate, "why, you'll get used to it!"

Bettina, though a little more sympathetic, was even more discouraging. "I never thought you'd feel like that," she said. "But it's too late to mend matters now. It could have been helped yesterday, but not today — what's done can't be undone. There isn't a respectable woman in the world who'd speak to you now!"

Alice walked away as if in a dream. "What's done can't be undone," she kept repeating to herself, as if to fasten the dreadful statement upon her mind and memory. Occasionally the words changed, and she repeated, "It's too late to mend matters now."

It was the old argument, used so successfully in thousands of cases — the argument that one step down the ladder of disgrace involves the whole distance, that there is no hope, no way of escape, after the first wrong-doing.

"There's no help for it — you are doomed now. You might as well take what pleasure you can out of this life." In almost every case someone is sure to come with this temptation to utter hopelessness, and the young girl whose better nature is fighting against the horror of the whole thing calls on that better nature to yield the battle. "It is no use trying to be good," she says despairingly.

So it was with Alice Sawyer. She knew of no one in the village to whom she could go for help, or even advice, and she gave up the struggle. "It isn't my fault," she said to herself once when her half-dormant conscience spoke out and would be heard. "There simply isn't any way out for me, or if there is, I can't find it, and that's the same thing."

Weeks passed by, during which no one would have suspected that Alice Sawyer felt any repugnance toward the careless, irregular sort of life she was leading.

"There, I knew she'd get used to it soon enough," exclaimed Kate one day.

But Bettina said nothing. Deep down in her heart there was a sort of sorrow for her youngest sister, but it was a sorrow she did not know how to put into words.

After a time Alice went away from home and found her way to Grand Rapids, where she began to search for work. Like many others, she imagined that it would be easy to hide her shame in the midst of a crowd.

She wanted to be lost, but instead she was found — found by the One who came to seek and to save that which was lost.

Almost at the beginning of her search for work, Alice discovered that at least one part of the disheartening prophecy of her sister was untrue, because she came across an earnest Christian lady who not only "spoke to her", but even took her into her own home for the night.

The next day this lady brought her to the Salvation Army Rescue Home in Grand Rapids. Alice wanted to stay and was very grateful. Yet it all seemed so strange, so unexpected, that it took the poor child some time to realize that "the way out" of her sin and misery had actually been found.

Kneeling by her bedside one night, Alice claimed for herself the power of that uttermost salvation which alone can take away the bitterness from the memory of such a past as hers, and which alone can make it possible to sing,

> He breaks the power of cancelled sin,
> He sets the prisoner free;
> His blood can make the foulest clean,
> His blood avails for me!

That night marked the last of Alice's unhappy days, the "black ones" as she sometimes called them in contrast to the "white ones" of the new life which then began. Her one sorrow was for those left behind in the village home, without any knowledge of Christ. She prayed for them all, especially for her father, then seventy-one years old.

"It will take something to touch my father's heart," she said one day to the Captain of the Home, "but I am praying for him, and I believe he will give his heart to God."

That "something" which should touch her father's heart

came sooner than was expected by some.

Alice had to go to the hospital, and after she had been there a short time it became evident that she would never be able to go out again. But she had no fear. Her only sorrow was that she had hoped to be able to go to others with the story of the wonderful salvation which had availed for her.

On the first evening of her stay in the hospital, the Captain and Lieutenant of the Rescue Home went with her and stayed a few hours. As they were saying good-night to her and the nurse who was to have her in charge, Alice suddenly dropped on her knees by the bedside.

It was indeed a striking picture. On the one side were the two Salvationists in their uniforms, on the other side the nurse in hers, while by the bedside knelt the girl of eighteen who had been saved *just in time* from a life of misery and sorrow. It seemed as if the very light of Heaven were striking through, illuminating the scene with divine radiance and blessing. It may indeed have been so, for Alice was rapidly nearing the very gates of Heaven.

* * * *

Suddenly the summons came — such a summons always seems sudden at the last, even when the possibility has been in view for some time.

Word was sent to the Rescue Home, and the Captain came at once to the hospital. "I do love you, Captain," said Alice. Then, with her eyes steadfastly fixed on the face of the one who had led her into the light of salvation through Jesus, the girl passed quietly and peacefully away to that land where there is no more pain, for the "former things are passed away".

This scene itself would have been a beautiful ending to a story which began in such sadness and gloom. It was indeed a bright, white, glorious day in Alice's experience, but it did not mark the end of her work on earth.

The "something" which was to touch her father's heart proved to be his youngest daughter's death. At the simple funeral service, he came forward like a child, knelt by the coffin, shaking with sobs, and asked God to help him meet his Alice in the great, wonderful land beyond the grave

—Adjutant Elizabeth M. Clark; from The War Cry

31

Napoleon Bonaparte A.D. 1821

This great emperor of France died in exile. His last recorded words were, "I die before my time, and my body will be given back to the earth to become food for worms. Such is the fate of him who has been called the great Napoleon. *What an abyss lies between my deep misery and the eternal kingdom of Christ!*"

—*Dying Words* by A. H. Gottschall

An Elephant Hunt That Opened Heaven

I heard an outstanding testimony from missionary Paul Landrus* when I was visiting in Liberia, West Africa.

Paul, whom I know personally, was out in the jungle with an eighteen-year-old African boy hunting elephants. He shot an elephant, but his gunsight was off and the animal was only wounded. The elephant charged, and though Paul tried to hide behind a tree, it reached around the tree with its trunk and began squeezing the life out of him. He took the elephant's snout and began to squeeze it, which somewhat loosened its grip around his midriff, but by this time the animal's trumpeting had stirred up a whole herd of elephants.

These came lumbering through the thick of the jungles, and in the providence of God, one of them hit the back end of the wounded elephant, spinning him around and loosening his hold. At that moment, the African boy came running out to help Brother Landrus, but one of the elephants got him. He was gored from his groin almost to his throat. As the elephants raced away, the poor boy was screaming *"Pa, I die! Pa, I die!"*

Brother Landrus followed to find where the elephant had taken him, as elephants often bury their prey in shallow graves. Sure enough, this elephant had scraped out a shallow grave and covered the boy over with leaves and dirt. Paul found him and uncovered him — and from that moment on he said nothing could ever dissuade him that there was a Heaven. This African boy, saved out of heathenism only a short while and not preconditioned to descriptions of Heaven, began to describe the angels and spoke of music like Landrus knew he had never heard in his lifetime. In a few moments the boy was gone, but in those

32

fleeting last moments he had clearly seen Heaven's glory and even heard its glorious sounds.

—Loren Cunningham, *Youth With A Mission*
Pasadena, California

* Unfortunately this marvelous testimony came to us late, and we were unable to contact Mr. Landrus in time for a first-hand account of the story. Perhaps a more detailed, first-hand account can be added in future editions.—*The Editor*

Mrs. Catherine Booth A.D. 1890

Wife of William Booth, founder of the Salvation Army

"The waters are rising, but so am I. I am not going *under,* but *over!* Do not be concerned about dying — go on living well and the dying will be right."

—*Dying Words* by A. H. Gottschall

Charles IX, King of France

"I am lost; I see it well."

This wicked young king died May 30, 1574. His character was a compound of passion, acuteness, heartlessness and cunning. The infamous massacre of St. Bartholomew, August 24, 1572, was the culmination of a series of treacheries toward the Huguenots which greatly disgraced his reign.

While he was yet a young man, death reached forth its awful hand. Its clutch tore away kingly robes, and as the crown which had given him such great authority over the lives of men fell from his brow, he slipped into the dark night of eternity, a *naked* soul.

No doubt, for the sake of a watching world, the Spirit of God opened his eyes to show him what awaited beyond that dark veil. History has recorded the remorse and cry of anguish that followed.

During his last hours he cried to his nurse, "Oh, my nurse, my nurse! What blood, what murders, what evil counsels have I followed!" Then a futile prayer — "Oh, my God, pardon me and have mercy on me if Thou canst. I know what I am — What shall I do? *I am lost; I see it well!"*

33

"Everyone that is godly (shall) pray unto Thee in a time when Thou mayest be found. Surely, in the floods of great waters *they shall not come nigh unto Thee.*" — Psalms 32:6

—*Dying Testimonies* by S. B. Shaw

Lady Jane Grey A.D. 1554

Lady Jane Grey was the Queen of England for ten days. Apparently through the uneasiness of Queen Mary, she and her husband were beheaded on the same day.

From the platform she addressed the bystanders, and there committed herself to God. Her beautiful throat was then bared, and after tying a handkerchief over her eyes and feeling for the block, she laid her head upon it.

Before the ax fell she exclaimed, *"Lord, into Thy hands I commend my spirit!"*

—*Dying Words* by A. H. Gottschall

Nishizawa, Notorious Japanese War Criminal

"Saved by the grace of God . . . to die is gain!"

A happy, vivacious young Irish girl set sail for Japan on October 9, 1916. She was Irene Webster-Smith, and came from an aristocratic family. Irish to the core, she bubbled over with a delightful wit that sometimes startled the ultra "prim and proper", but which attracted thousands of Japanese to her in after-years.

Little did that talented Irish girl realize that one day she would be used by God to transform the lives of fourteen of the toughest war criminals in Japan.

How did the miracle take place?

Nishizawa San was one of the Japanese military leaders convicted of war crimes. The International War Crimes Tribunal found him guilty and sentenced him to death by hanging. He was in Sugamo prison awaiting execution when he first met Miss Webster-Smith.

Nishizawa's wife was a Christian and was deeply concerned about her husband. Allowed to see him for only half an hour each month, she had taken him a Gospel of St. John on one of her visits. Nishizawa, however, was not interested. Hardened by sins of the deepest dye, he was completely indifferent to his wife's endeavor to bring him to Christ.

One day Miss Webster-Smith, called "Sensei" (which means "teacher" or "wise one") by the Japanese who knew her, went to speak at a women's meeting in Kashiwa. In that meeting was Mrs. Nishizawa. She introduced herself to Sensei and then pleaded with her to go to see her husband in prison.

"I am deeply concerned about my husband, and I want very much for him to become a Christian before he dies. If only you would go I would give up my visiting privilege for you."

Such a moving appeal was irresistible, and Sensei promised to do her best. She soon found, however, that Nish'zawa and the other war crimes prisoners at Sugamo prison were held under tight security. The authorities were taking no chances, especially since one prisoner's wife had smuggled poison into the prison when visiting her husband. She had smeared it on the wire mesh of the interview booth; the prisoner had licked it off and died.

At first it seemed impossible for Sensei to break through the regulations and red tape of officialdom. But a God-inspired enthusiasm and determination at last convinced the authorities that this charming old lady had a right to see the doomed Nishizawa. She was admitted to the great grey stone building known as Sugamo Prison.

The interview booth was heavily guarded as Sensei sat on one side of the heavy wire mesh which separated her from Nishizawa. With a silent prayer, she spoke to the man. "I have seen your wife and children, and they are well. I met your wife at a Christian meeting."

Nishizawa replied: "She told me she had been converted, and she left me a booklet." The tone of his voice showed no interest. But Sensei quickly seized her chance. The booklet must be the Gospel, she thought. So it was, and it gave Sensei the golden opportunity of telling the prisoner that the Christ of the Gospel had died on the Cross for the sins of men and that He would freely pardon all who would truly repent and believe in Him. She went on to explain that Christ would receive such believers into his glorious Kingdom where they would live eternally with Him.

Nishizawa was visibly moved by the earnest and confident preaching of the Gospel in that prison booth. Before the interview ended he asked the vital question: "Do you mean that He could forgive *my* sins? I have committed terrible sins. You cannot imagine what they are."

Quickly Sensei assured Nishizawa that there was hope for the worst sinner who trusts in the cleansing blood of Jesus Christ and believes on Him as his personal Saviour.

Deeply moved by the Holy Spirit, the poor prisoner then and there prayed with Sensei, crying to God for mercy. Afterwards there came into his heart a peace and joy he had never known before. Sensei heard him whisper, "Thank God, and thank you."

The great transaction was done! Nishizawa was a "new creature in Christ Jesus". At once he told Sensei that he believed Christ had saved him. The missionary then urged him to find some person in that prison and tell him what Christ had done for Nishizawa.

The prisoner's only chance was during exercise time, for he was in solitary confinement — and even then he was not supposed to talk to other prisoners. But Nishizawa promised he would do his best to witness for his newly-found Saviour. This he did with such amazing success that, one by one, thirteen other war criminals in Sugamo were brought to Christ. They asked for baptism and were immersed by the Baptist prison chaplain.

Then, one day, there came a deep sense of urgency to Sensei that she must go at once and visit Nishizawa again. But the officials at headquarters were adamant. She had used the one interview permitted; another clemency visit was completely out of the question.

Knowing that the urgent call had come from God, she felt she must at all costs see Nishizawa again before he was executed. And when Sensei made up her mind to do something for her Lord, all the powers of Hell could not stop her. She marched straight to the office of the only man in Japan who could then open the prison doors for her. He was the famous General MacArthur, the man who then virtually ruled all Japan.

The great man received her courteously and listened to her plea. He then gave her permission to see the prisoner once again, even providing a staff car to drive her to the prison.

In the interview room she looked keenly at Nishizawa as

36

he was brought in. His face was radiant with joy as he exclaimed, "Only this morning I asked God to send you to see me. He answered my prayer! I want to give you instructions for the care of my wife and children and a last message for them and for my parents." Thus Sensei and Nishizawa prayed together and said goodbye.

Just before Nishizawa was executed Sensei received a letter from him. It read:

"Mother Smith,

I appreciate you sincerely and that you saw me again and gave me kind encouragement, sharing your busy time. Thank you also by the name of the Lord, with the other brethren, hearing that the favor of baptism was realized by your unusual efforts.

I am living thankful days, believing that I may receive salvation of the Holy Ghost on my last day, and entirely trusting in Him, that for me — saved by the grace of God — 'to live is Christ and *to die is gain.*'

I pray your good health by the name of the Lord Jesus Christ and God the Father.

Yours sincerely,
A saved sinner
M. Nishizawa"

Two days later Sensei learned that Nishizawa and one of the other converts had been executed the previous night.

—Adapted from an article in The Flame

William Grimshaw A.D. 1763

When asked in his last moments how he felt, he replied, "As happy as I can be on earth, and *as sure of glory as if I were in it.* I have nothing to do but to step out of this bed into Heaven!"

—Dying Words by A. H. Gottschall

Reality Of The Spirit

What does science have to say about the immortality of man? A revealing article by Dr. J. B. Rhine, director of the Parapsychology Laboratory at Duke University.

Forty years ago my wife and I began to look into a question that has intrigued and troubled mankind since the dawn of history, the question of life after death. Having been educated as biologists, we approached it as scientists, respectful of religious teachings and beliefs, but primarily concerned with studying and testing scientifically claims that communication with the spirit world was possible.

This search took us to Duke University where, under Professor William McDougall, we established the Parapsychology Laboratory and continued our investigations. Our studies led us into intensive research on extrasensory perception, or ESP, for which the Duke Laboratory has become known. Eventually our experimental demonstrations of ESP were confirmed by scientists working in other laboratories in this and other countries.

What we learned, and proved experimentally, is that a part of the human personality is not wholly explainable by physical principles. It can receive knowledge without using sensory means. It can transcend the laws of time and space. Parapsychologists call this mysterious ability of the personality *"psi"*, a noncommittal term that we use for the time being, while its full explanation and characteristics are still unknown.

It now is known that *psi* ability includes different types of ESP — telepathy, clairvoyance and precognition (knowledge of things that are going to happen). Under these names, it has now been firmly proved that the human mind can transcend both space and time; and independent of material barriers, it can make contact with other minds.

Since this power is apparently non-physical, it may very well be called spiritual. And if it is non-physical, the question at once arises: does it belong to a part of man that can survive the physical process known as death?

This is a very difficult question, because many phenomena in this *psi* area that might seem to indicate survival after death also can be explained by one form or another of extrasensory perception.

Some years ago we were visited by a general and his wife whose son, a young officer, had died. Very soon after his death, his mother felt a hand on her shoulder. Looking up through her tears she saw — or thought she saw — her son. He looked splendid, immaculate as always in his uniform. "Cheer up, Mother," he said, "I'm all right. It's not like you to give way like this!"

And so this mother put her poignant question to me. "Doctor, was this really our son I saw?"

For one who works in science, there is only the known truth to tell. Even when one wishes it were otherwise, one can give only established knowledge. So my answer had to be, "I cannot give you a definite answer. Perhaps that experience of yours was projected by your own mind, as hallucinatory relief for your grief. I will add that I think it *possible* for such an experience to be the result of an outside agency, of your son's surviving personality. But it was so much what you wanted to hear, and it left no trace beyond that. And so as scientific evidence of anything beyond your own unconscious needs, I am afraid it does not qualify."

Occasionally people have experiences that *do* qualify as scientific evidence — of something. During World War II a man and wife were sleeping when suddenly the man sat up, wakening his wife. He said:

"I just dreamed that my brother Joe was killed in action. He wants me to break the news to Father."

"Oh, Honey, it's just a nightmare. Go back to sleep!" the wife replied.

This was July 26, 1945. A week later the telegram came. Joe was killed in action July 26, 1945.

Did Joe come to his brother after his own death with that message? The question is the same one the general's wife asked, but in this case the agony of grief was lacking, for the brother had not received the news until the experience itself brought it. As an example of extrasensory perception, at least, the case is valid. As evidence for the survival of the spirit, it is not enough for a scientific decision. But here too one can say, "It could have been" — and for those most intimately concerned, a "could be" is better than a "can't be."

The further research on this question progresses, the more man's mind and body appear to be one highly complex unity. But even if we cannot see at present any complete separability, still we *know* now that the spiritual side is no less real than the physical, and incomparably more important. It is the knowledge of its reach and independence that still is incomplete.

To the student of ESP, the most significant type of case

history where this question of survival is concerned is one in which the information transmitted to the living person was known only to the deceased, or one in which the *method* of transmission is beyond the capabilities of the person through whom the information comes.

A professor at Northwestern University received the following case from one of his students, which is noteworthy on both counts:

"One evening when I was a boy of four, before I knew anything of school or the alphabet, my mother was working at her desk in our hotel, and I got hold of a note pad and began scribbling on it. Mother, noticing what I was doing, told me to stop and play with something else.

"The next morning my mother saw the papers with my scribblings and was about to throw them away when the day clerk, who had taken shorthand at night school, told her they looked like shorthand. He insisted on taking the papers to a teacher for examination. They *were* shorthand, the old-fashioned square-type shorthand.

"On these papers was a message to my mother from my father who had died two weeks before in New York, while my mother and I were in Oregon. It started 'Dearest Beloved," and spoke of a letter that had not been posted. It was an urgent letter containing information about Father's safety-deposit box in the East. His death had been sudden, and mother had not known the location of that box.

"My father always had called my mother 'Dearest Beloved,' and as a young man had learned the old-fashioned method of shorthand. Mother still has those pieces of paper, and the message has been verified by other people too."

To a scientist, does such a story offer acceptable proof of life after death? No, but it is in line with scientific research that has proven that there is something in man that has a wholly different set of properties from those of his physical body — *and it is this finding that makes survival a logical possibility.*

We know now that man is, as he has long intuitively believed, a spiritual being. That much seems definite. Is this spiritual side of his nature sufficiently strong and independent to survive the death of the physical body? This we cannot demonstrate — at least, not so far.

The fact is, then, that it is the *living* human spirit about which we know most and it is that about which we most need to know. For it has been on the assumption of a spiritual aspect of man that religion, morality, free will and true democracy have been founded.

So let us get on with the discovery of this side of man's nature, both in its potential for human life and its destiny beyond the grave. We need this larger understanding.

—Reprinted from *Guideposts* Magazine
Copyright 1963 *Guideposts Associates, Inc.,* Carmel, N.Y.

I believe in an immortal soul. Science has proved that nothing disintegrates into nothingness. Life and soul, therefore, cannot disintegrate into nothingness, and so are immortal.

—Wernher von Braun

"Nothing Remains But The Bridge Of The Savior"

Byron Bunson, born in 1791, was one of the most distinguished statesmen and scholars of Germany. In 1841 he was sent on a special mission to London to negotiate the establishing of an Anglo-Prussian Bishopric in Jerusalem and was shortly afterward appointed ambassador at the English court. He is known in literature by many outstanding works such as *Constitution of the Church of the Future, Christianity and Mankind,* and *God in History.* He was a great statesman and philosopher.

He died at Bonn, Germany, in 1860. On his death-bed he cried out, "All bridges that one builds through life fail at such a time as this — nothing remains but the bridge of the Savior!"

—*Dying Testimonies* by S. B. Shaw

"It Is Easier To Get Into Hell Than It Will Be To Get Out."

In the village of Montgomery, Michigan, in the spring of 1884, an infidel, the husband of a spiritualist, was stricken down with disease. He had such a hatred for the cause of Christ that he had requested previously that his body not be carried to a church for funeral services or any pastor be called upon to officiate.

Now, as he was nearing the shores of eternity, he turned

41

his face toward the wall and began to talk of his future prospects. His wife saw that he was troubled in spirit and endeavored to comfort and console him by telling him not to be afraid. She told him that his spirit would return to her and they would commune together then as now. But this gave him no comfort in this awful hour.

With a look of despair, he said, *"I see a great high wall rising around me and am finding out at last — when it is too late — that it is easier to get into Hell than it will be to get out."*

In a few moments his spirit had departed from this world to "receive the reward of unrighteousness". This conversation was heard by my sister-in-law who was present at the time of his death.

—Rev. W. C. Muffit, Cleveland, Ohio

Anthony Groves A.D. 1853
"I who am utterly vile am going to be with Jesus!"

Archibald Campbell A.D. 1661

This man — the Marquis of Argyle — was executed in Edinburgh. On the morning of his death, while engaged in settling his worldly business, he was so overpowered with a sense of the Divine presence that he broke out in raptures, "I am now ordering my affairs, and God is just now saying to me, *'Son be of good cheer! Thy sins are forgiven thee.'*

—*Dying Words* by A. H. Gottschall

John Hunt—Apostle To Fiji
"I Want Strength To Praise Him Abundantly! . . ."

We turn now to the remarkable story of the conversion of Fiji. This name is given to a group of islands, some two hundred and twenty-five in number, of which about one hundred and forty are inhabited. The largest of these islands, Vitu Leyu, is about the same size as Jamaica.

The story of these fair and fertile islands, long the habitation of cruelty, is one of intense interest. That a Lincolnshire plowboy, who grew up to manhood with no educational advantages, should — before his thirty-sixth year — be the chief instrument in the conversion to Christianity and civilization of one of the most barbarous races of cannibals on the face of the earth, is one of the most remarkable events in the history of Christian missions.

We cannot take space here to relate the wonderful story of John Hunt's missionary life. One scene will have to suffice to touch our hearts with the depth of this humble man's exploits in the power of the Spirit.

As the glorious reward of Mr. Hunt's labors and deep devotion, a great spiritual awakening finally took place. Among the converts was the Queen of Viwa. "Her heart," says Mr. Hunt, "seemed literally to be broken, and though a very strong woman, she fainted twice under the weight of a wounded spirit. She revived only to renew her strong cries and tears, so that it was all that we could do to proceed with the service.

"The effect soon became more general. Several of the women and some of the men literally roared for the disquietude of their hearts . . . It was very affecting to see upward of a hundred Fijians, many of whom were a few years ago some of the worst cannibals in the group, and even in the world, chanting, 'We praise Thee, O God; we acknowledge Thee to be the Lord', while their voices were almost drowned by the cries of broken-hearted penitents."

Mr. Hunt's continuous toil at length told seriously upon his health. The man of iron strength, who had come up to London from the fields of Lincolnshire only twelve years before, was evidently dying. Of him, as it was with his Lord, might it be truly said, *"The zeal of thine house hath eaten me up."*

The converts from heathenism, with sad faces, flocked to the chapel and prayed earnestly for the missionary. "O Lord," Elijah Verani cried aloud, "we know we are very bad, but spare Thy servant! If one must die, take *me*! take *ten* of us! but spare Thy servant to preach Christ to the people!"

As he neared the end, the missionary confidently committed his wife and babes to God, but was sorely distressed for Fiji. Sobbing as though in acute distress, he cried out, "Lord, bless Fiji! save Fiji! Thou knowest my soul has loved Fiji — my heart has travailed for Fiji!" Then, grasping his friend Calvert by the hand, he exclaimed again, "Oh, let me pray once more for Fiji! Lord, for Christ's sake, *bless Fiji! save Fiji!"*

43

Turning to his mourning wife, he said, "If this be dying, praise the Lord!" Presently, as his eyes looked up with a bright joy that defied death, he exclaimed, "I want strength to praise Him abundantly!" and with the cry of triumph, "*Hallelujah!*" on his lips, he joined the worship of the skies.

— Adapted from *The Picket Line of Missions*

Miss Isabella Campbell A.D. 1827

"Oh, that I could tell you of the exceeding joy I have in the Lord Jesus Christ! How much is implied in those words, *'The peace of God which passeth all understanding.'* I wish those who seek satisfaction in the things of time could understand a little of it.

"Live alone to God . . . *Farewell!*"

—*Dying Words* by A. H. Gottschall

"Oh, Papa, What A Sweet Sight! The Golden Gates Are Open"

Through the kindness of L. B. Balliett, M.D., we furnish this touching incident. When ten-year-old Lillian Lee lay dying she spoke to her father thus: "Oh! papa, what a sweet sight! The golden gates are open and crowds of children come pouring out. Oh, such crowds!"

Later she cried, "They ran up to me and began to kiss me and call me by a new name. I can't remember what it was."

She then lay looking upwards, her eyes dreaming. Her voice died into a whisper as she said, *"Yes, yes, I come, I come!"*

—*Dying Testimonies* by S. B. Shaw

Death-Bed Scene Of David Hume, The Deist

David Hume, the deistical philosopher and historian, was born in Edinburgh in 1711. In 1762 he published his work, *Natural Religion.* Much of his time was spent in France, where he found many kindred spirits as vile and depraved as himself.

44

He died in Edinburgh in 1776, aged sixty-five years.

E. P. Goodwin, in his work on *Christianity and Infidelity* revealed Hume as dishonest, indecent and a teacher of immorality. Rev. Robert Hall, in his *Modern Infidelity,* says:

"Infidelity is the joint offspring of an irreligious temper and unholy speculation, employed, not in examining the evidences of Christianity, but in detecting the vices and imperfections of confessing Christians. It has passed through various stages, each distinguished by higher gradations of impiety, for when men arrogantly abandon their guide, and willfully shut their eyes on the light of Heaven, it is wisely ordained that their errors shall multiply at every step, until . . . the mischief of their principles works its own antidote.

"Hume was the most subtle, if not the most philosophical, of the deists. By perplexing the relations of cause and effect, he boldly aimed to introduce a universal skepticism and to pour a more than Egyptian darkness into the whole region of morals."

Again, in M'Ilvaine's *Evidences,* we read:

"The nature and majesty of God are denied by Hume's argument against the miracles. It is atheism. There is no stopping place for consistency between the first principle of the essay of Hume and the last step in the denial of God. Hume, accordingly, had no belief in the existence of God. He did not positively deny it, yet he could not assert that he believed it. He was a poor, blind, groping compound of contradictions. He was literally 'without God and without hope', 'doting about questions and strifes of words', and rejecting life and immortality out of deference to a paltry quibble, of which common-sense is ashamed.

"There is reason to believe that however unconcerned Hume may have seemed in the presence of his infidel friends, when not diverted by companions or cards, or his works and books of amusements, when left to himself and the contemplation of eternity, he was anything but composed and satisfied.

"The following account was published in Edinburgh, where he died. It is not known to have been ever contradicted. About the end of 1776, a few months after the historian's death, a respectable-looking woman, dressed in black, came into the Haddington stage-coach while passing through Edinburgh. The conversation among the passengers, which had been interrupted for a few minutes, was resumed, and the new passenger found it to be regarding the state of mind of persons at the prospect of death. In defence of infidelity, an appeal was made to the death

45

of Hume as not only happy and tranquil, but mingled even with gaiety and humor.

"To this the lady said, 'Sir, you know nothing about it; I could tell you another tale.'

" 'Madam,' replied the gentleman, 'I presume I have as good information as you have on this subject, and I believe what I have asserted regarding Mr. Hume has never been called in question.'

"The lady continued, 'Sir, I was Mr. Hume's housekeeper for many years and was with him in his last moments. The mourning I now wear is a present from his relatives for my attention to him on his death bed. Happy would I have been if I could have borne my testimony to the mistaken opinion that has gone abroad of his peaceful and composed end. I have never till this hour opened my mouth on this subject, but I think it a pity the world should be kept in the dark.

" 'It is true, sir, that when Mr. Hume's friends were with him he was cheerful and seemed quite unconcerned about his approaching fate. He even frequently spoke of it to them in a jocular and playful way. *But when he was alone, the scene was very different* — he was anything but composed. His mental agitation was so great at times as to occasion his whole bed to shake! And he would not allow the candles to be put out during the night, nor would he be left alone for a minute. I had always to ring the bell for one of the servants to be in the room before he would allow me to leave it.

" 'He struggled hard to appear composed, even before me. But to one who attended his bedside for so many days and nights and witnessed his disturbed sleep, and still more disturbed wakings — who frequently heard his involuntary breathings of remorse and frightful startings — it was no difficult matter to determine that all was not right within.

" 'This continued and increased until he became insensible. I hope to God I shall never witness a similar scene.' "

Thomas A. Edison

The late Mrs. Thomas A. Edison told me that when her famous husband was dying he whispered to his physician, "It is very beautiful over there." Edison was the world's greatest scientist. All his life he had worked with phenomena. He was

46

of a factual cast of mind. He never reported anything as a fact until he saw it work. He would never have reported, "It is very beautiful over there" unless, having seen, he knew it to be true.

—*Power of Positive Thinking* by Norman Vincent Peale
Prentice-Hall, Inc.

Michael Angelo Buonarotti A.D. 1564

In a brief will, the great Italian painter and sculptor said, "I commit my soul to God, my body to the earth, my possessions to my nearest relatives. I die in the faith of Jesus Christ and in the firm hope of a better life."

His last words were, "Throughout life *remember the sufferings of Jesus.*"

—*Dying Words* by A. H. Gottschall

Bishop Butler A.D. 1752

Upon his death-bed he sent for his chaplain, and said, "Though I have endeavored to avoid sin and please God, yet because of the consciousness of inner failure I am still afraid to die."

"My lord," answered the chaplain, "have you forgotten that Jesus Christ is a Saviour?"

"True," continued the Bishop, "but how shall I know that He is a Saviour *for me?*"

"It is written, 'Him that cometh to Me I will in no wise cast out.'"

"True!" exclaimed the dying man. Then he said, "I am surprised that, though I have read that Scripture a thousand times over, I never felt its virtue *till this moment.* Now I die happy."

The Beloved Physician Walter C. Palmer's Sunlit Journey To Heaven

Dr. Palmer's biographer, Rev. George Hughes, gives the following account:

At 5:15 p.m., July 20, 1883, Dr. Palmer's ransomed spirit

entered the triumphal chariot and, under a bright angelic escort, sped away to the world of light and blessedness. There was no dark river to cross — no stormy billows to intercept his progress. It was a translation from the terrestrial to the celestial — the work of a moment, but covered with eternal resplendency.

Heaven's pearly gates were surely opened wide to admit this battle-scarred veteran, laden with the spoils and honors of a thousand battles. The light of a conqueror was in his eye. His countenance was radiant. His language was triumphant. The angelic escort was near. The expanded vision was rapturously fixed on immortal objects and scenes. The ear was saluted with the songs of angels and redeemed spirits. The blood-washed soul was filled with high expectancy. Every avenue of the inner being was swept with rapture. Hallelujahs burst momentarily from his lips.

The aspect of such a departure was gorgeous indeed — no other word will express it. The splendors of the eternal state were gathered into a focus and burned intensely around the couch of the Christian warrior as he breathed his earthly farewell. He died only a few steps from his cottage-home, while the grand old ocean ceaselessly rolled its billows upon the sand, making solemn music and offering a deep-toned anthem of praise to the Creator. The clear blue heavens above were resplendent. The sun was declining, but glorious in its decline.

Not far away was the hallowed grove, the place of holy song and Gospel preaching, where multitudes congregated. And there, too, the "James Tabernacle" where such indescribable triumphs had been won. Even now we seem to hear the forest resounding with prayer and praise.

Oh, the glorious scenes which those trees had witnessed:

In yonder cottage there is one newly born into the kingdom of heaven. The first song of the new life is breaking upon the ears of surrounding friends. Hallelujahs rule the hour.

In a little tent there is a child of God who has just entered "Beulah Land!" He is inhaling its pure atmosphere. The fragrance of the land delights him. He is basking in the meridian rays of the "Sun of righteousness". What a heavenly glow there is upon his countenance! How the Beulah-notes burst from his lips!

Hark! Yonder is the shout of victory! What does it mean? Ah, one of God's dear saints has been sorely buffeted of Satan, but "Strong in the strength which God supplies through His eternal Son," she has just said, authoritatively, in overcoming faith, *"Get thee behind me, Satan!"* And, lo, the enemy is discomfited — he flies ingloriously from the field! Jesus, in the person of His tempted one, has driven the arch-foe to his native Hell.

And so we might go on and on. At each step new wonders rise upon our view. Heaven and earth were surely keeping jubilee in this sacred enclosure.

Can we conceive of a grander spot, in either hemisphere, from which a good man might make his transition from world to world? Is it not written, "My times are in Thy hand"? And are not the *places*, too, at the Divine disposal? Did not Jehovah conduct His servant of old to the Mount of transition, and Himself perform the funeral-rites and interment? And so secure was the entombment, so hidden from the rude gaze of men, that the ages have not discovered the burial-place.

Is it too much to think that the God of glory put forth His hand to designate the place for the departure of His honored servant, Dr. Palmer? And then, what a quiet hour — just as the sun was declining and the soft evening shades were being stretched forth! What an evening, after such a day!

All day long the beloved one had been quietly reclining upon his couch. A new light had been given to his languid eye. A radiant smile illuminated his whole countenance. Inspiring words dropped from his lips. Loving friends, who had kept sleepless vigils around him, rejoiced with great joy.

The day had been a festive one. The table of the Lord had been spread before him, and he had feasted upon its dainties. At the foot of his couch had been suspended the book, "The Silent Comforter", telling of the riches of the kingdom of heaven. It was open at the passage for the day, reading thus:

> *"But now thus saith the Lord that created thee, O Jacob, and He that formed thee, O Israel, Fear not: for I have redeemed thee, I have called thee by thy name; thou art mine.*
>
> *"When thou passest through the waters, I will be with thee: and through the rivers, they shall not overflow thee: when thou walkest through the fire, thou shalt not be burned; neither shall the flame kindle upon thee.*
>
> *"For I am the Lord thy God, the Holy One of Israel, thy Savior."* (Isaiah 43:1-3)

What beautiful words — beautiful words of life! Well might that prostrate one rise into new life as he gazed upon the glittering pages. Indeed, he had during the weeks of his suffering taken refuge in the precious Word, so that the wicked one had not dared to approach him!

About two weeks before, Mrs. Palmer said to him, "My dear, Satan has not troubled you much of late." Raising his arm, with emphatic voice he exclaimed, "No! He has not been allowed to come near me!"

So strong was the doctor's returning pulse that those with him were encouraged to have him dressed and seated in an easy chair where he could look upon the ocean and be invigorated by its breezes. Indeed, he walked out and took his seat on the upper piazza. The beloved of his life was by his side, and a letter written later to a friend beautifully describes what transpired at this particular juncture:

"About three in the afternoon, he walked out on the second-story balcony, sat there a half-hour or more and seemed unusually joyous. He talked of the beautiful landscape before him and the grand old ocean. Seeing our dear friend Mr. Thornly, who had so kindly relieved us of the care of the morning meetings, our loved one waved his hand again and again, with smiles of affectionate recognition. He then went into the room and wrote a business letter to his son-in-law, Joseph F. Knapp, and read it to me in a strong voice.

"About five o'clock he proposed lying down to rest. His head had scarcely reached the pillow, when I was startled by seeing those large blue eyes open wide, as if piercing the Heavens. Two or three struggles, as if for breath, followed.

"'Raise me higher,' he said, as I put my arm about him, holding him up. A moment's calm ensued. I said, 'Precious darling, it's passing over.' The dear one, putting his finger on his own pulse, looking so sweetly, said in a low tone, 'Not yet' — and almost in the same breath, in a clear, strong voice, said, *'I fear no evil, for Thou art with me.'* After a moment's pause, he continued, *'I have redeemed thee; thou art mine. When thou pass . . .'* Here his loved voice failed. The precious spirit was released to join the glorified above."

Calconis (about) A.D. 108

Calconis was a Pagan. However, while watching the martyrdom of two Christian brothers, their wonderful patience under terrible sufferings so struck him with admiration that he cried out, *"Great is the God of the Christians!"* He himself was then immediately put to death.

—*Dying Words* by A. H. Gottschall

"Oh! I Have Missed It At Last!"

Some time ago, a physician called upon a young man who was ill. He sat for a little while by the bedside, examining his patient, then honestly told him that he had but a very short time to live. The young man was astonished. He had forgotten that death often comes "in such an hour as ye think not".

At length he looked up into the face of the doctor and, with a most despairing countenance said, *"I have missed it — at last!"*

"What have you missed?" inquired the tender-hearted, sympathizing physician.

"I have missed it — at last," again he repeated.

"Missed *what*?"

"Doctor, I have missed the salvation of my soul."

"Oh, say not so — it is not so. Do you remember the thief on the cross?"

"Yes, I remember the thief on the cross. And I remember that he never said to the Holy Spirit, 'Go your way!' But I did. And now He is saying to *me*, 'Go your way!' "

He lay gasping a while. Then, looking up with a vacant, staring eye, he said, "I was awakened and was anxious about my soul a little time ago. But I did not want to be saved then. Something seemed to say to me, 'Don't put it off. Make sure of salvation.' I said to myself, 'I will postpone it.' I knew I ought not to do it. I knew I was a great sinner and needed a Savior. I resolved, however, to dismiss the subject for the present. Yet I could not get my own consent to do it until I had promised myself to take it up again, at a time more favorable. *I bargained away, resisted and insulted the Holy Spirit.* I never thought of coming to this. I meant to have made my salvation sure, but now — I have missed it!"

51

"You remember," said the doctor, "that there were some who came at the eleventh hour."

"My eleventh hour," he rejoined, "was when I had that call of the Spirit. I have had none since — shall not have. I am given over to be lost. Oh, I have missed it! I have sold my soul for nothing — a feather, a straw. Now I am undone forever!"

This was said with such indescribable despondency that the doctor said nothing in reply. After lying a few moments, he raised his head, and looking all around the room as if for some desired object. Then he buried his face in the pillow, and again exclaimed in agony and horror, *"Oh, I have missed it at last!"* and died.

"Now is the accepted time!" *"Today,* if ye will hear His voice, harden not your hearts" (Hebrews 3:7, 8).

—From *The Fire Brand*

Anne Camm A.D. 1705

"I am the Lord's! *His unspeakable peace I now enjoy.* I am full of assurance of eternal salvation. The Cross is the only way to the crown immortal. I have only *one* death to encounter."

—*Dying Words* by A. H. Gottschall

Augustus M. Toplady—
Author Of "Rock Of Ages"

Augustus M. Toplady died in London, August 11, 1778, at the age of thirty-eight. He was the author of those immortal words,

> *"Rock of Ages, cleft for me,*
> *Let me hide myself in Thee;*
> *Let the water and the blood,*
> *From Thy wounded side which flowed,*
> *Be of sin the double cure—*
> *Save from wrath and make me pure."*

He had everything before him to make life desirable, yet when death drew near, his soul exulted in gladness. He said, "It is my dying avowal that these great and glorious truths, which the Lord in rich mercy has given me to believe and enabled me

52

to preach, are now brought into practical and heartfelt experience. They are the very joy and support of my soul. The consolations flowing from them carry me far above the things of time and sense."

Frequently he called himself a dying man and yet the happiest man in the world; adding, "Sickness is no affliction, pain no curse, death itself no dissolution; and yet how this soul of mine longs to be gone — like a bird imprisoned in its cage, it longs to take its flight. Had I wings like a dove, then would I fly away to the bosom of God and be at rest forever."

About an hour before he died he seemed to awaken from a gentle slumber. "Oh, what delights! Who can fathom the joys of the third Heaven? What a bright sunshine has been spread around me! I have not words to express it. I know it cannot be long now till my Savior will come for me, for . . . " He burst into a flood of tears as he continued, "*Surely after the glories that God has manifested to my soul!* All is light, light, *light* — the brightness of His own glory! O come, Lord Jesus, come; come quickly!"

Then he closed his eyes, his spirit going to be "with Christ"; his body falling asleep, to be awakened with others of like precious faith on that great day "when the Lord Jesus shall be revealed from Heaven with His mighty angels, to be glorified with His saints and admired in all them that believe" (II Thess. 1:10).

— *The Contrast Between Infidelity and Christianity*

Clement Brown

When about to die he pointed with his finger and said, "I see one, two, three, four, five angels waiting their commission. I see them as plainly as I see you, Hester. How I wish you could see them! They are splendidly robed in white. They beckon me, and Jesus bids me come."

—*Dying Words* by A. H. Gottschall

To Heaven And Back

An older woman of our acquaintance told us a story that has greatly impressed me. She is perhaps around seventy now, but she tells of a time in her youth when she became very ill and was in the hospital for nine months with goiter and gland trouble. Her young husband watched over her with loving care, anxious that she should get well and be able to raise their little two year old child.

One day, however, she felt her spirit leaving her body, and looking back at the hospital room she saw her husband weeping uncontrollably and the doctor shaking his head as they looked at her body lying on the bed.

When she got to Heaven, she met an angel who, I suppose, was going to lead her. Then suddenly she saw a young man and said, "Why Tom, I didn't know you were up here."

He answered, "I didn't know you were here either."

She said, "I have just come."

"So have I," he replied.

Suddenly the angel said to the woman, "But you are going back to earth for a while."

For a moment she was disappointed, for she said Heaven was the most beautiful, peaceful, wondrous place — far beyond anything she had ever dreamed. Then she thought of her husband and little child and said, "Alright, I guess I should go back to them."

Suddenly she was back on the bed in the hospital room. The doctor opened one of her eyes and exclaimed to her husband, "Why this girl is going to live!" He was so excited that he kissed her cheek.

A little later her husband was called for a long distance call, and it was Tom's father. He said, "I have bad news for you. My son Tom has just been killed in an automobile accident."

—Mrs. F. W. Strine, Dallas, Texas (1967)

Return From Tomorrow

Is it possible to have a glimpse into the next life? Dr. George C. Ritchie, Jr. — a Richmond, Virginia, physician — answers this question with a step-by-step account of his amazing "return from tomorrow."

When I was sent to the base hospital at Camp Barkeley, Texas, early in December, 1943, I had no idea I was seriously ill. I'd just completed basic training, and my only thought was to get on the train to Richmond, Virginia, to enter medical

54

school as part of the Army's doctor-training program. It was an unheard-of break for a private, and I wasn't going to let a chest cold cheat me out of it.

But days passed and I didn't get better. It was December 19 before I was moved to the recuperation wing, where a jeep was to pick me up at four A.M. the following morning to drive me to the railroad station.

A few more hours and I'd make it! Then about nine P.M. I began to run a fever. I went to the ward boy and begged some aspirin.

Despite the aspirin, my head throbbed, and I'd cough into the pillow to smother the sounds. Three A.M. — I decided to get up and dress.

The next half-hour is a blur for me. I remember being too weak to finish dressing. I remember a nurse coming to the room, and then a doctor, and then a bell-clanging ambulance ride to the x-ray building. Could I stand, the captain was asking, long enough to get one picture. I struggled unsteadily to my feet. The whir of the machine is the last thing I remember.

When I opened my eyes, I was lying in a little room I had never seen before. A tiny light burned in a nearby lamp. For a while I lay there, trying to recall where I was. All of a sudden I sat bolt upright. The train! I'd miss the train!

Now I know that what I am about to describe will sound incredible. I do not understand it any more than I ask you to; all that I can do is relate the events of that night as they occurred. I sprang out of bed and looked around the room for my uniform. Not on the bedrail. — I stopped, staring. Someone was lying in the bed I had just left.

I stepped closer in the dim light, then drew back. He was dead. The slack jaw, the gray skin were awful. Then I saw the ring. On his left hand was the Phi Gamma Delta fraternity ring I had worn for two years.

I ran into the hall, eager to escape the mystery of that room. Richmond, that was the all-important thing — getting to Richmond. I started down the hall for the outside door.

"Look out!" I shouted to an orderly bearing down on me. He seemed not to hear, and a second later he had passed the very spot where I stood as though I had not been there.

It was too strange to think about. I reached the door, went through and found myself in the darkness outside, speeding toward Richmond. Running? Flying? I only know that the dark earth was slipping past while other thoughts occupied my mind, terrifying and unaccountable ones. The orderly had not seen me. What if the people at medical school could not see me either?

In utter confusion I stopped by a telephone pole in a town by a large river and put my hand against the guy wire. At least the wire seemed to be there, but my hand could not make contact with it. One thing was clear: in some unimaginable way I had lost my firmness of flesh, the hand that could grip the wire, the body that other people saw.

I was beginning to know too that the body on that bed was mine, unaccountably separated from me, and that my job was to get back and rejoin it as fast as I could.

Finding the base and the hospital again was no problem. Indeed I seemed to be back there almost as soon as I thought of it. But where was the little room I had left? So began what must have been one of the strangest searches ever to take place: the search for myself. As I ran from one ward to the next, past room after room of sleeping soldiers, all about my age, I realized how unfamiliar we are with our own faces. Several times I stopped by a sleeping figure that was exactly as I imagined myself. But the fraternity ring, the Phi Gam ring, was lacking, and I would speed on.

At last I entered a little room with a single dim light. A sheet had been drawn over the figure on the bed, but the arms lay along the blanket. On the left hand was the ring.

I tried to draw back the sheet, but I could not seize it. And now that I had found myself, how could one join two people who were so completely separate? And there, standing before this problem, I thought suddenly:

"This is death. This is what we human beings call 'death,' this splitting up of one's self." It was the first time I had connected death with what had happened to me.

In that most despairing moment, the little room began to fill with light. I say "light," but there is no word in our language to describe brilliance that intense. I must try to find words, however, because incomprehensible as the experience was to my intellect, it has affected every moment of my life since then.

The light which entered that room was Christ: I knew this because a thought was put deep within me, "You are in the presence of the Son of God."

I have called Him "light," but I could also have said *"love,"* for that room was flooded, pierced, illuminated by the most *total compassion* I have ever felt. It was a Presence so comforting, so joyous and all-satisfying, that I wanted to lose myself forever in the wonder of It.

But something else was present in that room. With the presence of Christ (simultaneously, though I must tell it one by one) also had entered every single episode of my ent're life. There they were, every event and thought and conversation, as palpable as a series of pictures. There was no first or last; each one was contemporary; each one answered a single question, "What did you do with your time on earth?"

I looked anxiously among the scenes before me: school, home, scouting and the cross-country track team — a fairly typical boyhood, yet in the light of that Presence it seemed a trivial and irrelevant existence.

I searched my mind for good deeds.

"Did you tell anyone about Me?" came the question.

"I didn't have time to do much," I answered. "I was planning to, then this happened. I'm too young to die!"

"No one," the thought was inexpressibly gentle, *"is too young to die."*

And now a new wave of light spread ·through the room already so incredibly bright, and suddenly we were in another world. Or rather, I suddenly perceived all around us a very different world occupying the same space. I followed Christ through ordinary streets and countrysides, and everywhere I saw this other existence strangely superimposed on our familiar world.

It was thronged with people — people with the unhappiest faces I ever have seen. Each grief seemed different. I saw businessmen walking the corridors of the places where they had been working, trying vainly to get someone to listen to them. I saw a mother following a 60-year-old man, her son I guessed, cautioning him, instructing him. He did not seem to be listening.

Suddenly I was remembering myself, that very night, caring about nothing but getting to Richmond. Was it the same for these people: had their hearts and minds been all concerned with earthly things, and now, having lost earth, were they still fixed hopelessly here? I wondered if this was hell. To care most when you are most powerless; this would be hell indeed.

I was permitted to look at two more worlds that night — I cannot say "spirit worlds" for they were too real, too solid. Both were introduced the same way; a new quality of light, a new openness of vision, and suddenly it was apparent what had been there all along. The second world, like the first, occupied this very surface of the earth, but it was a vastly different realm.

57

Here was no absorption with earthly things, but — for want of a better word to sum it up — with truth.

I saw sculptors and philosophers here, composers and inventors. There were universities and great libraries and scientific laboratories that surpass the wildest inventions of science fiction.

Of the final world I had only a glimpse. Now we no longer seemed to be on earth, but immensely far away, out of all relation to it. And there, still at a great distance, I saw a city — but a city, if such a thing is conceivable, constructed out of light. At that time I had not read the Book of Revelation, nor, incidentally, anything on the subject of life after death. But here was a city in which the walls, houses, streets, seemed to give off light, while moving among them were beings as blindingly bright as the One who stood beside me. This was only a moment's vision, for the next instant the walls of the little room closed around me, the dazzling light faded, and a strange sleep stole over me. . . .

To this day, I cannot fathom why I was chosen to return to life. All I know is that when I woke up in the hospital bed in that little room, in the familiar world where I'd spent all my life, it was not a homecoming. The cry in my heart that moment has been the cry of my life ever since: *Christ, show me Yourself again!*

It was weeks before I was well enough to leave the hospital, and all that time one thought obsessed me: to get a look at my chart. At last the room was left unattended. There it was in terse medical shorthand: Pvt. George Ritchie, died December 20, 1943, double lobar pneumonia.

Later, I talked to the doctor who had signed the report. He told me there was no doubt in his mind that I had been dead when he examined me, but that nine minutes later the soldier who had been assigned to prepare me for the morgue had come running to him to ask him to give me a shot of adrenalin. The doctor gave me a hypo of adrenalin directly into the heart muscle, all the while disbelieving what his own eyes were seeing. My return to life, he told me, without brain damage or other lasting effect, was the most baffling circumstance of his career.

Today, over 20 years later, I feel that I know why I had the chance to return to this life. It was to become a physician so that I could learn about man and then serve God. And every time I have been able to serve our God by helping some broken-hearted adult, treating some injured child or counseling

58

some teenager, then deep within I have felt that He was there beside me again.

—George C. Ritchie, Jr., M.D.

ABOUT DR. RITCHIE:

In doing research for the Life After Death series, Guideposts *came across many fascinating stories similar to this experience described by Dr. Ritchie. His story was chosen, however, because there is documentary evidence available supporting the circumstances surrounding it.* Guideposts *has in its possession affidavits from both the Army doctor and attending nurse on the case which attest to the fact that Dr. Ritchie was pronounced dead on the morning of December 20, 1943.*

Probably as remarkable as the story itself is the transformation it caused in Dr. Ritchie's life — a transformation which changed him from an indifferent Christian into a man whose life is centered in Christ. For 18 years he has been active in youth work in Richmond, Virginia, and in 1957 he founded the Christian Youth Corps of America *for the purpose of helping to develop Christian character in our young people. Dr. Ritchie's vision is "a world run by men who are run by God."*

—Reprinted from *Guideposts* Magazine
Copyright 1963 *Guideposts Associates, Inc.,* Carmel, N.Y.

Elizabeth B. Browning A.D. 1861

This famous English Poetess declared at one time, "We want the touch of Christ's hand upon our literature."
Her last words were, *"It is beautiful!"*

—*Dying Words* by A. H. Gottschall

The Dying Experience Of A Wealthy Man

"How shall we escape if we neglect so great salvation?"
Hebrews 2:3

A man, whom we shall leave anonymous, spent his life amassing a fortune without giving any attention to his soul's salvation. When he came to die his wealth was no satisfaction to him. In fact great anguish came upon him as he fully realized that he had spent his life in amassing wealth to the neglect of his soul.

In his dying condition he called in his brother-in-law to pray for him. This man said he called so loudly for mercy that he could scarcely hear himself pray or fix his thoughts on anything. After the prayer was over, the dying man took his friend's hand in both of his, and said as he shook it, "Good-by, John. Pray for me. I shall never see your face again." And he never did.

After he had gone away, a neighbor came in and seeing the condition he was in, said something must be done. "I would suggest that we do something to quiet his mind and fears." He then recommended a game of cards. "Cards!" the poor man exclaimed. "Cards for a dying man! How contemptible. I'm going into *eternity*! These are not what I want — I want *mercy*!"

A little later his son came into his room and said, "Father, what arrangements, if any, do you wish to make in regard to the property?" The dying man answered, "I have given all my life to gain property; I cannot take a dollar with me. The law and the family will have to take care of that. I want to take care of my soul. Property avails nothing — I want mercy!"

And so he died, calling upon God for mercy, though he left no evidence that he found it.

—*The Word*, as quoted in *Dying Testimonies*

Dying Without God

A youth at one of the large iron works in Sheffield, England, was accidentally thrown onto a red hot armor plate. When he was rolled off by his fellow-workmen, nearly all one side of his body was burned to the bone.

Some of the men cried, "Send for the doctor!" But the suffering youth cried, "Never mind the doctor! Is there anyone here that can tell me how to get saved? My soul has been neglected, and I'm dying without God. *Who can help me?*"

Three hundred men around him, but not one who could tell him the way of salvation. After twenty minutes of untold agony he died as he had lived — without God.

One man who saw this accident and heard the cries of the dying youth was a Christian who had fallen back into a sinful life. When I asked him about the incident, he said, "I have heard his cries ever since and so wished I could have stooped down and pointed him to Jesus — *but my life closed my lips."*

* * * *

Does our life tell the world that we are Christians — or does it close our lips when others need us most?

—Adapted from an article by William Baugh

Sir David Brewster A.D. 1835

This distinguished Scottish scientist (in the field of optics) died saying, "I shall see Jesus, and that will be grand. I shall see Him *who made the worlds."*

—*Dying Words* by A. H. Gottschall

A Young Man Returns To Tell Of Heaven

The following remarkable testimony was given by George B. Hilty to his daughter, Mrs. Carol Reeves of Hammett, Idaho. I've known the Hiltys for many years and even faintly remember David Hilty. I've heard this testimony several times, and in essence the re-telling has proved consistent.

—*Paul W. Miller, Hammett, Idaho*

In the year 1893 the Lord was speaking to David Hilty, a middle-aged, uneducated Mennonite farmer living in Hancock County, Ohio. God was calling him to yield himself for the service of ministering to his brethren, but David could not see how a Holy God would use such a man as he and would not surrender.

During this time that he was running away from God, David bought a different farm and moved into a house where, unknown to him, the former owners had died of tuberculosis. One member of the Hilty family after another became ill with this terrible disease. Two had bones in their legs infected, and the oldest son, Will, developed a lung infection.

One day they realized that Will, nearly twenty-one years old, was dying. His life was slipping away from his body, but his spirit was in such communion with his Lord that he told them he would be going Home in two weeks.

Then little Elizabeth, the baby of the family and just five

61

years old, told several members of the family one morning that she was going to Heaven too. "Jesus is going to take me Home *right away*," she said. It was as if she was happy to have received an invitation to go first on this journey her brother Will spoke of so often.

The parents had planned a trip by team and wagon up into Michigan, but decided to postpone it a few days, until their little girl got over her unnatural ideas about death. However, that very day Elizabeth was quiet and seemed unusually tired. Toward evening she became feverish and ill. About four o'clock the next morning she was gone — to be with her Jesus who told her He would be taking her home "right away".

As the last days of Will's life passed, he continued to praise and glorify God the Father and Jesus His Son, pleading with all who visited him to be converted and believe. Through cracked and bleeding lips he spoke of the surpassing joy of knowing Christ!

He longed to be released from his pain-filled body, and on the very day he had prophesied that he would go, he fell asleep in death.

But the mother's heart could not bear to say goodbye to another child. She refused to be consoled. The brother next to Will also felt torn with grief, and kneeling on the opposite side of the bed from his mother, he too wept and called, *"Will, don't die yet!"*

Moments passed, but the hearts of those who mourned Will's going could find no calm. Suddenly, a sister, standing at the foot of the bed, exclaimed, "Look, didn't Will's eyelids flutter?" All watched breathlessly as the still form stirred and breath again came through the blistered lips.

"Mother — John — don't weep for me. Don't call me back. *I've been with Jesus, and the glory and wonder of it is so great!* Your grief hurt me, and I asked permission to come and tell you to be glad. I had to promise not to tell you the secrets that God has prepared for His saints, but I want you to know *it is far, far more wonderful than anything you can imagine!"*

The boy's face shone with a heavenly light as he comforted his parents and brothers and sisters. When he again said, "Goodbye," and left, they were able to rejoice in his joy and believe that this was only a temporary separation.

David Hilty answered the call to be a minister and pastor. He allowed the power of God to change him into a new man

and an able teacher of the Word. The experience of this super-
natural act and the presence of the Holy Spirit that was so
evident in his resurrected son, Will, completely melted the unbelief that had held him bound.

John Brooks A.D. 1825

Governor of Massachusetts

"I see nothing terrible in death. In looking to the future
I have no fears, for I know in whom I have believed. I look
back upon my past life with humility and am sensible of many
imperfections that cleave to me, but I now rest my soul on the
mercy of my Creator, through the only Mediator, His Son, our
Lord Jesus.

"Oh, what a ground of hope there is in that saying of the
Apostle that *God is in Christ, reconciling the guilty world to
Himself, not imputing their trespasses unto them."*

He put out his hand and was asked, "What are you reaching for?"

A kingdom!" he whispered, just as he passed away.

—*Dying Words* by A. H. Gottschall

Carrie Carmen's Vision Of The Holy City

Young Carrie Carmen lay at death's door, perfectly conscious. Suddenly she gazed upward and exclaimed, "Beautiful!
beautiful! beautiful!"

Someone asked, "What is so beautiful?"

"Oh, they are so beautiful."

"What do you see?"

"Angels — and they are so beautiful."

"How do they look?"

"Oh, I can't tell you. They are so beautiful."

"Have they wings?"

"Yes — listen! They sing the sweetest of anything I have
ever heard."

"Do you see Christ?"

"No, but I see the Holy City that was measured with the

63

reed, whose length and breadth and height are equal, and whose top reaches to the skies. It is so beautiful; I can't tell you how splendid it is."

Then she repeated the verse beginning, "Through the valley of the shadow I must go." She also spoke of the loneliness of her husband, praying that he might have grace to bear his bereavement and that strength might be given him to go out and labor for souls. (They were expecting soon to enter the ministry.) She also prayed for her parents, asking that they might make an unbroken band in the beautiful city.

She closed her eyes and rested a moment, then looked up with beaming eyes and said, "I see Christ, and Oh, He is so beautiful!"

Her husband asked again, "How does He look?"

"I can't tell you; but He is so much more beautiful than all the rest." Again she said, "I see the Holy City." Then, after gazing a moment longer, she said, "So *many!*"

"What do you see, of which there are so many?"

"People."

"How many are there?"

"A great many — more than I can count."

"Any you know?"

"Yes, a great many."

"Who?"

"Uncle George and a lot more. They are calling me — they are beckoning to me."

"Is there any river there?"

"No, I don't see any."

Her husband then said, "Carrie, do you want to go and leave me?"

"No, not until it is the Lord's will that I should go. I would like to stay and live for you and God's work. *His will be done.*"

Presently she lifted her eyes and said, "Oh, carry me off from this bed." Her husband said, "She wants to be removed from the bed." But her father said, "She is talking with the angels." When asked if she were, she replied, "Yes."

She then thanked the doctor for his kindness and asked him to meet her in Heaven. She closed her eyes, and seemed to be rapidly sinking away.

Her husband tenderly kissed her and said, "Carrie, can't you kiss me?"

She opened her eyes again and kissed him, saying, "Yes, I

can come back to kiss you. *I was part way over."*

She said little more, but prayed for herself and for her friends. Frequently she would gaze upward and smile as though the sights were very beautiful.

—From an article written by her pastor in *Christ Crowned Within*

James Guthrie A.D. 1661

Just before being beheaded, this Scottish minister cried, "The Covenants shall yet be Scotland's reviving. I would not exchange this scaffold for the palace!"

—*Dying Words* by A. H. Gottschall

Caliph Abd-er-Rahman III. A.D. 961
(Ommyade, Sultan of Spain)

"Fifty years have passed since first I was Caliph. Riches, honors, pleasures — I have enjoyed all. In this long time of seeming happiness I have numbered the days on which I have been happy. *Fourteen."*

—*Dying Words* by Gottschall

The Supreme Moment

How many times I've nodded gratefully when I heard the statement, "He died quietly in his sleep." Then two years ago my husband passed away. He died awake. Alert. Participating in the momentous event with his whole mind. And in doing so he left me a legacy of faith that I want to pass on to all who fear to trust God in life's most supreme moment.

I wish I could relate some stirring event of my husband's 54 years on earth to make you understand how he was able to accept the challenge of death. But his simply was not a dramatic life. Fred seemed happiest working in his nursery which he called Chinquapin Farm. It was here, on a Mississippi Bayou beneath ancient streamers of Spanish moss, that he grew his surpassingly lovely camellias.

I used to get secret pleasure from watching this modest, deeply honest man struggling to write truthful advertising for his plants. He debated a long time before he settled on the slogan "Root Strength."

"All growth," he wrote, "comes from a good root stock."

I believe now that in these years on Chinquapin Farm he was sending down his own spiritual roots. He learned the farmer's respect for God's timing, the gardner's reverence for the power that can transform a little brown seed into a blossoming bush. Somehow the beauty of nature enabled him to see deep into the wonder of creation.

But it was only after a pain in his left arm was diagnosed as an inoperable malignancy that he was able to talk aloud about these things. All our married life he'd read the Bible each evening as his last act of the day. But now Fred was able for the first time to speak to me about his personal faith: a faith that extended to all life's processes, even to its pain and death.

Because he believed that even these things are part of a whole, acceptable to God, he was able to ease my anguish and come swiftly to terms with the physical ordeal of the illness. As a result, Fred rarely resorted to strong, pain-killing drugs through nearly two years of the disease.

As news of his illness spread, letters of concern poured in from people I had never heard of, and I learned something else: that he had been as much a giver-away of plants as a seller. Other people's pleasure meant a lot to him; I had never known how much. During a period of treatment in Texas we sat by a fire one night opening letters from people who were enjoying his flowers, and I looked up suddenly to see tears of sheer joy streaming down his face.

It was not until he entered the hospital for the last time, however, that he spoke of the wish closest to his heart. Paralysis had come overnight and unexpectedly. Then, as we waited for the ambulance needed to move him, he said suddenly, "Do you believe that if I ask God for something personal for myself He will grant it?"

"I know He will," I said.

"Then I'll ask Him." He closed his eyes and was silent so long that the words when they came startled me, "*I want to die in dignity.*"

One of the supreme moments of life was approaching, he said. He wanted to go into it with his mind clear, and his one fear was that someone would dope him and rob him of the

66

experience. "Don't you let them give me any high-powered drugs at the last to drag me back!"

I promised, not knowing exactly how I was going to influence a hospital staff. And in the end I did nothing at all. No one else knew of this last wish of his: a Power stronger than any human one worked to grant it to him.

The weeks passed. Fred gradually weakened. Late one afternoon he told me he thought I should go back to the motel and get a nap. "But be sure you come back before midnight," he concluded.

A little puzzled at these specific directions, I went back to the motel. After spending 18 hours a day at the hospital for two weeks, I was exhausted. I bathed, slept and had a quiet dinner. At 9:45 I wondered if I should write a letter, read, or go straight to the hospital. Suddenly I felt two strong hands on my shoulder turning me toward the door, compelling me to get to the hospital.

Soon I was tiptoeing down the quiet hall. The door stood ajar, and I peeped in, expecting Fred to be asleep. The nurse was standing with her back to the bed. Fred was wide awake, his eyes bright and alert.

In a perfectly normal voice he said, "I'm dying." The nurse seemed not to hear him. I walked in as if I hadn't heard either and said in a cheery voice, "Hello, Freddie, I've come to stay with you."

"That's fine, Sweetie, for I'm dying." And with that he closed his eyes, took four or five deep breaths and began talking in a low voice. I leaned closer to hear.

This is what he was saying, "I love God. I love my family. God, I'm coming." Over and over he said, *"God, I'm coming . . ."* his breathing getting shallower and shallower but always easy. Then his voice trailed off until he didn't breathe any more. I stood transfixed, my hand on his head.

Now the room was full of nurses, while an intern frantically slapped his hand. I remember hearing the hall nurse say, "We don't have anything on his chart to give him. He wasn't expected to die now." They were trying to get in touch with his doctors. "I don't understand how they could *both* be out," the intern kept saying.

But I understood, and kept a silent chorus of praise rising to God.

Now the intern was speaking to me, but he seemed to be on the other side of a cloud. I couldn't see any of them clearly;

67

everything was soft focus. I knew something beyond sense was happening in that room. I didn't try to understand it. I just let the impressions come into my being, believing I would be given the meanings later.

The intern took me to a small room to wait for the doctors. The room was utterly still. This was the first moment of inactivity in nearly two years of Fred's illness. I just laid my head down on the table and rested.

At last the two doctors came in together. They spoke the kindly phrases of sympathy and kept using words like "unusual" and "remarkable" and "unexpected." In effect, they were saying, "We've never known anyone to go in such an open, clear-eyed manner."

Our grown son and daughter hurried home, the funeral was held, and still I was haunted by the feeling that the most significant part of Fred's death lay just beneath the surface of my consciousness. Something immense and wonderful had happened in that hospital room — something I had known — and yet not quite known.

It was summertime before the answer was given to me. I was lying in the hammock one day, gazing up at a white oak tree when I noticed an empty cicada shell clinging to the bark. The yard was full of them at this time of year, yet I'd never seen an insect actually shedding its case. Perhaps, I thought, it happens in the very early morning.

The following morning I was outdoors before sunrise, waiting before the same tree. Sure enough, a fat gray cicada larva soon began to climb the trunk. A more purposeful act I've never seen; the cicada moved slowly up the tree, feeling with his claws for a suitable place.

At last about seven feet up the trunk he found the right spot. I ran for a stepladder, my heart beating with a strange excitement. Now the shell was firmly anchored to the solid tree, and a thin, barely perceptible line appeared down its back. Inside, the winged creature was struggling to be free. It would push forward, rest, push backward, rest. Then it twisted from side to side. At last it broke loose, and the new insect lay beside its old house, exhausted, new wings still folded.

I scarcely moved, for I had the uncanny feeling that I had watched it all before. The wings slowly expanded and grew as they moved back and forth gently in the breeze. When the wings dried in the sunlight, I caught my breath: they were all irridescent color and light. The glorious thing then soared off above me, and I was left staring at the tree trunk and the gray, earth-bound body which had housed that unimaginable splendor.

And still the feeling of familiarity persisted, the conviction that I had watched this miracle before. Several weeks later I remembered. It had taken place in the hospital room and *what I had watched was the eager, willful thrust of the soul toward a new beginning.*

What I actually saw in that room, I have never recaptured except in terms of the cicada. I only know that Fred's spirit struggled to be free from a body grown suddenly too small, that there was no break in his consciousness as the tremendous transition took place and that he was there in that room even after the shell was laid aside, but in a form too marvelous for me to grasp. I know that he stepped with God to the very door of death and found Him utterly trustworthy for that supreme moment and beyond.

—Ann Moreton, Powhatan, Virginia
—Reprinted from *Guideposts* Magazine

Thomas Hauks A.D. 1555

After being condemned to death at the stake, he agreed with his friends that if God would give him grace to so endure the pains of burning as to show some sign, he would raise his hands above his head before dying.

With a strong chain about his waist he addressed the crowd, and as the fire was kindled, he poured out his soul to God in prayer. Soon his speech was taken away by the violence of the flames, his skin drawn together and his fingers consumed. When everyone thought he was dead, suddenly, and contrary to all expectation, *he reached up his burning hands and clapped them three times together.* Then sinking down in the fire he gave up his spirit.

"I Am In The Flames—Pull Me Out, Pull Me Out!"

Mr. W—, the subject of this narrative, died in New York about the year 1883 at the age of seventy-four. He was an avowed infidel. He was a good neighbor in some respects, but he was very wicked and scoffed at Christianity. About seven years prior to his death he attended a revival and the Spirit strove with him, but he resisted to the last.

One Sunday after this, a local lay-preacher who related this sketch, while on his way to church, passed Mr. W—'s house and saw him standing by the gate. He said, "Come with me to church, Mr. W—."

The infidel, holding out his hand, replied, "Show me a hair on the palm of my hand, and I will show you a Christian."

When Mr. W— was stricken with his last sickness, it was this preacher who called on him often, sat up with him several nights and was even with him when he died. The infidel was conscious of his near-approaching end and now, when too late, was also conscious of the terrors of his lost condition.

On one occasion he said, "Warn the world not to live as I have lived, and escape my woe."

At another time when visited by a doctor, he was groaning and making demonstrations of great agony. The doctor said, "Why do you groan; your disease is not painful?"

"Oh, doctor," said he, "it is not the body but the *soul* that troubles me!"

On the evening of his death, as the burdened preacher, with a friend, entered the room, he felt that it was filled with an awful presence — as if he were near the region of the damned. The dying man cried out, *"Oh, God! — deliver me from that awful pit!"* It was not a penitential prayer, but the *wail* of a lost soul.

About fifteen minutes before his death, which happened to be at twelve midnight, he exclaimed, *"I am in the flames — pull me out, pull me out!"* He kept repeating this, though as his strength failed his words became more faint. At last, the preacher put his ear down close to catch his departing whispers, and the last words he could hear were, *"Pull me out! Pull me out!"*

"It was an awful experience," he said. "It made an impression on me that I can never forget. I *never* want to witness such a scene again."

Years later when talking to this preacher, he told me that those last terrible words, *"I am in the flames — pull me out, pull me out!"* were still ringing in his ears.

"Then shall he say also unto them on the left hand, Depart from me, ye cursed, into everlasting fire, prepared for the devil

and his angels: . . . And these shall go away into everlasting punishment: but the righteous into life eternal . . . there shall be weeping and gnashing of teeth." —Matthew 25:41, 46, 30

—Adapted from an article by Rev. C. A. Balch,
Cloverville, N.Y.

God's Grace To A "Weak Believer"

In December of 1966, my dear mother died of cancer. Mom was what might be termed a "weak" believer. By this I mean that her spiritual roots were not deep enough to enable her to face death with victory. It was obvious that she dreaded it and avoided every mention of the subject. This concerned us and we prayed definitely.

As the end neared she still clung to life, fearing to take the plunge into the unknown. However, when finally she was forced over the edge of that cliff she found that though she believed not, yet He abideth faithful, and underneath *were* those everlasting Arms. She died with a definite testimony.

The day before the end she said, "I asked the Lord to take me last night, but He said it wasn't time yet."* Then when the doctor came in, she simply said to him, "I am ready to die." When we asked if she had actually talked with the Lord, she answered in effect, "Of course" — as if there was nothing at all unusual about this!

To me this was a triumph of God's love and grace. If Mom had been a strong Christian and thus with great faith marched boldly into the jaws of death, one might have expected the Lord to so respond; but when He did so anyway, it revealed His great and tender heart of love — truly all the glory was His! Also, we thank Him and were so comforted that Mom's passing was not accompanied by the great pain which usually comes with cancer of this sort.

But the story doesn't end here, for the tidings of one victory always touch off others. The above account of my mother's passing was included in our Jan.-Feb. 1967 newsletter, and later we received the following note from one of the readers:

"Right after I received the newsletter in which Mr. Myers told about his mother's death, I went home to see my cousin who also was dying from cancer. He had just accepted the Lord since the beginning of his illness, and he didn't want to die so

71

young — only thirty-one. He kept telling his dad this, and I could not but remember the newsletter.

"I felt led to pray for him the same way Mr. Myers did for his dear mother. And you know, *from then on he wasn't afraid to die.* I could just feel the presence of the Lord and His great Love wrapping my cousin up in that Love. He was at peace from then on.

"Oh, it was such a blessing just to be able to know enough to ask the Lord to love him so much that he wouldn't be afraid. And it all came from remembering the newsletter. So may your hearts be lifted up in praise, too, for I'm sure many people have a share in these blessings!"

—John Myers, *Voice Christian Publications,*
Northridge, California

* Having been called away by business several days earlier, I was hastening to Mom's side at this time. She had been so very reluctant to see me go, and I'd promised that I would return — it would have been a crushing blow to me had she died before I arrived. Perhaps this is the reason for the Lord telling her it wasn't yet time. She remained conscious less than an hour after my arrival.

Dreadful Martyrdom Of Romanus

Romanus, a native of Palestine, was deacon of the church of Caesarea at the time of the commencement of Diocletian's persecution in the fourth century. He was at Antioch when the imperial order came for sacrificing to idols and was much grieved to see many Christians, through fear, submit to the idolatrous command and deny their faith in order to preserve their lives.

While reproving some of them for their weakness, Romanus was informed against and soon after arrested. Being brought to the tribunal, he confessed himself a Christian and said he was willing to suffer anything they could inflict upon him for his confession. When condemned, he was scourged, put to the rack and his body torn with hooks.

While thus cruelly mangled, he turned to the governor and thanked him for having opened for him so many mouths with which to preach Christianity — "For," he said, *"every wound is a mouth to sing the praises of the Lord."*

He was soon after slain by being strangled.

—*Foxe's Book of Martyrs*

"You'll Be A Duke, But I Shall Be A King"

Tuberculosis seized the eldest son and heir of the Duke of Hamilton and brought him to an early death. A little before his departure from the world, he lay ill at the family home near Glasgow. Two ministers came to see him. One of them, at his request, prayed with him.

After the minister had prayed, the dying youth put his hand back and took his Bible from under his pillow and opened it at the passage, *"I have fought a good fight, I have finished my course, I have kept the faith; henceforth there is laid up for me a crown of righteousness, which the Lord, the Righteous Judge, shall give me at that day; and not to me only, but unto all them also that love His appearing."*

"This, sirs," said he, "is all my comfort."

As he was lying one day on the sofa, his tutor was conversing with him on some astronomical subject and about the nature of the fixed stars.

"Ah," said he, "in a little while I shall know more of this than all of you together."

When his death approached, he called his brother to his bedside, and addressing him with the greatest affection and seriousness, he closed with these remarkable words, "And now, Douglas, in a little time you'll be a duke, *but I shall be a king!"*

—*Cheever*

An Atheist Said,

"There is one thing that mars all the pleasure of my life. I am afraid the Bible is true. If I could only know for a certainty that death is an eternal sleep, I should be happy. But here is what pierces my soul— *If the Bible is true, I am lost forever!"*

"The fool hath said in his heart, there is no God."

—*Psalm* 14:1

—*Dying Testimonies* by S. B. Shaw

73

Sir Philip Sidney

"I would not change my joy for the empire of the world."

Sir Philip Sidney was born in Kent, in the year 1554. He possessed shining talents, was well-educated and at the early age of twenty-one was sent by Queen Elizabeth as her ambassador to the Emperor of Germany.

He is described by the writers of that age as the finest model of an accomplished gentleman that could be formed, even in imagination. An amiable disposition, elegant erudition, and polite conservation rendered him the ornament and delight of the English court. Lord Brooke so highly valued his friendship that he directed to be inserted as part of his epitaph, "Here lies Sir Philip Sidney's friend." His fame was so widely spread that if he had chosen it, he might have obtained the crown of Poland.

But the glory of this Marcellus of the English nation was of short duration. When only thirty-two years old, he was wounded at the battle of Zutphen and died in about three weeks.

After receiving the fatal wound and being brought into a tent, he raised his eyes towards Heaven and acknowledged the hand of God in this event. He confessed himself a sinner and thanked God that "He had not struck him with death at once, but gave him space to seek repentance and reconciliation."

In the light of his new understanding of God, his former virtues seemed as nothing. When it was said to him that good men, in the time of great affliction, found comfort and support in the recollection of those parts of their lives in which they had glorified God, he humbly replied, "It is not so with me. I have no comfort that way. *All things in my former life have been vain.*"

On being asked whether he did not desire life merely to have it in his power to glorify God, he answered, "I have vowed my life unto God, and if He cut me not off, and suffer me to live longer, I shall glorify Him and give up myself to His service."

The nearer death approached, the more his consolation and hopes increased. A short time before the end, he lifted up his eyes and hands, and uttered these words, *"I would not change my joy for the empire of the world!"*

His advice and observations when saying farewell to his deeply afflicted brother are worthy of remembrance.

"Love my memory; cherish my friends. Their fidelity to me may assure you that they are honest. But, above all, govern your wills and affections by the will and Word of your Creator. *In me behold the end of the world and all its vanities.*

—Adapted from an article in the *Power of Religion*

"Jesus Will Take Care Of Me"

These were the last words uttered by twelve-year-old Ella Gilkey, as she passed away from earth to live with Him who said, "Suffer little children to come unto me, and forbid them not, for of such is the kingdom of heaven."

In the winter of 1860-61 I was holding a series of meetings in Watertown, Massachusetts, during which a large number found Jesus precious — many believing they found Him in my room, thus rendering that room ever memorable and dear to me.

Among those who there gave themselves to the Savior was Ella. Coming in one morning, with tears on her face, she said, "Mr. Earle, I came up here to give my heart to Jesus. I feel that I am a great sinner. Will you pray for me?"

I replied, "I will pray for you, Ella, and I can pray in faith if you see that you are a sinner — for Jesus died for sinners."

After pointing out the way of salvation, I asked her if she would kneel down by my side and pray for herself, and, as far as she knew, give herself to Jesus to be His forever.

She said, "I will; for I am a great sinner."

Could one so young and kind to everybody be a great sinner? Yes, because she had rejected the Savior until she was twelve years old. Whenever the Holy Spirit had knocked at the door of her heart, she had said, "No, not yet. Go Thy way for this time."

We kneeled down, and after I had prayed, she said, "Jesus, take me just as I am. I give myself to Thee forever. I will love and serve Thee all my life."

The door of her heart was now open, and Jesus entered and took possession. When she arose, the tears were gone from her face and .it was covered with a beautiful smile. I believe holy angels in that room witnessed the transfer of her heart to Jesus and then went back to Heaven to join in songs of thanksgiving, for the Bible says "joy shall be in heaven over one sinner that repenteth."

Ella then went downstairs, her face beaming with joy as

75

she thought of her new relationship to Jesus. She at once said to her mother, "I have given myself to Jesus, and He has received me. Oh, I am so happy!"

Little did we think that in only a few weeks she would be walking the "golden streets" with the blood-washed throng.

Like the Redeemer, who, when her age, said to His mother, "Wist ye not that I must be about My Father's business?" she seemed to long to be doing good.

> *"What can I do for Christ," she said,*
> *"Who gave His life to ransom me?*
> *I'll take my cross, and by Him be led,*
> *His humble, faithful child will be."*

Among other subjects of prayer there was one which particularly weighed upon her heart; it was for the conversion of an older brother. One day, after earnestly praying that this dear brother might be led to accept the Savior, she said to her mother, "Oh, I think he will be a Christian!" At another time she said, "I would be willing to die if it would bring him to Jesus."

Anxious to obey her Savior in all things, she obtained permission from her parents to present herself for baptism; and, in the absence of a pastor, I baptized her along with several others a few weeks after her conversion.

The next Tuesday after the baptism she was present at our evening meeting and gave her last public testimony for Jesus. Facing the congregation, she said in a clear, earnest tone, "If there are any here who have not given their hearts to Jesus, do it *now.*"

I was staying at the Gilkey home, and as I sat in my room that night after meeting, I heard Ella's sweet voice mingling with her father's in songs of praise until near the midnight hour.

Less than three days later she was called away from us to sing with the angels in Heaven the song of Moses and the Lamb.

As death drew near, she said to her parents, "I am going home," and commenced singing her favorite hymn,

> *O happy day, that fixed my choice*
> *On Thee, my Savior, and my God;*
> *Well may this glowing heart rejoice,*
> *And tell its raptures all abroad.*

"Yes," she whispered, "it *was* a happy day." Then looking up at her father, whose heart seemed almost broken, she slipped her arm around his neck and said, "Don't care for me, father — *Jesus will take care of me.*"

These were her last conscious words. The smile of affection on her face, the look of love in her eyes — and its pressure in her hand — lingered a little longer, and then her spirit took its flight.

On the first Sunday of February the church gave the hand of fellowship to a large number of new members, and Ella would have been with them had she lived. It so happened that near the place where she would have stood there was a vacant spot. I directed the attention of the large assembly to that opening and asked, "Where is Ella today?"

For a moment all was still, as the entire congregation appeared to be bathed in tears. Then I said, "Jesus seems to say, 'I have given Ella the hand of fellowship *up here.*'"

A few days after her death her parents were looking over her school things. In the middle of a blank book, unknown to anyone, as if intended only for God's eye, they found the following statement, which shows her depth of purpose and complete dedication to Christ:

"*December* 21, 1860. *This day I have given my heart to the Savior and have resolved to do just what He tells me to do and to take up my cross daily and follow Him — my eyes to weep over sinners and my mouth to speak forth His praise and lead sinners to Christ.*" — Ella J. Gilkey

In the vestry of the church at Watertown these words, printed in large type and beautifully framed, now hang upon the wall where all who enter may read them. So in the hours of Sunday school, the prayer meeting and social gatherings, little Ella, though in Heaven, still speaks and continues her work for Jesus.

—From *Bringing in Sheaves*

Adoniram Judson. A.D. 1850.

This famous American missionary to Burma died at sea. His last words were, "I go with the gladness of a boy bounding away from school. I feel *so strong* in Christ."

—*Dying Words* by A. H. Gottschall

"I Saw The Black Angel"

The following letter is from Mrs. Robert Snyder at Prairie Bible Institute in Three Hills, Alberta, Canada:

Because of a sad misunderstanding — perhaps because of pride on my part — I allowed my fifteen-year-old daughter to be in Southern California for a whole summer without visiting her grandmother.

This was such a terrible disappointment for my mother that she became very ill. I was told that she was in the hospital for three weeks hovering between life and death.

Can you imagine how I felt? The Word of God is needed at such a time to divide between soul and spirit. He showed me how much my motives needed purifying. But thank God for a merciful and faithful High Priest Who is touched with the feeling of our infirmities. What do you think that our loving and merciful God did? *He visited Mamma in that hospital room, raised her up and gave her a new song and a testimony that never wavered!*

Then three years later, when He took her Home, He united our family as never before. But let her tell it herself. I quote from a letter of November 11, 1962:

"Nita, I sure almost went over this time. I saw the black angel standing by my bed, but then someone else with a sweet, smiling face came, and I went to sleep. When I awakened I knew I'd get well, but it was the one with the lovely, sweet face who let me stay for a while longer. I wasn't one bit frightened. Indeed, I shut my eyes to say, "Thank you, Lord, for my release," then opened them, and this smiling one was there. A very wonderful experience. So now I must find out what I'm left over another time to do."

Then a very remarkable thing happened. The Holy Spirit recalled to Mamma's mind a song that she used to sing after her conversion in an old Methodist Camp Meeting in Texas. This was over sixty years before — think of the power of God's Spirit to recall memories! Mamma later got up and sang this song before about 100 people. It was also sung at Prairie Tabernacle for the Palm Sunday solo. Here are the words:

Night with ebon' pinions brooded o'er the vale
All around was silence, save the night wind's wail,
When Christ the Man of Sorrows with tears and sweat of blood
Prostrate in the garden raised His voice to God.

78

Smitten for offences which were not His own,
He for our transgressions had to weep alone;
No friend with words of comfort, no hand to help was there
When the Meek and Lowly humbly bowed in prayer.
"Abba, Father, Father, if it so might be,
Let this cup of anguish, oh, depart from Me!
But if it must be suffered by Me, Thine only Son,
Oh, Abba, Father, Father, let Thy will be done!"

Ann Knight. A.D. 1806.

"This has been a blessed night to me. I have seen Heaven, and they are all happy, so happy there. The Almighty has been so near to me. I feel that He was asking me to let go of all the world — which I can freely do — to possess that peace and happiness I have seen."

—*Dying Words* by A. H. Gottschall

The "Valley Of The Shadow" Was All Bridged Over

Sarah A. Cook, widely-known in the last century for her writings and evangelistic work, gives an account of the last days of her sister, who died in England during the spring of 1864. She says in her book, *Wayside Sketches:*

I was called to the sick bed of my eldest sister, Eliza, living in Melton Mowbray, Leicestershire. I found her suffering from intermittent fever and general prostration.

During the first stage of her sickness there seemed a strong clinging to life. Very happy in her marriage, surrounded by a circle of loving friends and being an earnest worker in the cause of the Redeemer, life for Eliza was full of attraction. Then, also, came the thought of her husband's loneliness without her, and she said, "I would be quite willing to go, but Harry would miss me so much."

Finally, however, faith triumphed over nature and she said, "The Lord could make Harry a happy home if He should take me."

Day by day the attraction Heavenward became stronger. Once, when all was fixed for the night and I was leaving the room, she called me to her. Looking earnestly into my face,

79

she said, "Sarah, don't pray for my recovery." I reminded her how much we all loved her, but she answered, "And I love you all very much, but it is so much better to depart and be with Jesus."

While with her during the day and listening to the doctor's cheery and hopeful words, I would think she might recover; but in prayer I could never take hold for her health. I could only breathe out, "Thy will, O Lord, not mine, be done."

The prayer of faith, in which at times our Father enables His children to take hold for the healing of the body, was never given. In His infinite love and wisdom He was calling her home; *"Where no storms ever beat on that beautiful strand, while the years of eternity roll."*

Every afternoon she liked to be left entirely alone for about an hour. The fever would then be off, and she chose it as the best time for secret communion with the Lord. When I opened the door one day, after the hour had passed, she sat upright in bed, her face simply radiant with joy as she exclaimed, "Oh, I have had *such* a view of God's love!"

Stretching out her hands, she said, "It seems to me like a *boundless* ocean — and as though *I were lost in that boundless ocean of love!"*

When suffering from extreme prostration, her favorite lines would be:

Christ leads us through no darker rooms
Than He went through before;
He that would to His Kingdom come,
Must enter by that door.

A dear friend said to her one day, "Do you have any fear of death?"

"Oh no," she answered, "I don't know that I have ever thought of it." The word "death" was never on her lips. The "valley of the shadow" *was all bridged over.* She did not see it, for the eye of faith swept over it and was fixed upon Him Who is the resurrection and the life. *"To be with Jesus!"* was her oft-repeated expression.

On Friday, with tenderest, deepest joy she repeated the whole of that beautiful hymn:

Forever with the Lord,
Amen, so let it be;
Life from the dead is in that word,
'Tis immortality.

80

Here in the body pent,
Absent from Him I roam;
Yet nightly pitch my moving tent
A day's march nearer home.

Sunday was her last day on earth. Seeing the end was very
near, I hesitated about leaving to teach her Bible-class at the
chapel, a large class of young women. I had been teaching them
every Sunday afternoon.

"Would you like me, dear, to take your class this afternoon?"
I asked softly.

"Yes," she answered with some surprise in her voice, "why
not?" It was a melting time as we together realized how near
the parting was. Finally she said, "Tell them all I have loved
and prayed for them very much."

The lesson that day was the words of comfort our Savior
had spoken to His disciples, as recorded in the 14th of John.
Afterwards I invited the whole class home, and they all passed
by the open door to take a last look at their loved teacher. Wonderfully all through the day the words which I had taught the
girls were applied to my own heart, "If ye loved me ye would
rejoice, because I go unto my Father." The thought of her exceeding blessedness in being so near the presence of Jesus
swallowed up all thoughts of sorrow at losing her.

Hour after hour passed, as the "silver cord was loosening."
An aunt who was present remarked, "You have had seven
weeks of peace."

"I have had seven weeks of *perfect* peace," she answered.
Truly, her peace flowed like a river all through the day.

With her head leaning on the bosom of her husband, the
last words that our listening ears caught were, "Though I walk
through the valley of the shadow of death, I will fear no evil, for
Thou art with me."

—Adapted from an article in *Wayside Sketches*

Judgment In A Young Man

A few years ago I was at a camp-meeting in Rockingham,
Vermont, when a gang of rowdies got together to break up
the meeting. They lived eight miles away, but on Thursday evening they came to the camp grounds to "have their fun," as they
told some of their friends. The plan was to lay trails of powder
into every tent and under the beds. When the town clock struck

twelve, all were to touch fire to the powder, then run to a distance and see the frightened women and children run and scream. At ten o'clock distant thunder was heard, and before midnight God sent one of the most terrific thunder storms I ever witnessed. It had been a warm day, and these young men had no coats with them. Now, with their powder all wet and their plans defeated, they were compelled to ride the eight miles back to their homes drenched with rain and chilled through and through.

The ringleader had to be carried into his house, benumbed with cold. His mother tried for hours to get him warm — then came a burning fever. He told her what he had done, saying, "Mother, I've got to die! Do pray! Do pray! What shall I do? Oh, how can I die?"

She said, "I never prayed."

"Then call Father," cried the dying man. But the father could not pray either.

Then he cried, clutching his hands and wringing them in agony, "I can't die so! I can't die so! Mother, Mother, do pray! *Do pray!*"

The father went to a Baptist deacon, but before he arrived the young man was past help. With distorted eyes, hands uplifted over his head and writhing in agony, he died raving. Among his last words were, "I'm going to Hell — I'm lost, lost, lost! I can't die so! I can't, I can't! Oh, Mother, it's awful to go to Hell this way!"

—Adapted from an article in *The Revivalist* by
Mrs. M. A. Sparling

Basilides (197-235)

Basilades was the captain of a party of heathen persecutors who executed the female martyr Potamiena. He had shown her some kindness in shielding her from the mob, and to repay his kindness the virgin girl said she would pray for him.

Soon afterwards he became a Christian and was beheaded. Before his execution, when asked the cause of his sudden decision to cast his lot with the saints, he said that Potamiena, three days after her martyrdom, stood by him in the night and put a crown upon his head. She said that she had entreated the Lord for him and that her request had been granted.

—*Dying Words* by Gottschall

"Ma, I Can't Die Till You Promise Me"

At the close of a series of meetings in Springfield, Massachusetts, a mother handed me a little girl's picture wrapped in two one-dollar bills, at the same time relating the following touching incident:

The picture was of her only child. At the age of six she gave her heart to the Savior, giving, as the pastor with whom I was laboring said, the clearest evidence of conversion.

At once she went to her mother and said, "Ma, I have given my heart to Jesus and He has received me; now, won't you give your heart to Him?" The mother replied, "I hope I shall some time, dear Mary." The little girl said, "Do it *now*, Ma!" urging the mother, with all her childlike earnestness, to give herself to the Savior right then.

Finding she could not prevail in that way, she sought to secure a promise from her mother, feeling sure she would do what she promised, since her parents had made it a point never to make her a promise without carefully fulfilling it. Time after time she would say, "Promise me, Ma"; and the mother would reply, "I do not like to make a promise to you, Mary, for fear I shall not fulfill it."

This request was urged at various times for nearly six years, and finally the little petitioner had to die to secure the promise. Several times during her sickness the parents came to her bedside to see her die. But she would say, "No, Ma, *I can't die till you promise me.*" Still her mother was unwilling to make the promise, lest it should not be kept. She intended to give her heart to Jesus sometime, but was unwilling to do it "now".

Mary grew worse and finally had uttered her last word on earth. Her mother was never again to hear that earnest entreaty, "Promise me, Ma." But the little one's spirit lingered, as if detained by the angel sent to lead the mother to Jesus — that the long-sought promise might be heard before it took its flight.

The weeping mother stood watching the countenance of the dying child, who seemed to say, by her look, "Ma, promise me, and let me go to Jesus!" There was a great struggle in her heart as she said to herself, "Why do I not promise this child? I mean to give my heart to Jesus; why not now? If I do not promise her now, I never can."

The Spirit inclined her heart to yield. She roused the child and said, "Mary, I *will* give my heart to Jesus." This was the last bolt to be drawn; her heart was now open. Jesus entered at once, and she felt the joy and peace of sins forgiven.

This change was so marked, that she felt constrained to tell the good news to her child, that she might bear it with her when she went to live with Jesus. So, calling her attention once more, she said, "Mary, I have given my heart to Jesus, and He is my Savior now!"

For six years Mary had been praying to God and pleading with her mother for these words. Now, as they fell upon her ear, a peaceful smile lighted up her face. No longer able to speak, she raised her pale little hand slightly, and pointing upward, seemed to say, "Ma, we shall meet up there." Her life's work was done, and her spirit returned to Him who gave it.

The mother's heart was full of peace, though her loved one had gone. But she now felt very anxious that her husband should have this blessing which she found in Christ. The parents went together into the room where the dead child lay, to look upon the face of her who slept so sweetly in death. The mother then said, "I promised our little Mary that I would give my heart to Jesus, and He has received me. Now, won't you promise?" The Holy Spirit was there. The strong man resisted for awhile, then yielded his will. Taking the little cold hand in his, he knelt and said, "Jesus, I will try to seek Thee."

The child's remains were laid in the grave. The parents were found in the house of prayer — the mother happy in Jesus, and the father, too, soon having some evidence of love of Christ.

When I closed my labors in Springfield, Dr. Ide said to his congregation, "I hope you will all give Brother Earle some token of your regard for his services before he leaves." As this mother heard these words, she said she could, as it were, see her little Mary's hand pointing down from Heaven, and heard her sweet voice saying, "Ma, give him my two one-dollars."

Those two one-dollars I have now, wrapped around the picture of that dear child, and wherever I go, little Mary will speak for the Savior.

—From *Bringing In Sheaves*

John Knox. A.D. 1572

As in the case of his friend Calvin, no tombstone marks the place where this great Reformer of Scotland is buried. When his body was laid in the grave the Earl of Morton said, "Here

lieth a man who in his life never feared the face of man."
Before dying he said, "By the grace of God I am what I
am. Live in Christ and the flesh need not fear death."

—*Dying Words* by A. H. Gottschall

"I Have Treated Christ Like A Dog All My Life And He Will Not Help Me Now"

About twenty years ago, when we were holding revival
meetings at G—, Mr. B—, a well-to-do farmer living near the
town, was in the last stages of tuberculosis. He was a wicked
man, all of his life having been spent in laying up treasures on
earth. The pastor of the Methodist church, whom we were assisting, had not as yet called on him because he was so ungodly.

The pastor said to me one day, "I am waiting until Mr. B—
is near his end, hoping he will then allow me to talk to him about
his soul." Thus, several days before his death, in company with
this pastor, we visited the man and talked with him about his
moral condition.

His mind was very dark and full of unbelief. We talked
earnestly with him about the saving of his soul but had to leave
him without receiving much encouragement.

In a day or two we called on him again and found him
more willing to converse, but he still seemed to be far away from
God. We pleaded with him, urging that he call on God to
have mercy on him for Jesus' sake.

"I cannot!" he cried. "I have never spoken the name of
Jesus except when using it in profanity, and I have used it that
way all of these years. *I have treated Christ like a dog all of my
life and He will not hear me now.* I would give all I am worth
if I could only feel as you say you feel."

We told him that God was no respecter of persons, that
He never turned any away that came to Him for pardon.

He continued, "*I cannot get any feeling. What can I do? My
heart is so hard.*"

Oh, how our hearts ached for him. He was afraid to die
without faith in God, but he seemed to have no ability to repent.

Before we left the town he went to meet his God, so far as
we know unprepared, as he gave no evidence of salvation. He

85

had treasures on earth; but, alas, that did not avail him anything when he came to face *eternity.*

Reader, how are you treating the Christ on whom you must depend if you are to be saved?

—Adapted from an article by S. B. Shaw in his book *Dying Testimonies*

Sir Walter Raleigh. A.D. 1618.

Just before being beheaded, this famous English admiral and courtier said, "It matters little how the head lies if the *heart* be right. Why dost thou not strike?"

—*Dying Words* by A. H. Gottschall

Triumphant Death Of John Calvin

Calvin's unremitting labors favored the inroads of a variety of distressing diseases which he suffered from for many years but bravely battled against or disregarded. He hated nothing so much as idleness.

On February 6, 1564, he preached with difficulty his last sermon. After that he left his house but a few times. In the midst of intense sufferings his spirit was calm and peaceful, and he occupied himself with the Bible and in prayer.

When the famed Farel, in his eightieth year, heard of his sickness, he wrote from Neuchatel that he would visit him. Calvin replied, in a letter dated May 2nd, "Farewell, my best and most right-hearted brother, and since God is pleased that you should survive me in this world, live mindful of our friendship, of which, as it was useful to the church of God, the fruit still awaits us in Heaven.

"I would not have you fatigue yourself on my account. I draw my breath with difficulty and am daily waiting till I altogether cease to breathe. *It is enough that to Christ I live and die . . . He is gain in life and death.* Farewell again — not forgetting the brethren."

On the 27th of May, as the sun was setting, he fell asleep in

Jesus. He was buried on the banks of the Rhone, outside of the city where he had so long labored in behalf of the Gospel of the Lord Jesus Christ. He asked that no monument be placed upon his grave; and the spot where the black stone was erected is only conjectured to be his burial-place.

Professor Tulloch well says of Calvin, "He was a great, intense and energetic character, who more than any other — even of that great age — has left his impress on the history of Protestantism."

His clear intellect and his logical acumen, together with his concise and crisp style, make his works, even in the present day, a power in the Church of God. He was needed in the church just as truly as Luther, Knox or Wesley, and we thank God for the gift of such a man.

—Heroes and Heroines

Captain John Lee. A.D. 1784

Captain Lee was executed for forgery. He had been an infidel, but before his death he said, "I leave to the world the mournful memento that however much a man may be favored by personal qualifications or distinguished mental endowments, his genius will be useless and his abilities avail little unless accompanied by religion and attended by virtue. *Oh, that I had possession of the meanest place in Heaven and could but creep into one corner of it!*"

—Dying Words by A. H. Gottschall

"I Am So Looking Forward To Seeing Jesus, I Would Be Disappointed Did Anything Happen To Prevent It"

My husband was a man very close to God. He often expressed a wish to be in the ministry but did not feel that was where God wanted him to serve. His was the quiet, personal ministry no one ever knew about except Jesus and the one approached.

In the spring of 1951 he was having trouble with his

87

stomach and thought he had ulcers. However, after a prolonged period of half-and-half with egg, the distress persisted, so he went in for a check. The doctors told us that nothing definite showed up on the examination and that they wanted to perform minor surgery.

Our daughter, in her junior year at high school, was programmed for the lead in a music festival, and he postponed the surgery a week so he might hear her sing.

On March 27th he went into surgery for what the doctor thought would be only a short period of time. After waiting in the lounge for better than two hours, I began to feel there was something more involved than just minor surgery. When the doctor finally came to see me he told me he had found a perforation in the top of the stomach of about 36 hours duration and that the lymph glands and other tissues showed some infection. He had removed four-fifths of the stomach, built a new elimination connection with the intestine and was sending the organs to the cancer lab at Houston. He added that he had no doubt the test would show positive malignancy.

He was right; the test showed malignancy. The glands had picked it up and scattered it throughout the system and blood stream. It was the most virulent type and would not respond to any type of treatment then known. It would recur within six to eight months, in the lungs — terminal within two months after that.

Homer seemed to accept the prognosis much easier than I. He began to heal and was able to accept food much sooner than the doctors expected. He regained his strength quickly, put on weight and felt very well. After returning to work May 28th, his co-workers and our friends even began to scoff at the idea he was living on limited time.

However, some of the men whom he had tried to witness to prior to his illness came to him and asked how he felt about the prospect of limited life. This time they were ready to listen to his declaration that life hereafter is more sure than life here. His witness bore fruit many times.

In September he began to tire easily and a slight cough developed. His monthly x-ray showed a slight shadow on the lung and at the next check the shadow was much larger. The doctor wanted to try radium in spite of the lab's verdict that it would not respond. They were correct; it didn't. Instead, it scattered, and he went downhill rapidly. By the first week in November he was no longer able to leave the bed, and the malignancy wrapped itself around the esophagus and he could not eat.

The men from the plant would drop in to cheer him up, but instead they would leave cheered themselves, for he expressed to them an actual *expectancy* at the prospect of seeing our Lord Jesus.

A close friend came one evening late in November and said, "Homer, I know you believe in God's healing power. Have you asked to be healed?"

His answer was simple and clear. "Mary, since I have come to feel that God has used this to reach people I had been unable to reach otherwise, I do not feel I have any right to ask Him to set aside His will. *Instead, I am so looking forward to seeing Jesus, I would be disappointed did anything happen to prevent it.*"

The following Tuesday he had a coughing attack, and the doctor suggested he get to the hospital. We went, and shortly after we reached there, after saying one more time, "Honey, never forget how much I love you!" he dropped off into a coma. In 48 hours he went home.

As I tell this story I want to thank God, for He was so merciful throughout the entire ordeal. At no time did Homer suffer.

—Hasula Hanna, Aurora, Colorado

Maggie Lindsay. A.D. 1874

Miss Lindsay was fatally injured in a railway collision in Scotland. After lying for several hours with both legs broken, her skull fractured and other internal injuries, she was at last rescued and removed to a cottage near by.

It was supposed she had been reading her much-loved hymn, "The gate ajar for me" since that page was stained with her blood. Lying upon a stretcher, with bleeding lips and dying breath she sang the two following stanzas:

> *Nothing, either great or small,*
> *Remains for me to do;*
> *Jesus died and paid it all,*
> *Yes, all the debt I owe.*
>
> *Oh, depths of mercy, can it be*
> *That gate stands open wide for me?*

—*Dying Words* by A. H. Gottschall

89

"It Was The Cursed Drink That Ruined Me"

To one of the Bellevue cells there came one morning a woman bearing the usual permit to visit a patient. She was a slender little woman with a look of delicate refinement that sorrow had only intensified. The physician was just leaving the patient as she approached. She looked at him with clear eyes which had wept often, but kept their steady, straight-forward gaze.

"I am not certain," she said. "I have searched for my boy for a long while, and I think this may be he. I want to see him."

The doctor looked at her pityingly as she went up to the narrow bed where a lad of hardly twenty lay, his face buried in the pillow. His fair hair, waving crisply against skin browned by exposure, had not been cut, for the hospital barber who stood there found it so far impossible to make him turn his head.

"He's lain that way ever since they brought him in yesterday," said the barber and then, moved by something in the agitated face before him, turned his own way. The mother stooped over the prostrate figure. She knew it, as mothers seem always to know their own, and laid her hand on his burning brow.

"Charley," she said softly, as if she had come into his room to rouse him from some boyish sleep, "mother is here."

A wild cry rang out that startled even the experienced physician, "For God's sake take her away! She doesn't know where I am. *Take her away!*"

The patient had started up and wrung his hands in piteous entreaty. "Take her away!" he still cried, but his mother gently folded her arms about him and drew his head to her breast.

"Oh, Charley, I have found you," she said through her sobs, "and I will never lose you again."

The lad looked at her a moment. His eyes were like hers, large and clear — but with the experience of a thousand years in their depths. His beautiful, reckless face was graven with lines by passion and crime. He burst into weeping like a child. "It's too late! *It's too late!*" he said in tones almost inaudible. "I'm doing you the only good turn I've ever done you, mother. I'm dying and you won't have to break your heart over me anymore. It wasn't your fault. *It was the cursed drink that ruined me, blighted my life and brought me here.* It's murder now, but the hangman won't have me — I'll save that much disgrace for our name."

As he spoke he fell back upon his pillow. His face changed and the unmistakable hue of death suddenly spread over his handsome features. The doctor came forward quickly, a look of anxious surprise on his face.

"I didn't know he was that bad," the barber muttered under his breath, as he gazed at the lad still holding his mother's hand. The doctor lifted the patient's head and then laid it back softly. Life had fled.

"It's better to have it so," he said in a low voice to himself, and then stood silently, ready to offer consolation to the bereaved mother, whose face was still hidden on her boy's breast. She did not stir. Something in the motionless attitude aroused vague suspicion in the mind of the doctor and moved him to bend forward and gently take her hand. With an involuntary start he hastily lifted the prostrate form and quickly felt the pulse and heart, only to find them stilled forever.

"She has gone, too," he softly whispered, and the tears stood in his eyes. *"Poor soul!* It is the best for both of them."

This is one story of the prison ward of Bellevue, and there are hundreds that might be told, though never one sadder or holding deeper tragedy than the one recorded here.

—*New York Press*

Louis IX. A.D. 1270

Louis IX, king of France, was noted not only for wisdom and justice, but also for piety and virtue.

His dying advice to his daughter contained these words: "My dear daughter, I conjure you to love our Lord with all your might, for this is the foundation of all goodness. I wish you could comprehend what the Son of God has done for our redemption. Never be guilty of any deliberate sin, though it were to save your life. Shun too familiar discourse except with virtuous persons. Obey, my dear daughter, your husband. *Aspire after a disposition to do the will of God, purely for His sake, independently of the hope of reward or the fear of punishment."*

—*Dying Words* by A. H. Gottschall

Queen Elizabeth

"All my possessions for a moment of time!"

Queen Elizabeth ascended the English throne at the age of twenty-five and remained in power for forty-five years. She was a Protestant but was far from being a true Christian in her life. She persecuted the Puritans for many years, and her cruelty was manifested throughout her reign.

We take the following from Schaff's Encyclopedia:

With Elizabeth, Protestantism was restored, and — in spite of occasional resistance from within, the Spanish Armada and papal deposition from without (1570) — became the permanent religion of the large majority in the land.

Two periods stand out in the history of the church of England under Elizabeth. In the early part of the reign the divorce of the National Church from the Roman Catholic See was consummated; in the latter part its position was clearly stated in regard to Puritanism, which demanded recognition, if not supremacy, within its pale.

The queen was no zealous reformer but directed the affairs of the church with the keen sagacity of a statemanship which placed national unity and the peace of the realm above every other consideration. In the first year of her reign the Acts of Supremacy and Uniformity were passed. By the former, all allegiance to foreign prince or prelate was forbidden; by the latter, the use of the liturgy was enforced.

The royal title of "Defender of the Faith and Supreme Head of the Church" was retained, with the slight alteration of "Head" to "Governor". But the passage was struck out of the Litany which read, "From the tyranny of the Bishop of Rome and all his detestable enormities, good Lord deliver us."

The queen retained, against the protests of bishops, an altar and crucifix, and lighted candles in her own chapel, disapproved of the marriage of the clergy, interrupted the preacher who spoke disparagingly of the sign of the cross and imperiously forced her wishes upon unwilling prelates.

She died in 1603 at the age of seventy. Her last words were, *"All my possessions for a moment of time!"*

Raymond Lull A.D. 1315

While seeking to convert the Mohammedans, he was stoned by a mob in Bowgiah, Africa. Although managing to get aboard a vessel, he died from the injuries he had received. His parting words were:

"I was once rich, lascivious and worldly, but willingly did I forsake everything to advance the glory of God and the good of mankind. I learned Arabic and departed to preach to the Saracens.

"For my religion I have been whipped and imprisoned. Now I am old and poor, yet steadfast in the same purpose, and through grace steadfast will I remain."

—*Dying Words* by A. H. Gottschall

Last Words Of The Great Commentator, Matthew Henry

Matthew Henry, a distinguished non-conformist and Biblical scholar, was born October 28, 1662, at Broad Oak, Flintshire, England, and died June 22, 1714, at Nantwich, England.

On the return journey from a visit to Chester he was seized with apoplexy. His old intimate friend, Mr. Illidge, was present, who had been desired by Sir Thomas Delves and his lady to invite him to their house at Doddington. Unable to proceed any further, they stopped at Mr. Mottershed's house, where he felt himself so ill that he said to his friends, "Pray for me, for now I cannot pray for myself."

While they were putting him to bed, he spoke of the excellence of spiritual comforts in a time of affliction and blessed God that he enjoyed them. To his friend, Mr. Illidge, he addressed himself in these memorable words: "You have been used to take notice of the sayings of dying men — this is mine: *That a life spent in the service of God and communion with Him is the most comfortable and pleasant life that one can live in the present world.*"

—*Memoirs of the Rev. Matthew Henry*

93

Miss Hannah More. A.D. 1833

An English authoress and philanthropist
An unusual brightness, followed by a smile, came over her face and she reached out her arms, as if grasping something. *"Joy!"* she exclaimed — then was gone. Joy was the name of a sister who had died some years previously.

—*Dying Words* by A. H. Gottschall

"You Cannot Run Away From The Spirit Of God"

Several years ago a gentleman, apparently in great haste, entered a certain city in one of the southern states on horseback. He rode up to the hotel, alighted, and after introducing himself, told the following story:

"I have been trying to run away from the Spirit of God, but it has followed me all of these many miles that I have traveled, and it is with me now. I had Christian training, and as I heard the Gospel proclaimed from time to time I became deeply convicted of sin. However, I was very rebellious and determined not to yield. The Spirit said, 'You must be born again,' but I said, 'I will *not* be born again.'

"I purchased this horse, a good, strong beast at the time, and I have worn it down poor, as you see; but I have not succeeded in outrunning the Spirit of God. I feel that I am about to die, and I have a request to make. I want you to sell this horse and bury me here in the street by this sign post, and put up a slab by my grave bearing this inscription, 'You cannot run away from the Spirit of God.'"

The man soon died. Physicians examined him and said there was no disease about him, but that he died of mental agony.

His strange request was granted, and the slab bearing this silent warning preached many a sermon to passers-by, and resulted in a revival of religion in the city of Tuscaloosa, Alabama.

—Mary E. Jenks, McBain, Michigan
—*Dying Testimonies* by S. B. Shaw

A Young Woman Looks Into Eternity

One of the predecessors of my last pastorate was Rev. A. D. Sandborn who related the following incident. He was president of a school at Wilton, Iowa, and while going back and forth to his school would usually stop for a few moments of conversation with a devoted young Christian woman who was seriously ill.

One morning he found the family gathered at her bedside. She was bolstered up in nearly a sitting position and was intently looking off into the distance. She seemed to see a glorious city, for she said, "Now, just as soon as they open the gate I will go in. They will be here very soon now."

As she looked, her eyes just danced. Suddenly she leaned her head forward with a happy, eager expression. *"There! There! They are coming now and I shall go!"* Then she sank back upon her pillow with a disappointed look and exclaimed, "They have let little Mamie in ahead of me." Then she added, "But next time they will let me in. Pretty soon they will open the gate again, and then I will go in."

Still gazing eagerly and expectantly into space, she lay quietly for a few minutes. Then starting up, with head leaning forward and eyes straining to see, she exclaimed, "There! There! They are going to open the gate. *Now* I shall go in!"

Again, however, she sank back on the pillows in sore disappointment. "They let Grandpa in ahead of me — but next time I will go in for sure. They will be back pretty soon."

She still kept looking far away and talking. No one spoke to her, and she said nothing to any one in particular. She seemed to see nothing save the sights of the beautiful city.

Doctor Sandborn could not remain from his duties longer and quietly left the house. Later in the day he learned that soon after he left she had died, just as he had seen her, so full of eager expectancy and waiting for the gate to open and give her entrance into the beautiful city.

The scenes of that morning made a profound impression upon Dr. Sandborn, and a few days after the funeral he called at the house to inquire who it was that the dying girl had called "Little Mamie". They replied that she was a little girl who had lived near them at one time. She had later moved to a town in New York State. To his question, "Who was Grandpa?" they replied that he was an old friend of the young lady and that he had moved to some place in the Southwest. They gave the name of the place.

All of the circumstances made such an impression on Dr. Sandborn that he at once wrote to each of the postmasters in the places referred to, asking for information on these people. One day, in the same mail, he received letters from the two postmasters replying to his questions. Both letters were worded very much alike and in each instance stated that the person referred to had lived there but had died on the morning of September 16, naming the hour. *This proved to be the very time when he witnessed that affecting deathbed scene.*

—*The Child of God Between Death and the Resurrection*
by Judson B. Palmer, Galveston, Texas

William Otterbein, Founder Of The United Brethren Church

Bishop Otterbein, founder of the United Brethren Church, ended a ministry of sixty-two years in great peace.

Dr. Kurtz of the Lutheran Church, for many years a devoted personal friend of the distinguished preacher, offered at his bedside the last audible prayer. The bishop responded, "Amen, amen! It is finished." Like good old Simeon, who was spared to take the babe of Bethlehem in his arms, he could say, "Lord, now lettest thou thy servant depart in peace, according to Thy word: for mine eyes have seen Thy salvation."

His grief-stricken friends, thinking at that moment he was dying, gathered about him to take the last look ere he smote with his sandals the waters of death's river; but rallying again for a moment, as if to finish his testimony and give still greater assurance of victory, he said, "Jesus, Jesus, I die — *but Thou livest, and soon I shall live with Thee.*"

Then, turning to his friends, he continued, "The conflict is over and past. I begin to feel an unspeakable fullness of love and peace divine. Lay my head upon my pillow and be still." All was then quiet. He simply awaited the approach of Heaven's chariot, and he did not wait in vain. "A smile, a fresh glow lighted up his countenance; and, behold, it was death."

—From *Life to Life*

Anne Askew (A.D. 1546)

Because of her adherence to the Protestant faith, her husband drove her violently from his house, though she was the mother of his two children. While imprisoned, an apostate named Shaxton advised her to recant. She replied by telling him that it would be well had he never been born.

Being placed upon the cruel rack, her joints and bones were pulled out of place. After recovering from a faint, she preached for two hours to her tormentors. On the day of execution she had to be carried on a chair, her bones being so dislocated that she could not walk.

After being fastened to the stake with a chain, a letter was brought offering pardon from the King if she would recant. She died praying for her murderers while in the very midst of the flames. Her last recorded words, an answer to the King's offer of pardon, were:

"I came not thither to deny my Lord and Master."

—*Dying Words* by Gottschall

"I Am In The Midst Of Glory!"

Bishop Hanby, a devoted preacher of the United Brethren Church, began to weep shortly before he died. His daughter noticed this and tenderly inquired, "What is it, Father?"

"Oh, I am *so happy,*" was the reply, "My long, toilsome journey is nearly ended; my life work is joyfully over; half of my children are already safe in heaven, and I am just as sure the rest will be. Half are safe at home, and all the rest are on the way. Mother is there (referring to his wife), and in a little while I shall be there too!"

Then he quoted the following lines:

The Lord My Shepherd is,
I shall be well supplied;
Since He is mine, and I am His,
What can I do beside?

After he had descended into the river, he suddenly shouted back, *"I'm in the midst of glory!"*

—Adapted from an article in *From Life to Life*

97

Agrippina—Mother Of The Roman Emperor Nero

This infamous woman once had a lady beheaded who was her rival for imperial dignity. The head being brought to her, she examined it closely with her own hands in order to be sure it was the one she wanted.

She was eventually condemned to death by her own son, the Emperor Nero. To the men sent to slay her she said:

"Strike *here!* Level your range against the womb which gave birth to such a monster!"

—*Dying Words* by Gottschall

"Too Late! Too Late! Too Late!"

When I lived in west Tennessee, I was well-acquainted with a noted infidel who neither feared God nor regarded man. He considered it an insult to his dignity for anyone to speak to him on the subject of religion. In fact, he had been known to fight some who dared approach him about his soul's salvation. Although favored with an abundance of the earthly possessions of this life, it seemed to me that he was the most unhappy man that I had ever seen.

When this man was dying, his weeping sister asked her husband, who also was a rough man and an infidel, to go get my uncle so that he might pray for her brother. Of course, my uncle responded, and when he entered the room the dying infidel said to him, "I can now see and realize that I am doomed to Hell. *Pray for me!*"

Uncle did all he could. I was along, and while uncle was praying and singing, I tried to keep the man's mind on the Lord by talking to him.

Nothing seemed to help, however, and the poor fellow kept warning all present not to live as he had lived and sink at last to a devil's Hell. Finally, he turned his face towards the wall and cried with an awful wail, *"Too late! Too late! Too late!"*

—J. Earnest of Searcy, Arkansas

From *Dying Testimonies* by S. B. Shaw

Oliver Cromwell

"The devil is ready to seduce us, and *I have been seduced.*"

Me

Me was an old blind warrior of the South Sea Islands. He had a plantation upon which he raised sweet potatoes and bananas, but when he was stricken with disease others seized his property. A missionary found him alone and suffering from the pangs of hunger, but he said, "I am not lonely for I have frequent visits from God. *God and I were talking when you came in.*"

—Above two selections from
Dying Words by A. H. Gottschall

A Victory Crossing

"I'll see you in the morning."

Those were the last smilingly confident words William G. Roll spoke to me, shortly before he passed from Time into Eternity.

Although we had been loathe to let him go — hoping the Lord's will might be to permit him to remain among us for yet a longer time — he had whispered: "My body is weary — I would like to go home." Then with a flash of his delightful smile he repeated his farewell — *"I'll see you in the morning."*

In those few words there was a world of faith, trust, hope, almost eagerness to be gone to meet his Saviour. There was no uncertainty, no fear — just a deep settled peace and unbounded confidence.

Nor were there any tears or regrets. His life in God's service, his triumphant passing, savors of the words of Saint Paul: "I have fought a good fight, I have finished my course, I have kept the faith . . ."

For the first time in the history of the Fellowship, Eternity has reached out to enfold a member of our International Board. We feel a great sense of loss. We shall miss his voice in our councils, his steady, unwavering faith in difficult days, his

99

prayers and his holding on to God for the Fellowship and its work. But what an abundant entrance for him!

Our Brother Roll has contributed more than any other one man to building the truly international stature of FGBMFI. For years a diplomatic representative of the United States in foreign courts, he has opened numerous doors in many nations through which we have been able to carry the Gospel into areas that otherwise might not have been available to us.

Though his earthly voice is now silent, he yet speaks to us through our memory of his faith and service.

—Demos Shakarian, *Full Gospel Business Men's Voice*
(March 1967)

Philip Melanchthon. A.D. 1799

Philip Melanchthon's ever-ready pen, clear thought and elegant style made him the scribe of the Reformation. His last known words in answer to his son-in-law's question as to whether he would have anything was: " 'The world knew Him not. But as many as received Him, to them gave He power to become the sons of God, even to them that believe on His name.' *I want nothing but Heaven,* therefore trouble me no more."

—*Dying Words* by A. H. Gottschall

"My Master Calls; I Am Going Home. It Is Well."

David Nelson, a noted Presbyterian clergyman, was born on September 24, 1793. In 1810 he graduated from Washington College, Virginia, and for some years practiced medicine. Several of these years were spent as a surgeon in the United States Army, and it was during this period that he became an infidel.

In the providence of God, however, his eyes were opened and he was saved from his "refuge of lies". Thrilled with new-found faith and love for God, Mr. Nelson then began to preach in the spring of 1825. Five eventful years of serving the Lord in Tennessee and Kentucky were climaxed with God's call to go to Missouri and establish Marion College. He was the school's first president and filled that position for six years.

Then, in 1836 he opened a training school for missionaries and in the suceeding years wrote the widely circulated book, *The Cause and Cure of Infidelity.*

Mr. Nelson died in 1844 and his last words were, "My Master calls; *I am going home. It is well.*"

—*Dying Testimonies* by S. B. Shaw

Francis Bacon

Lord Chancellor of England

"The sweetest life in this world is piety, virtue and honesty."

Lord Bacon (A.D. 1626)

One of the great men of England — a philosopher and statesman

"Thy creatures, Oh, Lord, have been my books, but Thy Holy Scriptures much more."

Edward Augustas (A.D. 1820)

Duke of Kent, father of Queen Victoria

In the prospect of death his physician strove to sooth his mind by referring to his honorable conduct. The Duke stopped him, saying:

"No. Remember, if I am to be saved, it is not as a prince, but as a *sinner.*"

—Above three testimonies from *Dying Words* by Gottschall

"I Am Going To Die. Glory Be To God And The Lamb Forever!"

There were the last words of the saintly Ann Cutler, one of John Wesley's workers in whom he had great confidence. She was converted under the famed William Bramwell, who wrote the following account:

Ann Cutler was born near Preston, in Lancashire, in the

year 1759. Until she was about twenty-six years of age, though very strict in her morals and serious in her deportment, she never understood the method of salvation by Jesus Christ. Then the Methodist local preachers visited that neighborhood. After hearing one of them she was convinced of sin, and from that time gave all diligence to obtain mercy.

In a short time she received pardon, and her new life evinced the blessing she enjoyed. It was not long, however, before she had a clearer insight into her own heart and, though she retained her confidence of pardon, she became sensitive to the need of perfect love. Upon hearing the doctrine of sanctification and believing that the blessing is to be received through faith, she expected instantaneous deliverance and prayed for the power to believe. Her confidence increased until she could say, "Jesus, thou wilt cleanse me from *all* unrighteousness!"

In the same year of her finding mercy (1785) the Lord said, "I will; be thou clean." She found a sinking into humility, love and dependence upon God. At this time her language was, "Jesus, Thou knowest I love Thee with all my heart. I would rather die than grieve Thy Spirit. Oh, I cannot express how much I love Jesus!" After this change something remarkable appeared in her countenance — there was a smile of sweet composure. It was noticed by many as a reflection of the Divine nature, and it increased to the time of her death.

In a few months she felt a great desire for the salvation of sinners and often wept much in private, drawn out to plead with God for the world in general. She would frequently say, "I think I must pray; I cannot be happy unless I cry for sinners. I do not want any praise — I want nothing but souls to be brought to God. Though reproached by most, I cannot do it to be seen or heard of men. I see the world going to destruction, and I am burdened till I pour out my soul to God for them."

Her great devotion to God is shown in the following account of her sickness and death by Mrs. Highfield:

"I will endeavor to give you a few particulars relative to the death of Ann Cutler. While she was with us, it seemed to be her daily custom to dedicate herself, body and soul, to God. She came to Macclesfield very poorly of a cold on the fifteenth of December. Being our preaching night, she had an earnest desire to have a prayer meeting. I told her that on account of preaching lasting so late as eight o'clock and the classes having to meet afterwards, it would not be convenient.

102

She was very importunate, however, and said she could not be happy without one. "I shall not be long here and I would buy up every opportunity of doing something for God — time is short."

Knowing she had an uncommon talent for pleading for such souls as were coming to God, we got a few together, to whom she was made a blessing.

A few days before her death she said, "Jesus is about to take me home. I think I shall soon have done with this body of clay; and, oh, how happy shall I then be when I cast my crown before Him, *lost in wonder, love and praise!*"

About seven a.m. the doctor, with those of us about her, thought she was gone, but to our great surprise she continued in an unconscious state till between ten and eleven o'clock. She then lifted herself up and looked about her, speaking just so as to be heard. She was very sensible and seemed perfectly composed, but her strength was nearly gone.

Finally, about three o'clock, she looked at her friends and said, "*I am going to die,*" then added, "*Glory be to God and the Lamb forever!*" These were her last words. Soon afterwards the spirit left this vale of misery."

—*Dying Testimonies* by S. B. Shaw

Mohammed I. A.D. 1421

King of Spain

"The path of kings is in appearance strewn with flowers, but thou seest not that roses have thorns. Is not the prince to leave the world as naked as the peasant?"

—*Dying Words* by A. H. Gottschall

The Sad Death Of A Lost Man

In Texas there lived a wealthy farmer, the son of a Methodist preacher, with whom the writer was intimately acquainted. He was highly respected in the community in which he lived and was a kind-hearted and benevolent man. However, he had one great fault. He was very profane. He would utter the most

103

horrible oaths without, seemingly, the least provocation.

Several times I remember having seen him under deep conviction during revival meetings. On one occasion, when under powerful conviction during a camp-meeting, he said he was suddenly frightened and felt as if he wanted to run away from the place. He was again brought under conviction, but he refused to yield.

Shortly after this he was suddenly taken ill and died in three days. I was with him in his last moments. He seemed to be utterly forsaken of the Lord from the beginning of his sickness. The most powerful medicines had no effect on him whatever, and just as the sun of a beautiful Sunday morning rose in its splendor over the eastern hills, he died — in awful agony.

All through the night prior to his death he suffered untold physical and mental torture. He offered the physicians all his earthly possessions if they would save his life, but was stubborn and would not acknowledge his fear of death until a few moments before he died. Then, suddenly, he began to look, then to stare into the vacancy before him. Horribly surprised and frightened, he exclaimed, *"My God!"*

The indescribable expression of his countenance at this juncture, together with the despairing tones in which he uttered these last words, made every heart quake. His wife screamed and begged a brother to pray for him; but the brother was so terror-stricken that he rushed out of the room. The dying man continued to stare in dreadful astonishment, his mouth wide open, till at last, with an awful groan,

> *Like a flood with rapid force,*
> *Death bore the wretch away.*

His little three-year-old son, the idol of his father's heart, was convulsed with grief. This little boy, then so innocent, grew up to be a wicked young man and died a horrible death.

How solemn to reflect that in Hell there are millions of fathers and sons, mothers and daughters, husbands and wives — hopelessly lost.

Realizing that the future state of those who know not God will never abate its fury but, in accordance with the natural law of sin, degradation and wretchedness, will grow worse and more furious as the black ages of eternity roll up from darker realms, we turn for relief to the Man of Sorrows, *who tasted death for every man.* Then we turn to the beautiful City, whose builder and maker is God, to the bliss of the glorified who will shine as the stars forever and ever. Then, with renewed efforts, we continue with gratitude to work out our own, and the salvation of others, with fear and trembling.

—The Ambassador

M. Homel. A.D. 1683

Almost every bone of his body was broken with the iron bar of the wheel upon which he suffered for forty hours before the executioner gave him a death-blow upon the breast.

Before dying he said, "Farewell, my dear wife. I know that your tears and your continual sighs hinder you from bidding me adieu. Do not be troubled at this wheel upon which I must die. It is to me a triumphal chariot which will carry me into Heaven. Farewell once more, my well-beloved spouse. I am waiting for you. But know, though you see my bones broken to shivers, my soul is replenished with inexpressible joys — *I see Heaven opened and Jesus with His outstretched arms!*"

—Dying Words by A. H. Gottschall

John Oxtoby's Wonderful Revelation

John Oxtoby, one of the great men of Methodism, was soundly converted to Christ in 1804 after spending many years of his life in sin. Soon after his conversion he began to preach the Gospel, and thousands of lives were transformed as a result of his ministry.

His biographer, Harvey Leigh, gives the following account:

That which gave lasting effect to the labors of John Oxtoby was the uncommon power of the Spirit which attended his words. Seldom did he open his mouth, either in preaching, praying or personal conversation, without those being addressed feeling the force of that unction.

Not infrequently during his preaching have numbers of people actually fallen to the ground crying for mercy, under the most striking apprehensions of their sin and danger. Others, who with great difficulty escaped home, were impelled to send for him or others to pray for them before they dared attempt to sleep. And, strange as it may seem, some have even fallen to their knees on their way home, and others at their work, from the effects of his preaching and prayers.

During the whole of the affliction which brought about his death, he had a most glorious experience of God's favor. He received such a baptism of the Holy Spirit that his soul was filled with peace and joy unutterable. Amidst the sinkings of mortality, he approached the vale of death as if—

Prayer was all his business,
And all his pleasure, praise.

A little while before his departure he said, "As great as have been my comforts from the Lord during the years of my life, yet all the former manifestations which I have had are *nothing* compared with those which I now feel."

To his sister he said, *"Oh, what have I beheld! Such a sight as I cannot possibly describe. There were three shining forms beside me, whose garments were so bright, and whose countenances were so glorious, that I never saw anything to compare with them before!"*

His dying prayer was, "Lord, save souls — don't let them perish." Shortly afterwards he shouted in holy triumph, *"Glory, glory, glory!"* and immediately soared on high.

—From *Shining Lights*

"Oh! Save Me! They Drag Me Down! Lost, Lost, Lost!"

The following incident concerns a young lady who, under deep conviction for sin, left a revival meeting to attend a dance arranged by a party of ungodly men for the purpose of breaking up the meeting. She caught a severe cold at the dance and before long was on her death bed.

When a local minister visited her, she stiffly repulsed his efforts to counsel, saying, "Mr. Rice, my mind was never clearer. I tell you all today that I do not wish to be a Christian. I don't want to go to Heaven — I would not if I could. I would rather go to Hell than Heaven; they need not keep the gates closed."

"But you don't want to go to Hell, do you, Jennie?" the minister implored.

106

She then broke down and replied, "No, Mr. Rice. *Oh, that I had never been born!* I am suffering *now* the agonies of the lost. If I could but get away from God — but no, I must always see Him and be looked upon by Him. How I hate Him — *I cannot help it!* I drove His Spirit from my heart when He would have filled it with His love; and now I am left to my own evil nature — given over to the Devil for my eternal destruction. My agony is inexpressible! How will I endure the endless ages of eternity? Oh, the dreadful thought of *eternity!"*

When asked by Mr. Rice how she got into this despairing mood, she replied, "It was that Friday evening last winter when I deliberately stayed away from the meeting to attend the dance. At the dance I felt so sad — for my heart was tender — I could scarcely keep from weeping. Yet I felt provoked to think that my last dance, as I somehow felt it to be, should be spoiled by these feelings. I endured it until I became angry; then with all my might *I drove the influence of the Spirit away from me.* It was then that I had the feeling that He had left me forever. I knew that I had done something terrible, but it was done. From that time I have had no desire to be a Christian, but have been sinking down into deeper darkness and more bitter despair. And now all around, and above and beneath me, are impenatrable clouds of darkness. Oh, the terrible gloom — when will it cease?"

She then sank away and lay like one dead a short time. Finally, she raised her hand slightly, her lips quivering as if in the agonies of death. Suddenly her eyes opened with a fixed and awful stare, and she gave a despairing groan that sent chills through every heart.

"Oh, what horror!" she whispered.

Then turning to Mr. Rice, she said, "Go home now — return this evening. I don't want you to pray for me. I don't want to be tormented with the sound of prayer."

About four o'clock she inquired the time and upon being told exclaimed, "How slowly the hours wear away. This day seems an age to me. Oh, *how* will I endure eternity?" In about an hour she again said, "How slowly the time drags. Why may I not cease to be?"

That evening she sent for Mr. Rice again. As he approached her bed, she said to him, "I want you to preach at my funeral. Warn all of my young friends . . . remember everything I have said and use it."

"How can I do this? Jennie, how I do wish you were a good

Christian and had a hope of eternal life."

"Now, Mr. Rice, I don't want to hear anything about that. I do not want to be tormented with the thought. I am utterly hopeless, my time is growing short — my fate is eternally fixed! I am dying without hope because I insulted the Holy Spirit so bitterly. He has just left me alone to go down to eternal night. He could not have borne with me any longer and retained His divine honor and dignity."

Soon after that she began to struggle in the agonies of death. She gasped, *"Oh, save me! They drag me down! Lost! lost! lost!"*

A moment later she rallied and with glazed eyes looked upon her weeping family and friends for the last time. Her eye lids sank partly down and pressed out a remaining tear as she whispered the strange yet knowing words, "Bind me, ye chains of darkness! Oh, that I might cease to be, but still exist."

The spirit fled, and Jennie Gordon lay a lifeless form of clay.

—From *The Unequal Yoke,* by J. H. Miller

"I Didn't Know It Was So Beautiful"

Hulda A. Rees was a successful evangelist of the Society of Friends. She was born October 15, 1855, and lived only forty-two years, but her life had made an impact upon her generation.

We saw from a distance the end approaching, but we could not fully realize the truth. It did not seem like "the valley of the shadow." We had read of the triumph of the saints when approaching the River, but surely this excelled anything of which we had ever heard. Such sweet resignation to all God's will, such divine unction in prayer, such holy tenderness in exhortation and admonition, such victory and gladness in the furnace of pain and agony!

Many visitors came to see her, and whenever her strength permitted, she always had them admitted to her room. Her words were ever full of cheer and eternal hope. On one occasion, when a minister called whom she had known for years, she said to him with the greatest exultation, *"The glory holds!"*

Yes, thank God, it did hold. The Gospel she had preached to so many thousands with emphasis and assurance was found true and unshakable in this time of earnest testing.

In one of her prayers she said: "Thou hast put, O Lord, a

great laugh in my heart. Glory! Glory be to Thy Name forever! No evil can come to me! All is turned to blessing!"

One afternoon the family were all gathered about her, when suddenly her face lighted up as if a candle were burning beneath the transparent skin. With the brightest, sweetest smile, and a far-away look as if she were gazing off in the distance, she said in a soft, reflective tone, "I didn't know it was so beautiful." Then after a moment or so, she exclaimed rapturously, *"Can it be that the glory of the Lord is risen upon me!"*

Thus this daughter of the Most High drew near to the exit from this world. It was indeed to her, as she said, "All bright and glorious ahead."

The night before she ascended she attempted to sing:

Fear not, I am with thee;
Oh, be not dismayed,
For I am thy God,
I will still give thee aid.

But she could only whisper the words. Her husband read the entire hymn to her.

In the evening of Friday, June 3, as the darkness was deepening about us, we watched her slip quietly away. There was no struggle. She passed away from us as calmly as a child falling asleep. We knew that she was *with the Lord,* both hers and ours.

—From *Hulda, The Pentecostal Prophetess*

A Dying Man's Regrets

A minister once said to a dying man, "If God should restore you to health, do you think that you would alter your course of life?"

The man answered, "I call Heaven and earth to witness, I would labor for holiness as I shall soon labor for life. As for riches and pleasure and the applause of men, I account them as dross. Oh, if the righteous Judge would but reprieve and spare me a little longer, in what spirit would I spend the remainder of my days! I would know no other business, I would aim at no other end, than perfecting myself in holiness. Whatever contributed to that — every means of grace, every opportunity of spiritual improvement — should be dearer to me than thousands of gold and silver. But, alas! Why do I amuse myself with fond imaginations? The best resolutions are now insignificant, because they are *too late!"*

Such was the language of deep concern uttered by one who was beginning to look at these things in the light of the eternal world, which, after all, is the true light. Here we stand on the little molehills of earthly life, where we cannot get a clear view of that other world; but what must it be to stand on the top of the dark mountain of death and look out upon our surroundings — knowing that from the top of that mountain, if angels do not lift us to the skies, we must take a leap into the blackness of darkness!

—Selected

"He Is Come! My Beloved Is Mine And I Am His Forever!"

Thomas Walsh is a great name in the history of early Methodism. Both preacher and scholar, he mastered not only his native Irish, but also was versed in Latin, Greek and Hebrew. It is said that he studied so deeply that his memory was an entire concordance of the whole Bible.

His soul was as a flame of fire. John Wesley says of him, "I do not remember ever to have known a man who, in so few years as he remained upon earth, was the instrument of converting so many sinners."

The ministry of Walsh was mostly in Ireland, and the Roman Catholic priests simply could not account for the extraordinary influence he possessed. Preaching on mountains and highways, in meadows, private houses, prisons and ships, he bore down all before him by a kind of absorbed ecstasy of ardent faith.

Dying at the early age of twenty-seven, he suddenly became oppressed with a sense of despair, even to doubting his own salvation. The sufferings of his mind were protracted and very intense, but at last he broke through and just before the end, exclaimed, "He is come! *He is come!* My Beloved is mine, and I am His — *forever!"*

—Adapted from an article in *The Great Revival*

110

"There Is Light All Around Me"

The noted evangelist of the nineteenth century, Mrs. Grace Weiser Davis, wrote this account of her mother's beautiful passing:

For five months past I have been a witness to the triumphs of the power of God to save amid suffering and to cast out all fear that hath torment.

My mother left us July 20th at the age of fifty-nine. She and my father were converted just previous to my birth in a revival that continued almost a year. After that our home was always open to ministers of the Gospel. Mother would give them the best she could get and then apologize because it was no better. Hundreds can testify to her loving ministrations.

When her last sickness came, we brought her to Bradley Beach, hoping for a prolongation of the precious life. She was cheerful, planning for a continued life here, and we shrank from telling her the truth. God Himself, however, gloriously revealed it to her. The doctor and other ministers bear testimony with my own that hers was the most glorious death bed we ever witnessed.

One day my mother prayed, "Dear Lord, prepare me for the country to which I am going!" Before the close of that day she was shouting the praises of God. From that time on she talked of her coming translation, and her faith was gloriously triumphant.

On Sunday, June 27, she had a day of wonderful exaltation. She said, "I have always hoped and trusted in God, but now I have a fuller realization than ever before." As we all wept, she said, *"I don't realize that this is death. It is His will, and is all right."* To the doctor she said, "Just think, doctor, *to be forever with the Lord!"*

After that no one could come into mother's room without being spoken to about the glory that was filling her soul. To me she said, "Grace, God has given you gifts that few others possess; let us pray that God will make you a weight of glory in the world. God has blest you and will still more."

One afternoon she said, "I am homesick for Heaven." To the doctor, "Sometimes my way has seemed dark, but it was like the ferris wheel — it always came round to a point of light." Again she said, "I believe I will awake sometime and find myself in a strange country, to which I shall be translated."

"Mother, it will not be so strange. Your father and mother

111

and husband and little boy are there, and we are on the way," I answered.

To one lately married, she said, "You are just beginning life. It pays to begin right. Everything you'll do for God is on compound interest — *compound* interest. It will be doubly repaid you. I commenced to serve Him in early life and consecrated my children to Him in infancy, and they are all Christians, and I am so happy."

As I kissed her one day she said, "We shall rejoice together in Jesus in Heaven." Her favorite words were, *"Surely goodness and mercy shall follow me . . . etc."* and her favorite hymn, "Jesus, Lover of My Soul." The night previous to her death she said, *"There is light all around me!"*

Until the last she gave evidence of hearing, seeing and understanding. I knelt within fifteen minutes of her passing and said, "Mother, though you walk through the valley of the shadow of death, you need fear no evil, for God is with you. Surely goodness and mercy shall follow you, and you are going to dwell in the house of the Lord forever."

There came a responsive smile. In a few minutes she drew a gentle breath and was gone.

—Adapted from an article in *The Christian Standard,*
July 10, 1898

Phillip J. Jenks

Just before he passed away a friend said to him, "How hard is it to die?"

"I have experienced more happiness in two hours today, when dying, than in my whole life. I have long desired that I might glorify God in my death, but I never thought that such a poor worm as I could come to such a glorious death."

—*Dying Words* by A. H. Gottschall

Triumphant Death Of George Edward Dryer

This young saint of God went to Heaven from Readsburg, Wisconsin, on February 1, 1896. His sister, Mrs. Evaline Dryer Green, wrote the following:

Dear readers, come with me for a little while as I look on memory's walls. See, there are many things written there! Here is one story, sweet and sacred, almost *too* sacred to relate; yet as with hushed voices we talk of this, our hearts shall melt and we shall feel that Heaven is drawing nigher.

I remember my baby brother — though I was a child of but four years when he came into our home. I well remember that little face and the chubby brown hands when he was a wee boy — always in mischief then. I was a frail girl, and he soon outgrew me. Then those sweet years of home life — and later the glad homecomings when I was away at school. On my return George was always the first to wave his hand and shout for joy. Often, he would toss his hat high in the air and give a certain "whoop" and three cheers that I loved to hear. We were right loyal friends, my brother and I.

But then it struck — ah, it's here I'd wish to draw the veil and forget. He was so strong, so full of life! But we will only glance at those long months of suffering and hasten to the last. Nearly eighteen months of weariness from coughing, and there he lay, the picture of patient endurance, saying from his heart's depths,

Farewell, mortality — Jesus is mine,
Welcome, eternity — Jesus is mine!

Often he would call me near him and say, "Oh, sister, the Lord does *so* save me!" To the doctor, the boys of his own age, to neighbors, and *all* who came, he testified how Jesus saved him, through and through.

The last hours were drawing near. One of the Lord's servants came and prayed. George prayed for father, mother, brothers and sisters. A little later in the evening a sweat, deathly cold, covered him. We thought he was going then — the poor, weak body seemed all but gone — but the spirit grew even more bright. Ah, that picture! His high, marble-white brow, either cheek glowing with fever intense; the great, expressive blue eyes, that peered earnestly, joyfully, all about him and *upward*.

Then, with heaven lighting his face, he lifted those dear hands high and said,

"Angels now are hovering round us!"

Even now I shall say, as I did then, "O *death,* where is thy sting? O *grave,* where is thy victory?"

Again he came back to us — to spend one more night of suffering on earth, and one more night working for God and

113

eternity. We watched all night while he praised God, often saying under his breath between awful fits of coughing, *"Precious Jesus!"*

Toward morning he asked a dear sister to sing "I saw a happy pilgrim."

Finally the morning came, a dark, rainy morning in February. The gray light was just dawning when we all gathered about his bed. We repeated beautiful texts and verses of hymns that he most loved and encouraged him to the very river's brink. His last spoken words were, "Eva, come on this side." Then, peacefully he closed his eyes and grew *so still.*

> *And with the morn, those angel faces smile,*
> *Which I have loved long since — and lost awhile.*

> —*Dying Testimonies* by S. B. Shaw

Jessie

Little Jessie's mother was dying. Her last words to the child were "Jessie, *find Jesus!"*

After the funeral Jessie started out in her simple child-like way to obey her mother's request. As a young man came out of a saloon and almost stumbled over her, she asked him, "Please tell me where Jesus Christ is."

"I don't know, child," he replied.

Upon one occasion, in her wanderings, she met a Jewess whom she asked, "Do you know Jesus Christ?" The woman turned fiercely upon her and exclaimed, "Jesus Christ is dead!"

Finally, one day a rough boy snatched her little basket and threw it into the street. While endeavoring to regain it the horses of a passing street car trampled her under foot. The doctors said she could not live till morning, but during the night she suddenly opened her eyes and her face lit up with a glad smile. Just before her lips were hushed in death, she said, *"Oh, Jesus, I have found you at last!"*

> —*Dying Words* by A. H. Gottschall

114

"Victory! Triumph! Triumph!"
John S. Inskip's Last Words

This great evangelist of full salvation was greatly used in bringing Christians from a life of wandering in the wilderness of doubts and fears to the "promised land" of perfect rest. For many years he was at the head of the great holiness movement in this country. His biographer says: "The agents whom God uses for special work are marked men — men who seem, by special enduement, to be leaders; and who at once, by their superior adaptation, command public attention and take their place, by general consent, in the front ranks. Such a character was Rev. John S. Inskip."

He was a great sufferer for many weeks before he died. On one occasion Mrs. Inskip said: "My dear, religion was good when you were turned from your father's home; it was good in the midst of labor, trials and misrepresentations; it has been good in the midst of great battles, and when the glorious victory came — *does it now hold in the midst of this great suffering?*"

He pressed her hand, and with uplifted eyes and a hallowed smile, responded, "Yes, oh yes! I am unspeakably happy." This was followed by "Glory! *Glory!*"

During his sickness he requested many of his friends to sing and pray with him. He was always cheerful, his face radiant with smiles and bright with the light of God. The last song sung on the day of his departure was "The Sweet By and By". While singing that beautiful and appropriate hymn, the dying man pressed his loving wife to his breast, and then, taking her hands in his, raised them up together, and with a countenance beaming with celestial delight, shouted, *"Victory! Triumph! Triumph!"* These were his last words on earth.

He ceased to breathe at 4 p.m., March 7, 1884; but so peacefully and imperceptibly did he pass away, that those who watched by him could scarcely perceive the moment when he ceased to live. On that day the Christian warrior, the powerful preacher, the tender husband, the world-renowned evangelist, was gathered to his fathers, and rested from his toil.

The battle's fought, the victory's won,
And thou art crowned at last!

—*The Life of John S. Inskip*

115

Clandious Salmasius A.D. 1653

A Distinguished French Classical Scholar

"*I have lost a world of time!* Had I one year more of life, it would be spent in pursuing David's Psalms and Paul's Epistles. I would mind the world less and God more."

—*Dying Words* by A. H. Gottschall

The Child Martyr

The noted evangelist, E. P. Hammond, supplied the following reliable and very touching article for this work:

I have been surprised to notice how many children have died a martyr death rather than deny Jesus. I want to tell you about one of these young martyrs. In Antioch, where the disciples were first called Christians, a deacon from the church of Caesarea was called to bear cruel torture to force him to deny the Lord who bought him with His precious blood. While he was being tortured he still declared his faith, saying: "There is but one God and one mediator between God and man, Christ Jesus."

His body was almost torn in pieces. The cruel emperor Galerius seemed to enjoy looking upon him in his suffering.

At length this martyr begged his tormentors to ask any Christian child whether it was better to worship one God, the maker of Heaven and earth, and one Savior, who had died for us and was able to bring us to God, or to worship the many gods and the many lords whom the Romans served.

There stood nearby a Roman mother who had brought with her a little boy, nine years of age, that he might witness the sufferings of this martyr from Caesarea. The question was asked the child. He quickly replied, "God is one and Christ is one with the Father."

The persecutor was filled with fresh rage and cried out, "Oh, base and wicked Christian, that you have taught this child to answer thus." Then turning to the boy, he said more mildly, "Child, tell me who taught you thus to speak? Where did you learn this faith?"

The boy looked lovingly into his mother's face and said, "It was God that taught it to my mother, and she taught me that Jesus Christ loved little children, and so I learned to love Him for His first love for me."

"Let us see what the love of Christ can now do for you," cried the cruel judge; and at a sign from him the officers who stood by with their rods, after the fashion of the Romans, quickly seized the boy and made ready to torture him.

"What can the love of Christ do for him now?" asked the judge, as the blood streamed from the tender flesh of the child.

"It helps him," cried the mother, "to bear what his Master endured for him when He died for us on the cross."

Again they smote the child, and every blow seemed to torture the agonized mother as much as the child. As the blows, faster and heavier, were laid upon the bleeding boy, they again asked, "What can the love of Christ do for him now?"

Tears fell from heathen eyes as that Roman mother replied, "It teaches him to forgive his tormentors."

The boy watched his mother's eye, and no doubt thought of the sufferings of his Lord and Savior. When his tormentors asked if he would now serve the gods they served, he still answered, "I will not deny Christ. There is no other God but one, and Jesus Christ is the redeemer of the world. He loved me and died for me, and I love Him with all my heart."

The poor child at last fainted between the repeated strokes, and they cast the torn and bleeding body into the mother's arms, supposing that he was dead. "See what the love of Christ has done for your Christian boy now!"

As the mother pressed him to her heart she answered, "That love will take him from the wrath of man to the peace of Heaven, where God shall wipe away all tears!"

But the boy had not yet passed over the river. Opening his eyes, he said, "Mother, can I have some water from our cool well upon my tongue?"

His eyes were closing in death when the mother answered, "Already, dearest, thou hast tasted of the well that springeth up unto everlasting life. Farewell! Thy Savior calls for thee. Happy, happy martyr! For His sake may He now grant thy mother grace to follow in thy bright path."

To the surprise of all, after they thought he had breathed his last, he again raised his eyes and looked to where the elder martyr was. In almost a whisper, he said, *"There is but one God, and Jesus Christ whom He has sent."* With these words upon his parched lips, he passed into God's presence, "where is fullness of joy," and to His right hand, "where are pleasures forevermore."

Are you, my dear reader, a Christian? If not, you can be-

117

come one now. That same Jesus who bled and died to save that little Roman boy suffered on the Cross for you. He is ready to give you a new heart, so that you will love Him so much that you would be willing to die a death of suffering rather than deny Him.

—Dying Testimonies by S. B. Shaw

Phillip III A.D. 1621

King of Spain

"Ah, how happy would it have been for me had I spent these twenty-three years that I have held the kingdom *in retirement!"*

—Dying Words by A. H. Gottschall

"I Can See The Old Devil Here On The Bed With Me"

"How shall we escape, if we neglect so great salvation."

—Hebrews 2:3

There lived at one time in our neighborhood a man whom we will call Mr. B—. He was intelligent, lively, a good conversationalist and had many friends. But Mr. B— loved strong drink and was not friendly to Christianity. He would not attend church and would laugh and make fun of religion. Some of his neighbors he called "Deacon so-an-so" for fun.

But Mr. B— was growing old. His head was frosted over with many winters, and he had long since passed his three score and ten years.

At the close of a wintry day, in a blinding snow-storm, a neighbor called at our home saying Mr. B— wished to see my husband. Knowing Mr. B— was ill, my husband was soon on his way. On entering the sick room, he asked what he wished of him.

"Oh, I want you to pray for me," he replied.

"Shall I not read a chapter from the Bible to you first?"

He assented, and the chapter selected was the fifth of St. John. While reading, Mr. B— would say, "I can see the old

118

devil here on the bed with me, and he takes everything away from me as fast as you read it to me. There are little ones on each side of me."

After the reading, prayer was offered for him, and my husband urged him to pray for himself.

"I have prayed for two days and nights and can get no answer," he answered. "I can shed tears over a corpse, but over this Jesus I cannot shed a tear. It is too late, *too late!* Twenty-five years ago, at a camp-meeting held near my home — that was the time that I ought to have given my heart to Jesus."

"Oh," he cried, "see the stream coming up! See the river rising higher and higher! Soon it will be over me and I will be gone."

The room was filled with companions of other days; not a word was spoken by them. Fear seemed to have taken hold of them, and one said after that, "I never believed in a Hell before, but I do now. Oh, how terrible!"

Mr. B— lived but a short time after this. He died as he had lived, a stranger to Jesus, with no hope in His cleansing blood.

—Mrs. E. A. Rowes

Philip III A.D. 1285

King of France

"What an account I shall have to give to God! How I should like to live otherwise than I have lived."

—*Dying Words* by A. H. Gottschall

"I Am Ready, For This (My Heart) Has Been His Kingdom"

Through the kindness of L. B. Balliett, M.D., we furnish our readers with the following incident:

A boy lay dying of his wounds in one of our hospitals during the Civil War. Realizing his near end, a Christian nurse asked, "Are you ready to meet your God, my dear boy?"

The large dark eyes opened slowly, and a smile passed over the young soldier's face as he answered, "I am ready, dear lady,

119

for *this* has been His kingdom." As he spoke he placed his hand upon his heart.

"Do you mean," questioned the lady gently, "that God rules and reigns in your heart?"

"Yes," he whispered, then passed away. His hand still lay over his heart after it had ceased to beat.

—*Dying Testimonies* by S. B. Shaw

Andronicus (393 A.D.)

The martyr Andronicus, after being imprisoned, was most cruelly scourged and his wounds rubbed with salt. Later he was brought out and tortured again, then thrown to wild beasts and afterward killed with a sword.

"Do your worst. I am a Christian. Christ is my help and supporter, and thus armed I will never serve your gods — nor do I fear your authority or that of your master, the Emperor. Commence your torments as soon as you please. Make use of every means that your malignity can invent, and you shall find in the end that I am not to be shaken from my resolution!"

—*Dying Words* by Gottschall

The Sainted Frances E. Willard

On February 17, the last day God let us have her with us, Mrs. Hoffman, the national recording secretary of our society, entered the room for a moment. Miss Willard seemed to be unconscious, but as Mrs. Hoffman quietly took her hand she looked up and said, "Why, that's Clara; good Clara! Clara, I've crept in with mother, and it's the same beautiful world and the same people. Remember that — it's *just the same.*"

A few moments later, a message of tenderest solicitude and love was received from dear Lady Henry. As I read the precious words I heard her voice, "Oh, how sweet, oh, how lovely, good — *good!*"

Quietly as a babe in its mother's arms she now fell asleep, and though we knew it not, "the dew of eternity was soon to fall upon her forehead. She had come to the borderland of this closely curtained world."

120

Only once again did she speak to us. About noon the little, thin, white hand — that active, eloquent hand — was raised in an effort to point upward, and we listened for the last time on earth to the voice that to thousands had surpassed all others in its marvelous sweetness and magnetic power.

She must have caught some glimpse of that other world for which she longed, for she said in tones of utmost content, *"How beautiful it is to be with God!"*

As twilight fell, hope died in our yearning hearts, for we saw that the full glory of another life was soon to break o'er our loved one's "earthly horizon". Kneeling about her bed, with the faithful nurses who had come to love their patient as a sister, we silently watched while the life immortal — the life more abundant — came in its fullness to this dear soul, whose cherished wish from her youth, that she might go, not like a peasant to a palace, but as a child to her Father's home, was about to be fulfilled.

Slowly the hours passed with no recognition of the loved ones about her. Then there came an intent upward gaze of the heavenly blue eyes, a few tired sighs, and at the "noon hour" of the night Frances Willard was:

> *"Born into beauty*
> *And born into bloom,*
> *Victor immortal*
> *O'er death and the tomb."*

—Adapted from *The Beautiful Life of Frances E. Willard*

Pastor Samuel Pierce A.D. 1799

"Blessed be His name who shed His blood for me! Now I fully see the value of the religion of the Cross. It is a religion for a dying *sinner*. It is all that the most guilty and most wretched can desire.

"Yes, I taste its sweetness and enjoy its fulness, even with all the gloom of a death-bed before me. Far rather would I be the poor emaciated creature that I now am than be an emperor with every earthly good, if without God."

121

Sudden Death

At one time during a prayer meeting my attention was directed towards an unsaved lady who was present, who appeared to be trifling. The pastor in charge of the meeting made the remark that as a watchman upon the walls of Zion, he felt that there was danger for someone there. He could not understand why he was impressed with this thought, and repeated that he felt drawn out to say that there was danger and someone there ought to get saved, *then and there.*

This irreligious lady appeared unconcerned and oblivious to his remarks and laughed when the minister shook hands with her at the close of the meeting. However, just as she was preparing to leave the church, she was taken very ill, so ill that she could not go home, neither could she be taken home by friends. Everything that could be done for her relief was done, but in less than one short hour she passed into eternity.

Before she died she tore her hair, cast aside the trashy ornaments which adorned her person — of which she had been very fond — and throwing up her hands cried aloud for mercy, *"Oh, Lord, have mercy on me! Oh, Lord, help me!"*

In this distress of body and soul she passed into eternity without leaving any hope to those that stood around her dying form.

This sad experience is a striking illustration of the danger of putting off the day and hour of salvation. *"For in such an hour as ye think not, the Son of Man cometh."*

—Julia E. Strail, Portlandville, New York

John Hus—Famous Bohemian Martyr

The great Bohemian reformer and martyr, John Hus, was born in 1369. He was burned at the stake as a heretic in Constance, Germany, July 6, 1415.

When arriving at the place of execution, he prayed, "Into Thy hands, O Lord, do I commit my spirit. Thou hast redeemed me, O most good and faithful God. Lord Jesus Christ, assist and help me that, with a firm and present mind, by Thy most powerful grace, I may undergo this most cruel and ignominious death to which I am condemned for preaching the truth of Thy most holy Gospel."

122

When the wood was piled up to his very neck, the Duke of Bavaria asked him to recant. "No," said Hus, "I never preached any doctrine of an evil tendency, and *what I taught with my lips, I now seal with my blood*." The fagots were then lighted, and the martyr sung a hymn so loud as to be heard through the crackling of the flames.*

—*Dying Testimonies* by S. B. Shaw

* It is also recorded that Hus said, "You may cook the goose today, but God shall raise up a *gander* and him you'll never roast!" Hus in Bohemian means "a goose," whereas *Luther* is derived in German from the word "gander." Luther was not even born at this time.

—*William Booth Clibborn*

William Pitt A.D. 1778

English Statesman, and First Earl of Chatham

"I have, like other men, neglected spiritual matters too much to have any ground of hope that can be efficacious on a death-bed. However, I now throw myself on the mercy of God through the merits of Christ."

—*Dying Words* by A. H. Gottschall

"I Die In Peace; I Shall Soon Be With The Angels"

Rev. J. M. Morris was born in Campbell County, Virginia, February 15, 1807, and died when he was nearly eighty-four years old at Mores Creek, California, February 4, 1891.

When Morris was twelve his father died, leaving him to be the main support of his mother. He had thirty days' schooling all told. By the aid of shell bark hickory as a substitute when out of candles, he devoted his evenings to study. He went through English grammar, arithmetic and part way through an advanced algebra without a teacher. When a man he was rarely surpassed in sound Biblical learning and doctrine.

In early life he was deprived of attending church and Sunday school, but he was impressed with the necessity of a change of heart. We give his experience in his own words:

"When a lone boy, having hardly ever heard anyone pray or preach, while all alone in the cotton field, with my hoe in hand, I became powerfully convicted that I was a sinner. I tried

123

to pray as best I could, and the Lord came down in mighty power and blessed my soul. I did not know what to do or say, but God put it into my mind to praise His name; so there, with hoe in hand, both arms outstretched, I shouted, *'Glory to God!'* All looked beautiful. The sun and sky never looked so bright as when I was alone in that cotton patch with no one near but God."

In meetings he would get shouting happy while relating this experience, and the holy fire would spread. Everyone would go home saying, "We had a good meeting; Morris was in the cotton patch today."

He crossed the plains in 1857 with ox teams to Trinity County, California. Going into a hotel near the mines, he demolished the bar where the grog was sold and preached for two years in the bar room, as it was called, where a class (church) of twenty-five or thirty was formed.

Though he preached and labored as colporteur in California, for about thirty years, he crossed the plains three times with ox teams and four times by rail. On these trips he preached in Iowa, Missouri and Kansas.

Disposing of all his little earthly effects in his last sickness, he said, "I die in peace with all men; I shall soon be with the angels. *All I want is to be a little twinkling star.*"

On calling Mother Morris, he said, "The other day you came to my bed and said, 'I want you to get well and pray as you used to once.' I have not been able to pray since, and I shall never be any better, but I want you to write to all the grandchildren and tell them I'd rather leave this request of their grandmother as a legacy *to them* than all the gold of Ophir."

He made us promise him that we would bury him in a plain coffin on the farm where he had lived for twelve years. No flowers or parade were to be given in his honor.

For thirty days we had watched day and night, taking four persons each night. All agreed that they did not know that anyone was capable of suffering so much as he did, but his patience and resignation held fast. He would say, "I am in the hands of the great God of the universe, *He knows best.*" Often he would pray, "Oh, help me to be patient. The will of the Lord be done."

After suffering thus for thirty days from asthma, lung trouble and something like the grippe, he drew his last breath just as if he were going to sleep, in his right mind and without a struggle or a groan.

—Adapted from an article in *The Earnest Christian*

Probus A.D. 303

Accused of being a Christian, he was scourged until the blood flowed, loaded with chains and consigned to prison. Some days later he was brought out and commanded to sacrifice to the heathen gods.

"I come better prepared than before, for what I have suffered has only strengthened me in my resolution. Employ your whole power upon me, and you will find that neither you, nor the Emperor, nor the gods you serve, nor the devil who is your father, shall compel me to worship idols!"

After much further torture and imprisonment he was finally killed with the sword, but his resolution held firm.

—*Dying Words* by A. H. Gottschall

He Saved His Face And Lost His Soul

A young man by the name of Smith was seen looking on with interest during a prayer meeting at a camp-meeting in Rootstown, Ohio. One of the ministers noticed him and spoke to him on the subject of his salvation. His eyes filled with tears and he seemed inclined to seek Christ.

One of his wicked companions, however, perceived this and stepped up.

"Smith, I would not be a fool." Poor Smith could not resist such influences. Dashing the tears from his eyes, he turned on his heel and went away.

He lingered about the camp ground until the meeting closed and then went off with his company. They bantered him on the subject of his feelings. To show them that he had not the feelings they supposed, he commenced cursing and blaspheming in a most awful manner, making all imaginable sport of religious things.

Suddenly a large limb from a tree fell on him and without one moment's warning—with a curse on his tongue—he was forced into the presence of the God whom he had thus been blaspheming.

—Rev. Thomas Graham

Jonathan Raine A.D. 1773

"Oh, the condescension of the Almighty, and *the unutterable love which fills my heart!*"

—*Dying Words* by A. H. Gottschall

"You Will Let Me Die And Go To Hell Before You Will Suffer A Negro To Pray For Me"

Mr. H——, a wealthy planter in South Carolina about 1860, came to his dying hour. He had made this world his god and used his influence and money against Christianity. When the last hour came he felt that he was a ruined man and requested his wife, who was as sinful as he, to pray for him.

Her reply was, "I can't do it. I don't know how. I never prayed in my life."

"Well, send for one who is a Christian to pray for me."

She replied, "For whom shall I send?"

"Send at once," said he, "for Harry, the coachman. He is a man of God."

"No," she replied, "I'll never do that. It would be an everlasting disgrace to have a Negro pray for you in your house."

"Then you will let me *die* and *go to hell* before you will suffer a Negro to pray for me!" And she did.

"Pride goeth before destruction, and a haughty spirit before a fall." — Prov. 16:18

—Rev. E. G. Murrah in *Dying Testimonies*

I Can Now Die Happy

A Young Woman Wins Her Lover to Christ at the Last Moment

Addie Asbury was dying. The doctor said that she could not live but a very short time, perhaps only minutes. She called her friends around her bedside and one by one bade them good-by, asking them to meet her in Heaven.

All at once she opened her eyes and said, "I want to see Tom." She had been engaged to marry Tom for several years, but would not marry him because he was not a Christian.

Being told that he was not there, she insisted that she had a message for him, whereupon she was assured that Tom would be sent for.

Knowing that she had but a short time and that Tom lived at quite a distance, her friends doubted whether he could arrive before she died. Seeming to read their thoughts, she said, "The God that I have loved and served can keep me here until he comes. I have a message for him, so please send at once."

We went for him, and although fully an hour elapsed before we returned, she was still alive and waiting. At once she reached out and took him by the hand, saying, *"Tom, I want you to be a Christian.* I am going to leave you and I want to know before I go that you are a child of God."

"Why, Addie," said he, "I can't say that I am a Christian when I am not. I would like to be, but I can't."

She then took her Bible and showed him from its sacred pages that he *could* be if he would repent and believe on the Lord Jesus Christ, who could forgive his sins. Right then and there the miracle took place — he accepted God's Word and opened his heart to the Saviour. What a blessed sight it was!

After bidding all good-by once more, the dying saint then closed her eyes and murmured, "I can now die happy. *Soul, take thy flight!"*

A few years later we saw Tom ordained a deacon in the Presbyterian Church not far from the place where his betrothed had died. He is now one of the pillars of the church and is a faithful defender of the cause of Jesus Christ.

—Rev. C. P. Pledger, Chicago, Illinois

John Randolph A.D. 1833

An American Orator and Statesman

"Remorse! Remorse! Remorse! Let me see the word — show it to me in a dictionary — write it on paper. Ah! — remorse! — *You don't know what it means!* I cast myself on the Lord Jesus Christ for mercy!"

—*Dying Words* by A. H. Gottschall

Thomas Paine

"My God, my God, why hast Thou forsaken me?"

Thomas Paine was born at Thedford, England, in 1737. He is widely known by his connection with the American and French revolutions and by his infidel writings. In 1791 he published his work, entitled, *"The Rights of Man.* In 1793, while in a French prison, he wrote his famous work, *The Age of Reason,* against atheism and against Christianity and in favor of Deism. In 1802 he returned to the United States where he "dragged out a miserable existence, indebted in his last illness for acts of charity to disciples of the very religion that he opposed." He died in 1809.

We quote from *M'Illvaine's Evidences:*

"Paine's first wife is said to have died by ill usage. His second wife was rendered so miserable by neglect and unkindness that they separated by mutual agreement. His third companion, not his wife, was the victim of his seduction while he lived upon the hospitality of her husband.

"Holding a place in the excise of England, Paine was dismissed for irregularity; restored and dismissed again for fraud, without recovery. Unable to get employment where he was known, he came to this country, commenced as a politician and pretended to some faith in Christianity. Congress gave him an office, from which, being soon found guilty of a breach of trust, he resigned in disgrace.

"The French revolution allured him to France. Habits of intoxication made him a disagreeable inmate in the American minister's house, where out of compassion he had been received as a guest. During all this time, his life was a compound of ingratitude and perfidy, of hypocrisy and avarice, of lewdness and adultery. In June 1809, the poor creature died in this country."

The Roman Catholic bishop Fenwick says: "A short time before Paine died I was sent for by him. He was prompted to do this by a poor Catholic woman who went to see him in his sickness and who told him if anybody could do him any good it was a Catholic priest.

"I was accompanied by F. Kohlmann, an intimate friend. We found him at a house in Greenwich (now Greenwich Street, New York), where he lodged. A decent-looking elderly woman came to the door and inquired whether we were the Catholic priests, 'for' said she, 'Mr. Paine has been so much annoyed of late by other denominations calling upon him that he has left express orders to admit no one but the clergymen of the Catholic Church.'

"Upon informing her who we were, she opened the door and showed us into the parlor. 'Gentlemen,' said the lady, 'I really wish you may succeed with Mr. Paine, for he is laboring under great distress of mind ever since he was told by his physician that he cannot possibly live and must die shortly. He is truly to be pitied. His cries when left alone are heart-rending. "O Lord, help me!" he will exclaim during his paroxysms of distress; "God, help me! Jesus Christ, help me!" — repeating these expressions in a tone of voice that would alarm the house. Sometimes he will say, "O God! what have I done to suffer so much?" Then shortly after, "But there is no God"; and then again, "Yet, if there should be, what would become of me hereafter?" Thus he will continue for some time, when on a sudden, he will scream as if in terror and agony, and call for me by my name. On one occasion I inquired what he wanted. "Stay with me," he replied, "for God's sake! I cannot bear to be left alone." I told him I could not always be in the room. "Then," said he, "send even a child to stay with me, for it is a hell to be alone." 'I never saw,' she continued, 'a more unhappy man. It seems he cannot reconcile himself to die.'

"Such was the conversation of the woman, who was a Protestant, and who seemed very desirous that we should afford him some relief in a state bordering on complete despair. Having remained some time in the parlor, we at length heard a noise in the adjoining room. We proposed to enter, which was assented to by the woman, who opened the door for us.

"A more wretched being in appearance I never beheld. He was lying in a bed sufficiently decent in itself, but at present besmeared with filth. His look was that of a man greatly tortured in mind, his eyes haggard, his countenance forbidding, and his whole appearance that of one whose better days had been but one continued scene of debauch. His only nourishment was milk punch, in which he indulged to the full extent of his weak state. He had partaken very recently, as the sides and corners of his mouth exhibited traces of it, as well as of blood which had also followed in the track and left its mark on the pillow.

"Upon making known the object of our visit, Paine interrupted, 'That's enough, sir, that's enough. I see what you would be about. I wish to hear no more from you, sir! My mind is made up on that subject. I look upon the whole of the Christian scheme to be a tissue of lies, and Jesus Christ to be nothing more than a cunning knave and impostor. Away with you, and your God too! Leave the room instantly! All that you have uttered are lies, filthy lies, and if I had a little more time I would prove it, as I did about your impostor, Jesus Christ.'

"Among the last utterances that fell upon the ears of the attendants of this dying infidel, and which have been recorded in history, were the words, *'My God, my God, why hast Thou forsaken me?'* "

—*Dying Testimonies* by S. B. Shaw

The Final And Greatest Proof

By Catherine Marshall

Recently, I was deeply moved by a plea from a broken-hearted mother. A short time ago her golden-haired three-year-old daughter was hit by a car in the street and killed instantly.

"Who is God, and where is He that He would allow this thing to happen?" she asked. "How do we know there is anything beyond death? I must *know,* somehow, that Jan is not dead, but just gone for awhile, and that I will see her again some-day. . . ."

Out of my own experience I understand this need of knowing. It always comes when death invades one's personal world. Prior to my husband Peter Marshall's sudden death in January, 1949, I had never seriously considered the subject of immortality. In fact, for years I had been doing what many do — ducking, pretending that I and the members of my family had a long lease on life. We were still young. Why should we even think about such gloomy matters?

But then came that day when, like the young mother, I needed answers. And I wanted them to be authoritative answers, not just someone's opinions. So I went directly to the most authoritative source I knew — the Scriptures, "the only infallible rule of truth and conduct." Here I found solid help.

My first discovery was that the Scripture writers never argued about immortality any more than Jesus argued about the existence and the love of His Father in Heaven. *The reason for these assumptions is that wise men knew that certain matters can never be proven by logic. They must be experienced. Then we know, and not until then.*

130

During His last talk with the Apostles on the night of His betrayal, Jesus pointed them to the path that they should follow in order that they might know. *"Because I live, ye shall live also,"* was His confident statement (John 14:19). Watch Me, He seemed to be saying. Watch what happens to Me on the third day. Then you will know finally and forever that there is no death.

And they did watch, and they did know. They knew so surely that they became utterly changed men. From timid, fearful creatures who had crept away into hiding following the crucifixion, after they had seen the risen Christ they became courageous men whose flaming declarations of faith nobody could silence . . .

"That which we have heard with our own ears, seen with our own eyes, handled with our hands, declare we unto you." (I John 1:1)

Then we find Paul picking up the joyous tidings and re-iterating the same line of reasoning, that the resurrection is the real proof of immortality:

"And if Christ did not rise, then those who have slept the sleep of death . . . have perished after all.

"But it is not so!

"Now is Christ risen from the dead. . . . He was seen of Cephas, then of the twelve.

"And after that He was seen of about five hundred brethren at once; of whom the greater part remain unto this present . . .

"After that, He was seen of James; then of all the Apostles.

"And last of all He was seen by me . . ." (Chapter 15 — I Corinthians)

Yes, but what if He has not been seen by us in this 20th century? How then would Jesus' resurrection be proof of immortality for us?

When I look back over the years of my own seeking, I know that once again the New Testament has not misled us. For I have come full circle in my thinking about immortality. A variety of evidential experiences have been granted me, but I know that they are just that — evidence, not the final word.

Nevertheless I am grateful for them, and have shared most of them in some detail in my books: like the comfort of the ever-lasting arms some four hours before Peter Marshall was to step over into the next life. It happened in the midst of churning emotions of fear from the realization that Peter was suffering another massive heart attack. Quite unexpectedly, a strange, all-pervading peace replaced the fear. *Love, of a quality that I never had felt before, flowed through and around from Someone who cared tenderly for Peter, for me, for our small son.* Only later did I realize that this was granted me, so that when the blow fell, I would have this proof that God's love had been with us every step of the way, in death as in life.

Then there was to come a dream in which I was allowed to see Peter briefly in his new setting. I spied him at a distance working in a rose garden. He looked as he always had; I would have recognized his characteristic gestures anywhere. As I sped to him, running with a lightness and freedom I had not known since childhood, he held out his arms to me. And yet, my impression was that Peter was preoccupied, bewildered by the swiftness of events that had dropped the curtain on his earthly life. He had not expected his own death. And the work in the rose garden had been lovingly provided to give him time to get his bearings, to make a difficult transition. For me there were so many new concepts implicit in this dream that to this day I cannot doubt its relevance.

Years later there was to be my father's death at 76, a gentle shepherding into the next life with every circumstance surrounding his going a series of blessed providences.

I even have had, all unsought, some psychical experiences through a Christ-centered couple who have gifts in this direction. The wife, in particular, has an extraordinary ability to see through the curtain which separates this world from the next.

There was that evening shortly after Easter, 1962, when we were chatting in their living room. Suddenly, apropos of nothing, the wife said, "Catherine, your father is here with us now. There are some things he wants to relay to you."

She spoke in a matter-of-fact voice. The room was fully lighted. There was not a trace of the atmosphere that one associates with seances or the like. In fact, I had come seeking nothing of the sort . . . "Your father wants you to know that he has had a reunion with his family. It has been a time of rejoicing."

I sat there thinking how typical this was of Dad.. He adored family reunions more than anyone I've ever known. But my friend had no way of knowing that. She never had met him in this life.

Then she went on, "He says that he has had many adjustments to make, rigid ideas to shed . . . He is a part of a little group which gets together frequently to check one another out on spiritual progress. At intervals, they are allowed the privilege of sitting at Jesus' feet for fellowship with Him.

"He says he is tremendously happy . . . "

I was moved by this experience, but to those who feel they *must* have this kind of confirmation of immortality, I point to the Parable of Lazarus and Dives in the New Testament. When Dives pleads that someone return from the dead to warn his five brothers, we have Christ's surprising statement that this kind of evidence would not convince or make them repent. (Luke 16:31).

Jesus was making an important point, namely that a psychical experience can be fascinating, even sometimes dangerously compelling, but it is periphery evidence. It is like seeking out medical advice from a nurse or midwife rather than making direct contact with the physician. Jesus Himself is the door . . . the way, even as He said (John 14:6).

There is another point that should be mentioned. The most valuable adventures in immortality usually come unexpectedly. Those whom I have known who went out deliberately seeking contact with their beloved dead, or messages from them, or proof, almost always have been disappointed.

Psychical or spiritualistic experiences fall short on another level, too. They may convince the mind, but to me they cannot satisfy the deep needs of a bereaved heart. So this is why I have come full circle right back to the path to assurance pointed out in the New Testament.

For if the resurrection really happened, then Christ is alive today. And if He is alive, then we, free spirits that we are, can choose to become His disciples. Then we, too, can get in touch with Him. *When that personal contact is made, then we shall be convinced that He is, in fact, who He said He was.* We can then trust what He told us — including His quite definite and clear-cut promises about immortality.

This means that Paul's argument as given in the 15th chapter of I Corinthians is just as valid in our century as it was in his. The alternative is stark . . . If Jesus did not rise from the dead, then He is dead like any other man, merely an historic figure with a fine ethic. He is a memory, a melody that has haunted succeeding generations — nothing more. The New Testament therefore is false. Christian preaching has been in vain. Generations of men have been deluded; we have no basis for our faith. We are, as Paul said, still in our sins. All who have died, have perished, and we shall perish, too. Eternity is a nothingness. All that — if Jesus did not, in fact, rise from the dead.

Then how can I be so sure that He is alive today? Because I decided to follow those New Testament signposts to see if they did bring proof of immortality. The signposts said, *Make Jesus Christ the center. Turn your life over to Him. He will tell you and show you and teach you what He wants you to know.*

The turning over of my life came in June, 1944. The teaching and the showing have been going on ever since. For since 1944 I have been living out one of the Bible's basic teachings about immortality: that we do not wait for physical death to enter into eternal life; rather it happens the moment we are *"born again."*

Thus every time I have known God's guidance . . . or an incisive answer to prayer . . . or have watched the miracle of His taking disappointments and frustrations and turning them into joys and blessings, I have had a foretaste of immortality.

Every time I have had depth-dimension fellowship with a friend . . . or have even seen a modicum of love let in to transform a sour human relationship, I have had a preview of immortality. For all of these are attributes of the life to come.

Therefore eternal life can be partially realized here and now. And in these daily realizations of a personal contact with Jesus Christ lie the real proof of immortality.

—Reprinted from *Guideposts* Magazine

Last Words Of Dr. Wakeley

"I shall not be a stranger in Heaven"

The death-scene of this saintly man was in harmony with his life-experience. Taken suddenly and violently ill, he was composed amid his acute sufferings and without alarm as to the issue. When the doctors informed him they had no hope of his recovery, he received the information without agitation and continued tranquil and happy.

I have seen many Christians die happily, but I never witnessed such perfect naturalness in the face of death. He conversed and acted in the same manner, with the same tone of voice, the same pleasant countenance and the same cheerful spirit which had characterized him in health. In his sickness, from first to last, everything he said and did was perfectly Wakeleyan. It really did not seem like a death-scene. It appeared more like the breaking of morning and the advancing of day than the approach of evening and the gathering of the night shadows.

At my first interview with him he said, "The doctors tell me there is no hope of my recovery; but I can say with Paul, *'I am now ready to be offered, and the time of my departure is at hand. I have fought a good fight; I have finished my course; I have kept the faith.'* "

He then added, "I see my crown and mansion and inheritance."

I said to him, "Yes, but you must die to possess them."

He instantly responded:

*"By death I shall escape from death
and life eternal gain."*

At another time he said, "I have fought long, fought honorably, fought heroically, fought successfully, fought for God, fought for Jesus, fought for Methodism, fought for Christianity. I have not gained all I wished; but, through Christ, I have taken great spoils."

He quoted, *"I am the Resurrection and the Life. He that believeth in Me, though he were dead, yet shall he live; and whosoever liveth and believeth in Me shall never die."* Looking at me very earnestly, he said, "Believest thou this?"

I said, "With all my heart."

He responded, with much emotion, *"So do I!"* Then, lifting up his hand, he said,

*The Head that once was crowned with thorns
Is crowned with glory now;
A royal diadem adorns
The mighty Conqueror's brow.*

"The spiritual kingdom of Christ in the earth is a mighty one. It must be set up in all the earth. It will over all prevail."

A few hours before his death I said to him, "What shall I say to your brethren in the ministry?"

"Preach the Word!" he replied firmly, *". . . be instant in season, out of season — reprove, rebuke, exhort, with all longsuffering and doctrine."* He repeated the words, *"with all longsuffering and doctrine"* three times.

After a moment's rest, while panting for breath, he added, "Tell them to preach the old Gospel — we want no new one. It cannot be improved upon. One might as well attempt to improve a ray of sunshine while vivifying a flower. The grand old Gospel forever!"

Speaking of his whole case, he said, "I leave *all* with God. I want it distinctly understood that I do so without any fear, without any cowardice, without any alarm. I do it with the boldness of an old soldier and with the calmness of a saint."

He added, "They will inquire in the morning, 'Is Brother Wakeley dead?' Dead? *No!* Tell them he is better, and *alive forevermore!*"

I said, "Yes, and a higher and nobler life."

He replied, "Wonderfully enlarged! Oh, wonderfully enlarged! I know the old ship. The Pilot knows me well. He will take me safe into port. Heavenly breezes already fan my cheeks. *I shall not be a stranger in Heaven.* I am well known up there.

"Like Bunyan, I see a great multitude with white robes, and I long to be with them. *'To depart and be with Christ is far better.'*

"When you go to the grave, don't go weeping. Death hath no sting. The grave hath no terror. Eternity hath no darkness. For many years neither death nor the grave had any terrors for me. Sing at my funeral:

> *Rejoice for a brother deceased;*
> *Our loss is his gain.*

"Listen! Hear ye not the song? Victory is ours! There is great rejoicing in Heaven. Roll open, ye golden gates, and let my car go through!"

Then, he added, "I must wait until the death-angel descends."

Soon the death-angel came — the silver cord was loosed and his freed spirit ascended to glory and to God.

—Bishop Janes of the Methodist Church
From *Dying Testimonies* by S. B. Shaw

John Randon

John Randon was a British soldier who fell in the battle of Bunker Hill. He said, "Bright Angels stand around the turf on which I lie, ready to escort me to the arms of Jesus. Bending saints reveal my shining crown and beckon me away. Yea, *Jesus* bids me come! *Adieu!"*

—*Dying Words* by A. H. Gottschall

The Sorrowful Testimony Of Cardinal Wolsey

Thomas Wolsey, one of the most distinguished men during the reign of Henry VIII, was born in the year 1471. When he became chaplain to the king, he had many opportunities to gain royal favor. These he used to the utmost. He successively obtained several bishoprics and at length was made archbishop of York, lord high chancellor of England and prime minister, and for several years the arbiter of Europe.

Emperor Charles the fifth and the French king, Francis the first, courted his interest and loaded him with favors. With immense revenues and unbounded influence, his pride and ostentation were carried to the greatest height. He had eight hundred servants, amongst whom were nine or ten lords, fifteen knights and forty esquires.

From this great height of power and splendor he was suddenly precipitated into complete ruin. His ambition to be pope, his pride, his exactions and his opposition to Henry's divorce occasioned his disgrace. Such a great reverse affected his mind and brought on a severe illness, which soon put a period to his days.

A short time before he died, after reviewing his life and the misapplication of his time and talents, he sorrowfully declared, "Had I but served God as diligently as I have served the king, He would not have given me over in my gray hairs. But this is the just reward that I must receive for my incessant pains and study, not regarding my service to God, but only to my prince."

—*Power of Religion*

Charles M. Talleyrand A.D. 1838

(Sometimes written DeTallyrand)

When dying, this great French statesman was asked by King Louis how he felt. He replied: "I am suffering, sire, the pangs of the damned!"

—*Dying Words* by A. H. Gottschall

"Mother, I'm Going To Jesus, And He's Here In This Room, All Around Me"

The noted evangelist of the last century, Rev. E. P. Hammond, supplied the following experience:

A lady from Brooklyn, New York, has just sent me a most touching story about a little cousin of hers, only nine years old. I could scarcely keep the tears from my eyes while reading it.

This little boy's praying mother had been called to part with five of her children. This, her youngest, she dearly loved, and when he showed signs of having learned to trust and love the dear Jesus she loved him all the more.

I will let you read a part of this kind lady's letter, just as it was read to me:

"One Sunday evening, last spring, he was left alone with his older sister, whose husband had died a few weeks before. After endeavoring to comfort her in various ways, he suddenly said, 'Sister, have you heard me tell a lie for a long time? I used to tell a great many, but I don't think I have now for six months, and I don't think God will let me tell any more. I don't want *ever* to do another wrong thing.' When he went to bed that night, she heard him pray that God would soon make him fit for those mansions that eye had not seen, nor ear heard about.

"On Thursday of that week he went with two other boys to get some fireworks — that he might 'amuse sister' on the fourth of July. The railway train was going very slowly up a long hill, and for fun the boys stepped off the back platform and onto the front one. Charley slipped, and the wheel of the carriage passed directly over his hip, crushing the bone to powder. He uttered one scream, and then never complained again.

"When a policeman was lifting him from his dreadful position, he opened his eyes and said, 'Don't blame anybody; it was my fault. But tell my mother I'm going right to my Savior.'

"The rough policeman in telling of this said, 'We all felt that there must be some reality in that boy's religion.'

"The sad news was told to his mother by two little street children, who expressed it in these terms: 'Does Charley live here? Well, he's smashed.'

"She followed the children and literally tracked her child by his blood to the hospital. When she entered the room where he lay, he opened his eyes and said, 'Mother, I'm going to Jesus, and *He's here in this room, all around me.* Oh, I love Him so much! Don't let them cut off my leg; but, if they do, never

138

mind — it won't hurt me as much as Jesus was hurt.'

"When his father arrived, he looked up and said, 'Papa, I am going to my Savior. Tell my brother Eddy if he feels lonely now — because he has no brother — to learn to love Jesus. He will be his brother and love him so much.' These were the last words he said, for in about two hours he bled to death.

"The hospital nurse was deeply touched, and as she closed his eyes said, 'He has gone to that Savior he talked so much about — *and I will try to love Him too.*'

"When his mother returned home, her only words were, 'The Lord has taken my Charley. Though He slay me, yet will I trust in Him.'"

—Dying Testimonies by S. B. Shaw

Francis Spira A.D. 1548

Francis Spira, a Venetian lawyer of wealth, learning and eloquence, was attracted by the fame of Luther and the principles of the Reformation. He even preached the evangelical doctrine for six years, but he could not bear the persecutions of that day. Again acknowledging Roman Catholicism, he publicly recanted in the presence of 2,000 people.

After making this public recantation he fainted and was ever after that a stranger to peace. Later, when sick and dying, he frequently called for water to quench his burning thirst and implored someone to kill him. When his friends began to bid him farewell, he declared that he felt his heart full of cursing and blasphemy against God. His last statement is recorded as follows:

"I have denied Christ voluntarily and against my convictions. I feel that He hardens me and will allow no hope. It is a fearful thing to fall into the hands of the living God; I feel the weight of His wrath burning like the pains of Hell within me. I am one of those whom God has threatened to 'tear asunder'.

"Oh, the cursed day! Would I had never been at Venice. I am like the rich man who, though in Hell, was anxious that his brethren should escape torment. Judas, after betraying his Master was compelled to own to his sin and to declare the innocence of Christ, and it is neither new or singular that I do the same.

"The mercy of Christ is a strong rampart against the wrath

of God; *but I have demolished that bulwark with my own hands.*
Take heed against relying on a faith which does not work a holy
and unblamable life, worthy of a believer. It will fail! I pre-
sumed I had the right faith; I preached it to others. I had all
places in Scripture in memory that might support it. I thought
myself sure, and in the meantime lived impiously and carelessly.
Now the judgment of God hath overtaken me, not to correction,
but to damnation."

—*Dying Words* by A. H. Gottschall

Clarence Darrow

"Intercede for me with the Almighty"

I was interested to read in a syndicated newspaper column
by a medical doctor that even Clarence Darrow, the famed ag-
nostic lawyer, was troubled in his soul as he lay on his death bed.

"Get me three clergymen," Darrow said to his law clerk.

When the ministers arrived, Darrow, who had laughed at
the Bible beliefs of William Jennings Bryan during the heated
Scopes Trial in Tennessee, this same Darrow said: "Gentlemen,
I have written and spoken many things against God and the
churches during my lifetime. Now I wish I hadn't! For I realize
it is entirely possible that I may have been wrong. So I should
like to ask a final favor — that each of you intercede for me
with the Almighty."

The ministers did pray for Clarence Darrow — and I trust
that he himself prayed the sinner's prayer.

—*The Log of the Good Ship Grace*
Vol. 33, No. 14, 1967

A Reproof From The Scaffold

In the year 1877, in Newark, New Jersey, a young man
was hanged for murder. Just before the fatal hour he said to
the Christian people about him, *"If in my early life I had received
one-half the attention and care from the good people of this city
that has been shown me since this trial commenced, I should
never have been a murderer."*

A few years ago we held a meeting in a certain town in Illinois. Two men had met their death on the scaffold just before our meetings commenced, and the excitement had not yet died away. We were told that two of the most prominent pastors of the city had shown considerable interest in these young men before they were executed. They visited them often, talking and praying with them, and both of them professed to be saved before they died.

One of the doomed men exhorted the people from the scaffold to take warning by his example, and urged them to seek the Lord before they became guilty of some sin which would cause them and their families disgrace.

If the interest of Christians had been brought to bear upon these criminals before their crime, they might have been saved in their youth.

—S. B. Shaw, *Dying Testimonies*

"Here She Is, With Two Angels With Her"

The following experience is taken from *A Woman's Life Work,* written by the saintly Laura S. Haviland:

One day on the street I met a sister White who was much distressed about her son. He was almost gone with tuberculosis; yet was unwilling to see any minister or religious person.

"Do, please, go with me now to see my son Harvey," she implored. "Maybe he'll listen to you."

I went to her house and found the young man too weak to talk much. Taking his emaciated hand, I said, "I see you are very low and weak. I do not wish to worry you with talking, but from your appearance I would judge that you have little hope of being restored to health."

He turned his head on his pillow as he said, "I can never be any better — *I can't live.*"

"Then your mind has been turned toward the future. May the enlightening influence of the Holy Spirit lead you to the Great Physician of souls who knows every desire of the heart and is able to save to the uttermost — even at the eleventh hour."

Still holding his feverish hand in mine, I saw the starting tear as he looked earnestly at me.

"Will it be too much for you in your weak condition if I should read a few of the words of our Lord and Savior?"

"Oh, no, I'd like to hear you."

I opened to the fourteenth of John and after reading a few verses I saw that the impression made was deepening. I asked if it would weary him too much if I should spend a few moment in prayer.

"Oh, no, I'd like to hear you pray," he answered.

Placing my hand on his forehead, I implored divine aid in leading this precious soul to the cleansing fountain. I asked that his faith might increase and that in its exercise he be enabled to find "the pearl of great price."

As I arose from his bedside, he reached out both hands for mine and said, "I want you to come tomorrow." He wept freely; and I left with the burden of that precious soul upon my heart.

The mother and sister, who were both Christians, stood near the door weeping for joy over the consent of the dear son and brother to listen to the reading and prayer.

The following day I returned, and as soon as I entered, his mother said, "Oh, how thankful to God we are for this visit to my poor boy! He seems in almost constant prayer for mercy. Early this morning he spoke of your coming today."

As I entered his room he threw up both hands, saying, "God will have mercy on poor me, won't He?"

"Most certainly," I responded; "His word is *nigh* thee, even in thy heart, and in thy mouth."

"Do pray for me," he requested.

I read a few words from the Bible and followed with prayer in which he joined with a few ejaculations. I left him much more hopeful than on the previous day.

The next morning his sister came for me in great haste, saying, "Brother Harvey wants to see you, *quick.*" It was not yet sunrise, but I hastened to obey the message as I supposed he was dying. But upon our opening the door he exclaimed, "Glory to God, Mrs. Haviland! Come to me quickly—I want to kiss you, for God brought me out of darkness this morning about the break of day! Oh, *hallelujah!* He shed His Blood for poor me! Oh, how I wish I had strength to tell everybody that I am happier in one minute than I ever was in all my life put together."

He became quite exhausted shouting and talking, and I advised him to rest now in the arms of the beloved Savior.

He answered, "yes, *I am* in His arms."

About two hours before Harvey died he suddenly looked at his mother, smiling, and said, "There's Mary! Don't you see her — standing at the foot of my bed?"

"No, my son, mother doesn't see her."

"Beautiful, beautiful she is. There, she's gone again."

Then, just as the soul took its flight, he raised both hands, with a smile, and said, "Here she is, with two angels with her. *They've come for me.*" The hands dropped as the breath left him, but the smile remained on his countenance.

The sister, Mary, had died a number of years previously at about the age of four. His mother told me that she had not heard her name mentioned in the family for months.

The Awful Death Of William Pope

"Once I could and would not; now I want and cannot."

The following is a short account of the life and death of William Pope, of Bolton, in Lancashire. He was at one time a member of the Methodist Church and seemingly a saved and happy man His wife, a devoted saint, died triumphantly. After her death, however, his zeal for religion declined, and by associating with backslidden hypocrites he entered the path of ruin. His companions even professed to believe in the redemption of devils. William became an admirer of their scheme, a frequenter with them of the public-house, and in time a common drunkard.

He finally became a disciple of Thomas Paine and associated himself with a number of deistical persons at Bolton. They would assemble together on Sundays to confirm each other in their infidelity and often amused themselves by throwing the Word of God on the floor, kicking it around the room and treading it under their feet.

But one day God laid His hand on William Pope, and he was seized with tuberculosis. Mr. Rhodes was requested to visit him. He says: "When I first saw him he said to me, 'Last night I believe I was in Hell and felt the horrors and torment of the damned — but God has brought me back again and given me a little longer respite. The gloom of guilty terror does not sit so heavy upon me as it did, and I have something like a faint hope that, after all I have done, God may yet save me.'

"After exhorting him to repentance and confidence in the Almighty Savior, I prayed with him and left him. In the evening he sent for me again. I found him in the utmost distress, overwhelmed with bitter anguish and despair. I endeavored to encourage him. I spoke of the infinite merit of the great Redeemer and mentioned several cases in which God had saved the greatest of sinners, but he answered, 'No case of any that has been mentioned is comparable to mine. I have no contrition; I cannot repent. God will damn me! I know the day of grace is lost. God has said of such as are in my case, *"I will laugh at your calamity, and mock when your fear cometh"* '

"I asked him if he had ever really known anything of the mercy and love of God. 'O yes,' he replied; 'many years ago I truly repented and sought the Lord and found peace and happiness.' I prayed with him and had great hopes of his salvation; he appeared much affected and begged I would represent his case in our church prayer meetings. I did so that evening and many hearty petitions were put up for him."

Mr. Barraclough gives the following account of what he witnessed. He says: "I went to see William Pope, and as soon as he saw me he exclaimed, 'You are come to see one who is damned forever!' I answered, 'I hope not; Christ can save the chief of sinners.' He replied, 'I have denied Him; therefore He has cast me off forever! I know the day of grace is past, gone — gone, never more to return!' I entreated him not to be too hasty, and to pray. He answered, 'I cannot pray; my heart is quite hardened. I have no desire to receive any blessing at the hand of God,' and then cried out, 'Oh, the Hell, the torment, the fire that I feel within me! Oh, eternity! eternity! To dwell forever with devils and damned spirits in the burning lake must be my portion — and justly so!'

"On Thursday I found him groaning under the weight of the displeasure of God. His eyes rolled to and fro; he lifted up his hands and with vehemence cried out, 'Oh, the *burning flame* — the *Hell* — the *pain* I feel! I have done the deed, the horrible, damnable deed!' I prayed with him, and while I was praying he said with inexpressible rage, 'I will not have salvation at the hand of God! No. — no! I will not ask it of Him!' After a short pause, he cried out, 'Oh, how I long to be in the bottomless pit — in the lake which burns with fire and brimstone!'

"The day following I saw him again. I said, 'William, your pain is inexpressible.' He groaned, and with a loud voice cried out, 'Eternity will explain my torments. I tell you again, I am damned. I will not have salvation.' He called me to him as if to speak to me, but as soon as I came within his reach he struck me on the head with all his might. Then, gnashing his teeth, he cried out, 'God will not hear your prayers!'

"At another time he said, 'I have crucified the Son of God afresh, and counted the blood of the covenant an unholy thing! Oh, that wicked and horrible deed of blaspheming against the Holy Spirit which I know I have committed!' He was often heard to exclaim, 'I want nothing but Hell! Come, O devil, and take me!'

"At another time he said, 'Oh, what a terrible thing it is! Once I could, and would not; *now I want and cannot!*' He declared that he was best satisfied when cursing.

"The day he died, when Mr. Rhodes visited him and asked the privilege to pray once more with him, he cried out with great strength, considering his weakness, *'No!'* That evening he passed away — *without God.*"

"There is a line by us unseen
That crosses every path,
A line that marks the boundary between
God's mercy and His wrath."

— From *Remarkable Narratives*

Little Springett Penn A.D. 1696

"All is mercy to me, dear father — all is mercy to me. Though I cannot go to meeting, yet I have good meetings. The Lord comes in upon my spirit. *I have heavenly meetings with Him by myself.*"

—*Dying Words* by A. H. Gottschall

Beulah Blackman, Teacher

"Oh, Ma, the Lord is here and I have the victory!"

Beulah Blackman was a girl of unusual loveliness and strength of character. As a school teacher, she held up the light of a pure and holy life, often bringing persecution upon herself by her unyielding adherence to the principles of Christianity and righteousness. On one occasion, while under the pressure of severe criticism, tears were streaming down her face as with a smile she told me, "This is good for me!"

145

She and my son, Lewis, were married in the summer of 1897, but on Easter Sunday of the following year — the resurrection day — her pure spirit took its flight to be forever with the Lord.

For months before she died she was unable to get out to church services, but she had her own "Bethel" (house of God). Her little red Bible was always near, and the young girls who helped in her housework received advice and admonitions which they will remember forever.

We were called to her home on Saturday evening, and when we entered the room she held up her hands for loving greeting as she said, *"Oh, Ma, the Lord is here and I have the victory!"* The Spirit came upon her, and she laughed and cried as we praised God together.

Upon the arrival of the doctor, she told him that a greater Physician than he had been there and had encouraged her so much. Since he was not a Christian, she added, "You don't understand it."

All through that long night she manifested such patient endurance. As her strength failed, she said again, "I am *so glad* I have the Lord." Just as the morning broke bright and beautiful, she welcomed her infant son into the world — with only time for one long kiss, and then to leave him motherless."

Her heart, naturally weak, failed, and she appeared to be paralyzed. An effort was made to arouse her so that she could look again at her babe, but she could neither move nor speak. Her husband begged her to speak once more but there was no answer. Then he asked her to smile if she still knew him. She did, and as he kissed the dear pale lips they parted in an effort to return the demonstration of love.

After that, like a weary child going to sleep in its mother's arms, she leaned her head on Jesus' breast and breathed her life out sweetly there.

As we wept she lifted her eyes upward and gazed an instant as if surprised, then a smile illuminated her face. A holy influence filled the room. There seemed to be angelic visitors waiting to conduct her home. The "terror" of death had fled and our tears were dried. It seemed as if the gates of Heaven were ajar, and a glimpse of the glory which awaits the faithful was given.

A moment more and all was over. A look of peaceful

victory rested on the lovely features. Truly God *is* our Father. *He is love.*

—Mrs. Anna M. Leonard, Manton, Michigan

Auld Peggy

After the gospel of God's Grace had been faithfully presented to the aged "Auld Peggy," she put down her pipe and anxiously weighed the matter. In a little while she resumed her pipe. Her face was callous and unmoved as she slowly uttered the words, "Na! Na! I've lived without Him seventy years, and I can live without Him the rest o' my days!"

Shortly afterwards she was found dead in bed, the pipe broken on the floor and the withered arms thrown above her head as if there had been a conflict with a foe.

—*Dying Words* by A. H. Gottschall

"Mother, You Never Taught Me How To Die"

More than 8,000 University of California at Berkeley students thronged the Greek Theater on campus to hear Billy Graham a few months ago.

So long as he referred to such subjects as LSD and the sexual revolution, loud cheers went up from this crowd of students. But when he touched on the issues of death and eternity, a respectful silence reigned.

Mr. Graham told them the true story of a campus queen who had been fatally injured in an auto accident. He quoted the dying girl's last words to her mother:

"Mother, you taught me everything I need to know to get by in college. You taught me how to light my cigarette, how to hold my cocktail glass . . . but Mother, you never taught me how to die. You better teach me quickly, Mother, because *I'm dying.*"

Yes, shipmate of mine, no person is prepared to live until he is prepared to die. It is impossible to live a truly joyful life unless you know for certain that you are ready to meet God.

—*The Log of the Good Ship Grace*
Vol. 33, No. 14, 1967

Sir Thomas Scott A.D. 1821

Sir Thomas Scott was Privy Councillor of James V of Scotland and a noted persecutor of the reformers. When dying, he cried out to the priests who sought to comfort him: "Begone you and your trumpery; until this moment I believed that there was neither a God nor a Hell. *Now I know and feel that there are both, and I am doomed to perdition by just judgment.*"

—*Dying Words* by A. H. Gottschall

He Saw The Other World

My father, William Foster, died near Chico, Texas, April 2, 1887, at the age of seventy-one years. He was one of the purest Christians I had ever known and was often made happy in the Savior's love. He died praising God. His last words were, *"My Heaven! Heaven! Glory!"*

I had often heard him remark that he did not believe that Christians ever saw departed spirits, while dying. I believed they did, so to satisfy myself I made the request during his sickness that if he came to die and should see spirits near him he would tell me. If he couldn't speak I told him to raise his hand in token that he saw them. Sure enough, just before consciousness left him, *he raised his right hand and pointed upward.*

I do praise the Lord for the dying testimony of one in whom I had so much confidence. Dear precious one! My mother also went home with the praise of God on her lips.

—Mrs. Dorcas Eskridge, Blue Grove, Texas

from *Dying Testimonies*

Miss Catherine Seeley A.D. 1838

"It has been eleven years since I opened my eyes to the full light of day or borne my weight on my feet. But my darkened room has been cheered by the smiles of Jesus, the Sun of Righteousness, whose blessed countenance sheds a luster upon everything that surrounds me and causes gratitude and praise to fill my soul. *Death has no terrors!*"

—*Dying Words* by A. H. Gottschall

Frances Ridley Havergal

There now, it is all over! Blessed rest."

This holy Woman of God was born at Astley, England, December 14, 1836. She was the youngest daughter of Rev. William H. and Jane Havergal, her father being a distinguished minister of the Episcopal Church. She bore the name of Ridley in memory of the godly and learned Bishop Ridley who was one of the noble army of martyrs. Many have been greatly helped by Miss Havergal's writings in both prose and verse. She died at Caswell Bay, England, on June 3, 1879. A short time before her death she said to her sister Ellen, "I should have liked my death to be like Samson's, doing more for God's glory than by my life. But He wills it otherwise."

Ellen replied, "St. Paul said, 'The *will of the Lord* be done,' and, 'Let Christ be magnified, *whether by my life or by my death.*'"

I think it was then my beloved sister whispered, "Let my *own* text, *'The blood of Jesus Christ, His Son, cleanseth us from all sin,'* be on my tomb. All the verse if there is room."

She said to her sister, "I do not know what God means by it, but no new thoughts for poems or books come to me now." At another time she said, "In spite of the breakers, Marie, I am *so* happy God's promises are so true. *Not a fear!"*

When the doctor bid her good-by and told her that he thought she was going, she answered "Beautiful, too good to be true! Splendid to be so near the gate of Heaven! So beautiful to go!"

The Vicar of Swansea said to her, "You have talked and written a good deal about the King, and you will soon see Him in His beauty. Is Jesus with you now?"

"Of course," she replied; "it is splendid! I thought He would have left me here a long while, but He is so good to take me now."

At another time she said, "Oh, I want all of you to speak bright, bright words about Jesus. Oh, do, do! It is all *perfect peace.* I am only waiting for Jesus to take me in."

Then, a little later, she sang the following stanza:

Jesus, I will trust Thee,
Trust Thee with my soul:
Guilty, lost and helpless,
Thou hast made me whole.

There is none in heaven,
Or on earth like Thee;
Thou hast died for sinners,
Thou hast died for me."

With deep feeling she emphasized that last word, "me." The parting scene is graphically described as follows: There came a terrible rush of convulsive sickness; it ceased, the nurse gently assisting her. She nestled down in the pillows and folded her hands on her breast, saying "There, now it's all over. Blessed rest!"

Then, all at once, she looked up steadfastly, as if she saw the Lord — and surely, nothing less heavenly could have reflected such a glorious radiance upon her face. For ten minutes we watched that almost visible meeting with her King. Her countenance was *so glad,* as if she were already talking to Him.

She tried to sing; but after one sweet, high note, "He—," her voice failed. As her brother commended her soul into her Redeemer's hand, she passed away. Our precious sister was gone — *satisfied* — *glorified* — *within the palace of her King!*

—From *The Life of Frances R. Havergal*

Girolamo Savonarola A.D. 1498

The Great Italian Reformer

When the Bishop announced the words, "I separate thee from the church," a sudden hope lit up the martyr's face, and he exclaimed:

"From the church *militant,* but not from the church *triumphant!* My Lord died for my sins — shall not I gladly give my life for Him?"

—*Dying Words* by A. H. Gottschall

The Atheist, Thomas Hobbes

"I am about to take a leap in the dark."

Thomas Hobbes was born at Malmesbury, in Wiltshire, England, April 5, 1588 and died at Hardwick Hall, in Devonshire, December 4, 1679. He was educated at Magdalen Hall,

150

Oxford, and the first part of his life, up to 1637, worked as a tutor in various noble families, often traveling on the Continent with his pupils. The remainder of his life was spent in a comprehensive and vigorous literary activity, first in Paris (1641-52), then in London, or in the country with the Hardwick family. The philosophical standpoint of Hobbes may be described as an application to the study of man of the method and principles of the study of nature. The results of this process were a psychology and a code of morals utterly antagonistic, not only to Christianity, but to religion in general.

On account of the merely preliminary stage which the science of nature had reached in the time of Hobbes, his conception is premature. However, he carried it out with great vigor, and it happens, not infrequently, that the materialistic psychology and utilitarian morals of today return to his writings and adopt some modification of his paradoxes.

—Adapted from an article in the *Encyclopedia Britannica*

We take the following from *Guide to the Oracles*: When the atheist, Hobbes, drew near to death, he declared, *"I am about to take a leap in the dark!"* The last sensible words that he uttered were, "I shall be glad to find a hole to creep out of the world. . . ."

Sir Thomas Smith A.D. 1577

Secretary of State to Queen Elizabeth

"It is a matter of lamentation that men know not for what end they were born into the world until they are ready to go out of it."

—*Dying Words* by A. H. Gottschall

An Infidel's Life Spared A Few Days

During the summer of 1862, I became acquainted with a Mr. A—, who professed infidelity, and who was, I think, as near an atheist as anyone I've ever met. I had several conversations with him but could not seem to make any impression on his

151

mind, and whenever I pressed a point strongly he would become angry.

In the fall he was taken ill and seemed to go into a rapid decline. I, with others, sought kindly and prayerfully to turn his mind to his need of a Savior, but we only met with rebuffs. However, as I saw the end drawing near, one day I pressed the importance of preparing to meet God. He became angry and said I need not trouble myself any more about his soul, as there was no God, the Bible was a fable, and when we die that is the last of us. He was unwilling that I should pray with him, so I left him, feeling very sad.

Some four weeks later, on New Year's morning, I awoke with the distinct impression that I should go see Mr. A—. I could not get rid of the impression, so about nine o'clock I went to see him.

As I approached the house I saw two doctors leaving. I rang the bell, and when his sister-in-law opened the door for me, she exclaimed, "Oh! I am so glad you have come. *John is dying!* The doctors say he cannot possibly live more than two hours, and probably not one."

I went up to his room and found him bolstered up in a chair. He appeared to have fallen into a doze. I sat down about five feet from him, and when in about two minutes he opened his eyes and saw me, he started up. There was agony on his face and in the tones of his voice as he exclaimed, "Oh, I am not prepared to die! There *is* a God; the Bible *is* true! Oh, pray for me! Pray God to spare me a few days till I shall know I am saved!"

These words were uttered with the most intense emotion, while his whole physical frame quivered from the intense agony of his soul. I replied in effect that Jesus was a great Savior, able and willing to save all who would come unto Him, even at the eleventh hour as He did the thief on the cross.

When I was about to pray with him, he again entreated me to pray especially that God would spare him a few days, till he might have the evidences of his salvation. In prayer I seemed to have great assurance of his salvation and asked God to give us the evidence of his salvation by granting him a few more days in this world. Several others joined in praying God to spare him in this way.

I called again in the evening. He seemed stronger than in the morning, and his mind was seeking the truth. The next day as I entered, his face expressed the fact that peace and joy had taken the place of fear and anxiety.

He was spared some five days, giving very clear evidence that he had passed from death to life. His case was a great mystery to the doctors. They could not understand how he lived so long; but we who had been praying for him all knew it was in direct answer to prayer.

—From *Wonders of Prayer*

St. Stephen A.D. 33

The first Christian martyr — stoned to death
"*I see the heavens opened, and the Son of Man standing on the right hand of God.* Lord Jesus, receive my spirit! Lord, lay not this sin to their charge."

—*The Bible*

"Seeing Him Who Is Invisible"

My beloved friend, Gertrude Belle Butterfield's last day on earth was May 24, 1898, and then she passed on to that fairer country whose inhabitants count not the days nor the years.

Only twenty-four years of the earth-life were given her; but, "*How long we live, not years, but actions tell.*"

In early girlhood she learned the beauty of a life in God's service and became willing "to spend and be spent for Him." Part of her service was evangelistic work, and only the last great garnering-time will tell how many soul-sheaves ripened from seeds of her sowing. When she saw the field of labor widening, she consecrated her life to mission work in foreign lands should God lead the way.

Upon graduating from the Evansville (Wisconsin) Seminary, a little less than a year before her death, she returned to her home near Reedsburg, Wisconsin. She was weary and worn from work and study, but thought rest was all that was needful. She felt that life was before her and that she was just ready to live. Love from one worthy — life's richest gift — had come to her, and her heart was satisfied.

But it was not long ere she knew that the weariness was

153

tuberculosis and that life's plans must be put aside. In a letter written in January she said, "Oh, it would be easy to go, so easy, if it were not for my life-work all undone. I cannot but feel that it would please Him to let me live and work for souls who know not my Jesus."

Later, however, even that unfinished work was given up to Him, and all was at rest. Dreams of Heaven came to her, and she was ready, yes, *glad* to go.

The last months of her life were very full of suffering, but there was no complaint. "Everyone is so kind," often fell from her lips at some attention from those who tenderly ministered to her wants.

Very precious is the memory of some days spent with her three weeks before her death. She was so pure, so gentle, so thoughtful of others, so like Him who had put upon her "The beauty of the Lord."

As the end approached, her sufferings became intense. The Sunday night before she went home, all thought the death-angel very near. She asked her friends to sing the beautiful hymn,

> *Fade, fade each earthly joy,*
> *Jesus is mine!*

For days she had scarcely spoken above a whisper, but now the Spirit of the Lord came upon her in blessing, and as she raised her hands she repeated, in a voice clear and strong, " *'O death, where is thy sting? O grave, where is thy victory? . . . Yea, though I walk through the valley of the shadow of death, I will fear no evil; for Thou art with me; Thy rod and Thy staff they comfort me.' "*

She was so eager for the release, asking those near her if they thought it the last, and saying, "Oh, I hope I won't be disappointed." But not until Tuesday afternoon did the end come and the soul escape as a bird from its prison of pain.

And we who await this "dawning light" that so thrilled her soul, treasure the memory of one "faithful unto death," our sainted Gertrude.

—Cora A. Niles

Isaac Shoemaker A.D. 1779

"Oh that I could tell you what I have seen and undergone! It would pierce the hardest heart among you. Perhaps some may think there is no Hell, but I have to tell you that there

154

is a Hell, and dreadful one too. And there *is* a Heaven where angels clothed in white robes sit at the right hand of God, singing praises to His great Name."

—*Dying Words* by A. H. Gottschall

"You Gave Me Nothing To Hold On To"

In a country village of Pennsylvania a physician gave books on infidelity to a young man and persuaded him to deny his Savior.

In about 1875 when the young man was fifty years of age he died. The infidel teacher was his physician, and as the end was approaching, the doctor told him to die as he had lived — a rejector of God and Christ.

"Hold on to the end," urged the doctor.

"Yes, doctor," said the dying man, "there is just my trouble — *you gave me nothing to hold on to.*"

The doctor did not reply.

—*Dying Testimonies* by S. B. Shaw

"Look At The Little Children — O Ma, I Must Go!"

My little sister, Minnie Chatham, was born in 1861 and died in the spring of 1873 at the age of twelve.

She was always of a sweet, gentle and religious nature and dearly loved Sunday school and her teachers. Her constant prayer was, "O God, give me a new heart." Sometimes her older friends would say to her, "Why, Minnie, you are a *good* little girl; you don't need to pray for a new heart." But she would reply, "Yes, I do. There is *none* good; we are *all* sinners."

During her sickness, which lasted two weeks, she suffered greatly, and father and mother stayed with her constantly night and day. One day she managed to get out of bed and kneel down at the footboard on the floor. With her hands clasped and eyes lifted toward Heaven, she prayed the most earnest prayer that I have ever heard. Her petitions were, *"O Lord, give me a new heart,"* after which she repeated the Lord's Prayer through. She then arose, clapped her hands and said, "Oh, I am *so*

155

happy!" Returning to her bed, she lay down and was as peaceful and quiet as though she had never experienced any pain.

Her mother had told her that Jesus could ease her pain; therefore, often when she was suffering we saw her little hands clasped in prayer. Sometimes she would sing a verse or two of her Sunday school songs that she loved so well. She called for her Testament and Sunday school papers, which she placed under her pillow and kept there until she died.

Shortly before she breathed her last she sat up in bed and said, "The angels have come for me, I must go! They are at the door waiting for me. Do, Ma, let me go! Why do you want to keep me here in this wicked world? I would not want to stay here for anything." And then she looked up toward Heaven and continued, "Look at the little children! Oh, Ma, I must go! I would not want to do anything to displease my dear Savior."

After this she called her father to her bedside, requested him to be good and meet her in Heaven and then added, "I want you all to be good." The next morning she said to her mother, "Now, Ma, if you had let me go, *I would have been with the angels this morning.*"

The day before she died, she sang her favorite Sunday school song:

> *There is no name so sweet on earth,*
> *No name so sweet in Heaven,*
> *The name, before His wondrous birth,*
> *To Christ, the Savior, given.*

> CHORUS
> *We love to sing around our King,*
> *And hail Him blessed Jesus,*
> *For there's no word ear ever heard*
> *So dear, so sweet as Jesus.*

Not long after this she closed her eyes and breathed her last as peacefully as though she had just fallen asleep.

Her public school teacher came to see her the day after she died. As she gazed at the little silent face in the coffin, she wept as though her heart would break. She said Minnie was the brightest and sweetest child she had ever met and was a perfect example for all her classes.

—Mrs. T. W. Roberts, East Nashville, Tennessee

Margaret Wilson

In the reign of Charles II, Margaret Wilson, a girl of 18, and a widow of 63 were condemned to be drowned because of being Protestants.

Two stakes were driven deep into the sand, but the one for the widow was placed further down the beach. The persecutors hoped that the young girl's fortitude might be shaken by watching the older woman's sufferings.

The tide rose and the widow struggled in her drowning agony. A heartless ruffian asked Margaret, "What do you think of your friend now?"

The undaunted young martyr answered, "What do I see but *Christ*—in one of His members—wrestling there. Think you that *we* are the sufferers? No, *it is Christ in us!* He does not send us to warfare at our own charges."

—*Dying Words* by A. H. Gottschall

Triumphant Death Of Jerome, The Martyr

This great Bohemian reformer and martyr, of the family of Prague, was born about 1365. He was an intimate friend of Hus, and suffered martyrdom at the stake in Constance, May 30, 1416, at the same place where Hus was burned.

Upon arriving at the place of execution he embraced the stake with great cheerfulness, and when the fagots were set on fire behind him, he said, "Come here and kindle it before my eyes, for if I had been afraid of it I would not have come to this place."

We take the following from *Schaff's Encyclopedia*:

Jerome studied at Oxford, probably in 1396 and returned to Prague with Wyclif's theological writings. In 1398 he took the degree of bachelor of arts at Prague, and subsequently that of master in Paris. Upon his return to Prague in 1407, he entered into hearty sympathy with the plans of Hus. In 1410 he went, on the invitation of the king of Poland, to assist in putting the University of Cracow on a secure basis, and from there he traveled to preach before Sigismund, king of Hungary. Being suspected of heretical doctrines, however, he fled to Vienna, but was put in prison, from which he was only released on the requisition of the university of Prague.

When, in October, 1414, Hus was about to leave for Constance, Jerome encouraged him to fortitude, and promised to go to his assistance if necessary. On April 4, 1415, he fulfilled his promise, but, on the advice of the Bohemian nobles, fled from Constance the day after his arrival. He was recognized at Hirschau by his denunciations of the council, taken prisoner and sent back in chains to Constance.

After Hus' death the council attempted to induce Jerome to retract — and succeeded on September tenth. However, the day following he withdrew his retraction. The council instituted a second trial, but not until the following May (1416) was he granted a public hearing. All attempts to move him again were unavailing. On May 30 he was condemned by the council as a heretic.

As the flames crept about him, he sang the Easter hymn, "Hail, festal day," and repeated the three articles of the Apostolic Creed concerning God the Father, Son and Holy Ghost.

The last words he was heard to say were, *"This soul in flames I offer, Christ, to Thee!"*

A Dying Mother Warns Her Children

"I have been leading you on the wrong road!"

A mother who denied Christ and sneered at religion came to her dying bed. Looking up from her restless pillow at the group of weeping sons and daughters gathered at her bedside, she said, "My children, I have been leading you on the wrong road all of your lives. I *now* find that the 'broad road' leads to destruction — I did not believe it before. *Oh! seek to serve God and to find the gate of Heaven,* though you may never meet your mother there."

So, amidst clouds and darkness, set the sun of her life.

—Dr. L. B. Balliett, of Allentown, Pennsylvania

The Testimony Of Norman Vincent Peale

Mr. H. B. Clarke, an old friend of mine, was for many years a construction engineer, his work taking him into all parts of the world. He was of a scientific turn of mind, a quiet, re-

158

strained, factual, unemotional type of man. I was called one night by his physician, who said that he did not expect him to live but a few hours. His heart action was slow and the blood pressure was extraordinarily low. There was no reflex at all. The doctor gave no hope.

I began to pray for him, as did others. The next day his eyes opened, and after a few days he recovered his speech. His heart action and blood pressure returned to normal.

After he recovered strength he said, "At some time during my illness something very peculiar happened to me. I cannot explain it. It seemed that I was a long distance away. I was in the most beautiful and attractive place I have ever seen. There were lights all about me, beautiful lights. I saw faces dimly revealed, kind faces they were, and I felt very peaceful and happy. In fact, I have never felt happier in my life.

"Then the thought came to me, 'I must be dying.' Then it occurred to me, 'Perhaps I have died.' Then I almost laughed out loud, and asked myself, 'Why have I been afraid of death all my life? There is nothing to be afraid of in this.' "

"How did you feel about it?" I asked. "Did you want to come back to life? Did you want to live, for you were not dead, although the doctor felt that you were very close to death. Did you want to live?"

He smiled and said, "It did not make the slightest difference. If anything, I think I would have preferred to stay in that beautiful place."

Hallucination, a dream, a vision — I do not believe so. *I have spent too many years talking to people who have come to the edge of "something" and had a look across, who unanimously have reported beauty, light, and peace, to have any doubt in my own mind.*

The New Testament teaches the indestructibility of life in a most interesting and simple manner. It describes Jesus after His crucifixion in a series of appearances, disappearances, and reappearances. Some saw Him and then He vanished out of their sight. Then others saw Him and again He vanished. It is as if to say, "You see me and then you do not see me." This indicates that He is trying to tell us that when we do not see Him, *it does not mean He is not there.* Out of sight does not mean out of life. Occasional mystical appearances which some experience indicate the same truth, that He is near by. Did He not say, " . . . because I live, ye shall live also" (John 14:19). In other words, our loved ones who have died in this faith are also near by and occasionally draw near to comfort us.

—From *Power of Positive Thinking,* Prentice-Hall, Inc.

Peace In The Storm

Some years ago a steamer was sinking with hundreds of persons on board. Only one boat-load was saved. As a man was leaping from the ship's side, a young girl who could not be taken into the boat handed him a note, saying, "Give this to my mother." The man was saved. The girl, with hundreds of others, was drowned.

The mother got the note. These were the words written: "Dear mother, you must not grieve for me; *I am going to Jesus.*"

—L. B. Balliett, M.D., Allentown, Pennsylvania

Governor Duncan Prays

"Oh, if I had only known. . . ."

Joseph Duncan was born in Kentucky about 1790. He served in the War of 1812, after which he moved to Illinois. As a member of the Senate of Illinois, he originated a law establishing common schools. He was elected a member of Congress in 1827 and Governor of Illinois in 1843. He died January 15, 1844. We take the following from *The Higher Christian Life* by Rev. W. E. Boardman:

For many years the Governor was distinguished as a Christian — a consistent member of his church. He was a rare and shining mark, both for the jests of ungodly politicians and for the happy references of all lovers of Jesus.

It is a very lovely and remarkable thing to see one occupying the highest position of honor in a State, himself honoring the King of kings. Happy is the people who exalt such a ruler to the places of power, and happy such a ruler in his exaltation — more, however, in the humility with which he bows to Jesus than in the homage which the people pay to him.

His conversion was clear. He renounced all merit of his own as grounds for his acceptance with God. The blood of

160

Jesus, the Lamb of Calvary, was all His hope. And all went well until death and the judgment drew near.

About three weeks before the hour of his death he was seized with the illness which he himself felt would end his life. With the premonition of death came the question of fitness for Heaven. He became troubled. The fever of his mind was higher than the fever in his veins—and, alas, he had not yet learned that Jesus is the Physician of unfailing skill to cure every ill to which the spirit is heir.

He saw plainly enough how he could be justified from the law, that it should not condemn him; for its penalty had been borne already by the Savior Himself, and its claims on the score of justice were all satisfied. But he did not see that the same Hands which had been nailed to the Cross would also break off the manacles of sin, wash out its stains and adjust the spotless robe of Christ's perfect righteousness upon him, investing him with every heavenly grace.

His perplexity was great. The night thickened upon him, his soul was in agony, and his struggles utterly vain. The point of despair is sure to be reached, sooner or later, by the struggling soul, and the point of despair to him who abandons all to Jesus is also the point of hope.

The Governor at last gave over and gave up, saying in his heart, "Ah! well. I see it is of no use. Die I must. Fit myself for Heaven I cannot. O, Lord Jesus, I must throw myself upon Thy mercy, and die *as I am*."

This hopeless abandonment was the beginning of rest to his soul. Indeed, it was the victory that overcometh, and soon the loveliness of Jesus began to be unfolded to him. He saw that the way of salvation from sin's *power* is just the same as with salvation from sin's *guilt*—through simple faith in the Savior.

The fire in his veins burned on, steadily and surely consuming the vital forces of his manly frame, but the fever of his spirit was all allayed by the copious and cooling draughts given him from the gushing fountain of the waters of life flowing from Jesus, the smitten Rock—*and his joy was unbounded.*

As his stricken and sorrowing family gathered around his bed for the last words of the noble man, he told them, with a face radiant with joy, that he had just found what was worth more to him than riches, or honors, or office, or anything else upon earth—*"the way of salvation by faith in the Lord Jesus Christ."* He then charged them as his dying mandate, by the love they bore him, not to rest until they too — whether already Christians as he himself long had been or not — had found the same blessed treasure.

They mentioned the name of a distinguished fellow officer and special friend of the governor's, living in a distant part of the state, and asked if he had any message for him.

"Tell him that I have found the way of salvation by faith in the Lord Jesus Christ, and if he will also find it for himself it will be better than the highest offices and honors in the reach of man upon earth."

So he died. "If he had only known this before," you say. Yes, that was *just* what he himself said: "Oh, had I only known this when I first engaged in the service of God, how happy I should have been! And how much good I could have done!"

Dr. Wingate

In his last moments Dr. Wingate of Lake Forrest College in North Carolina was heard personally talking to the Master, as follows:

"Oh, how delightful it is! I knew You would be with me when the time came, and I knew it would be sweet — *but not as sweet as it is!*"

—*Dying Words* by A H. Gottschall

"I Am Going To Hell!"

A preacher in the west sends us the sad account of his grandfather's death. He says:

My grandfather spent three years on the plains with the noted Indian scout, Kit Karson, but he had always been an unsaved man.

During the last three months of his life, when he was sick, he would often send for me to talk with him on the subject of religion. However, when pressed to seek the Lord at once, he would say, "I have got along so long, I think I will wait a while longer."

He died July 3, 1883 and almost (if not) the last words he uttered were these: *"I am going to Hell!"*

162

Awfully sad — fearfully true. He put off the most important duty of this life until it was too late, *forever too late.*

—From an article in *Dying Testimonies* by S. B. Shaw

Triumphant Death Of Martin Luther

This great German reformer was born at Eisleben (a town in Saxony not far from Wittenberg), November 10, 1483. He died at the same place, February 18, 1546. We take the following from *Schaff's Encyclopedia*:

Luther stands forth as the great national hero of the German people and the ideal of German life. Perhaps no other cultivated nation has a hero who so completely expresses the national ideal. King Arthur comes, perhaps, nearest to Luther among the English-speaking race.

He was great in his private life as well as in his public career. His home was the ideal of cheerfulness and song. He was great in thought and great in action. He was a severe student and yet skilled in the knowledge of men. He was humble in the recollection of the power and designs of a personal Satan, yet bold and defiant in the midst of all perils. He could beard the Papacy and imperial councils, yet he fell trustingly before the Cross. He was never weary, and there seemed to be no limit to his creative energy.

Thus Luther stands before the German people as the type of German character. Goethe, Frederick the Great, and all others, in this regard, pale before the German reformer. He embodies in his single person the boldness of the battlefield, the song of the musician, the joy and care of the parent, the skill of the writer, the force of the orator and the sincerity of rugged manhood — but also the humility of the Christian.

His last words were, *"O my Heavenly Father, my eternal and everlasting God! Thou hast revealed to me Thy Son, our Lord Jesus Christ! I have preached Him! I have confessed Him! I love Him and I worship Him as my dearest Savior and Redeemer! Into Thy hands I commit my spirit."*

—*Schaff's Encyclopedia*

John Wilmot A.D. 1680

Second Earl of Rochester

John Wilmot was saved from a life of deep sin and infi-.delity. When dying he laid his hand upon the Bible and said in earnestness and solemnity:

"The only objection against this Book is a bad life; I shall die now; but *oh, what unspeakable glories do I see!* What joys beyond thought or expression am I sensible of! I am assured of God's mercy to me through Jesus Christ. *Oh, how I long to die!"*

—*Dying Words* by A. H. Gottschall

Dying In Despair

About 1880, while we were doing some evangelistic work, early one morning a little boy with a very sad heart called at our room to say that his mother was dying and wished to see us. We hurried to his home, and as we opened the door we beheld a sorrowful sight — a woman in complete despair. The expression on her face and the sad look in her eyes told of great agony.

We were at a loss to know just what to say or do. Our heart was full. We said to her, "You are in great pain."

With a wild look she replied, "Yes, I am in great pain; but that is nothing compared with the thought of going to meet God unprepared. What is this physical suffering compared to the remorse of conscience and the dark future before me!"

Then she cried out in agony, " 'All is vanity!' I have lived for self and tried to find pleasure at the dance and other places of amusement. I have neglected the salvation of my soul! I am unprepared to meet God! Pray for me — *Oh, pray for me!"*

While we prayed she would say, "God help me! What shall I do? Is there any hope for a poor sinner like me?" and many other similar expressions. Her ungodly husband cried bitterly while she told of their past sinful life. Her heart was hardened with sin, her ears were dull of hearing and her eyes too blind to see the light of God.

Her friends were coming in from the village and surrounding country to see her die. As they entered the room, she would take each one of them by the hand and plead with them not to

164

follow her example and live as she had lived. Holding an uncle by the hand, a man deep in sin and who seemed to be far from God, she said, "Uncle, prepare to meet your God. Don't wait until you come to your dying day, as I have done. When you plow your ground, *pray*. When you plant your corn, *pray*. When you cultivate, *pray*. Whatever you do, *pray!*"

Many of her friends wept and promised to live better lives. Her mental agony was so far beyond her physical pain that she seemed to be unconscious of her intense bodily suffering. Her sins seemed to loom up before her as a great mountain, hiding from her the presence and love of God.

As long as she was able to speak, she prayed and requested others to do so, but finally the voice that had been pleading so pitifully for mercy and warning others by the example of her ungodly life, was hushed in the silence of death.

Soon after her death we called on her husband and reminded him of his wife's dying testimony, urging him to attend the evangelistic meetings we were holding in the town. But he was full of prejudice against Christianity and gave us no encouragement. He still continued to walk in the same sinful path as before.

—Rev. S. B. Shaw, from *Dying Testimonies*

"I Am So Glad I Have Always Loved Jesus"

Miss Orphie B. Schaeffer, daughter of Rev. G. F. Schaeffer, a Lutheran minister, who at that time was President of the North Carolina Lutheran College, was visiting at our home, and we soon became very warm friends. Suddenly, however, Orphie was taken ill, her sickness developing into a serious case of typhus fever which resulted in her death two weeks later.

During her illness she would often speak of her loved ones, far away in Easton, Pennsylvania. We had not wired them of her illness, as we did not realize that it was of such a serious nature until the end drew near.

She loved her Savior and put her utmost confidence in God. Often she would say, "It is so sweet to love Jesus. I have always loved Him."

As I stood at her bedside as she was dying, she called me to come closer to her and said, "Mollie, I hear the *sweetest music.*"

165

I asked her where the sound of the music came from, and she replied, "Oh, just over the hill. Do you not hear them say, 'Peace on earth, good will toward men'?"

Again her wan features lighted up with the very light of Heaven, and she said, "Oh, can't you hear them singing? Do listen."

I strained my eager ears to catch the sound to which I knew she was listening, but I could hear nothing save her labored breathing.

Soon after she said, "Good-by mamma! Good-by Florence! Good-by, papa!" and just then was seized with a hemorrhage which caused her to grow weaker and weaker.

Finally, just before the last, we heard her say once more, *"I am so glad that I have always loved Jesus."*

—Adapted from a letter by Mollie J. Herring,
Clear Run, North Carolina

Chief Vara

A Warrior

In the days of his ignorance Chief Vara was a mighty warrior and had offered human sacrifices. After his conversion, however, he became a devoted Christian.

"I have been very wicked, but a great King from the other side of the skies sent His ambassadors with terms of peace. We could not tell for many years what these ambassadors wanted, but at length Pomare invited all his subjects to come and take refuge under the wings of Jesus. I was one of the first to do so.

The blood of Jesus is my foundation, and I grieve that all my children do not know Him. My *outside* man and my *inside* man differ — let the one rot till the trumpet shall sound, *but let my soul wing her way to Jesus!*

—*Dying Words* by A. H. Gottschall

"Murder! Murder! Murder!"

When Mr. R—, from Baltimore, was seized with cholera, he sent for me. When I entered the room, he said, "My wife, who is a Christian woman, has been writing to me ever since

166

I came here, urging me to make your acquaintance and attend your church. But I have not done it; and what is worse, I am about to leave the world with no preparation to meet God."

He was a noble-looking man, and since I knew many of his friends in Baltimore, I felt the greatest possible sympathy for him. My soul loved him, and I determined, if possible, to contest the Devil's claim on him to the last moment of his life.

But he was in despair, and after laboring with him about an hour, urging him to try to fix his mind on some precious promise of the Bible, he said, "There is but one passage in the Bible that I can call to mind, and that haunts me. I can think of nothing else — it exactly suits my case: *'He that being often reproved, hardeneth his heart, shall suddenly be destroyed, and that without remedy.'* Mr. Taylor," he continued, "it's no use to talk to me or to try to do anything further. I am *that* man, and my doom is fixed."

The next day when I entered his room he said to a couple of young men present, "Go out, boys, I want to talk to Mr. Taylor." Then he said, "I have no hope, but for the warning of others I want to tell you something that occurred a few months ago when I was in health and doing a good business. A man said to me, 'Dick, how would you like to have a clerkship?' I replied, 'I wouldn't have a clerkship, even under Jesus Christ.' Now, sir, that is an example of the way I treated Christ when I thought I did not need Him. Now, when I'm dying and can do no better in this life, it's presumption to offer myself to Him. It is no use; He won't have me."

Nothing that I could say seemed to have any effect toward changing his mind.

A few hours afterward, when he felt the icy grasp of death upon his heart, he cried, "Boys, help me out of this place!"

"No, Dick, you're too sick," they replied, "We cannot help you up."

"Oh, do help me up! I can't lie here!"

"Please, Dick, don't exert yourself so; you'll hasten your death."

"Boys!" gasped the poor fellow, "if you don't help me up I'll cry Murder!" — and with that he cried at the top of his voice, *"Murder! — murder! — murder!"* till life's tide ebbed out, and his voice was hushed in death.

How dreadful the hazard of postponing the great object

for which life is given to the hour when heart and flesh are failing!

—Adapted from an article in *California Life Illustrated*

"It Is I, Be Not Afraid"

"Say ye to the righteous, that it shall be well with him."

So it was with the devout Bishop Glossbrenner when he had reached the end of his earthly pilgrimage, January 7, 1887. Mr. John Dodds, of Dayton, Ohio, a warm personal friend of the bishop, spent a day or two with him shortly before his death and found him in a most blessed frame of mind. When the subject of preaching was referred to, he said, "If I could preach again just once more, I would preach *Jesus*. I would preach from His words to the disciples on the Sea of Galilee, '*It is I, be not afraid.*'"

As Mr. Dodds was leaving, he looked back and to his surprise the bishop had gotten out of bed unassisted and was standing by the door. He was visibly affected, and with hand uplifted and tears running down his cheeks, said, "Tell my brethren it is all right. *My home is over there!*"

To another he said, "My title is clear, but not because I have preached the Gospel, but *alone* by the love and mercy and grace of our Lord Jesus Christ. Rely upon *nothing* but Jesus Christ and an experimental knowledge of acceptance with God through the merits of Jesus."

In view of his rapidly approaching end, he said to his pastor, "I shall not be here much longer." When asked about the future his reply was, "Everything is as bright as it can be. What a blessing it is to have a Savior at a time like this."

His last whispered words were, *"My Savior!"*

—From an article in *Life to Life*

Hugh Latimer, Martyr Of The English Reformation

"We shall light a candle in England today as will never go out!"

Hugh Latimer, one of the most influential preachers, heroic martyrs and foremost leaders of the English reformation, was born at Thurcaston, Leicestershire, in about 1491, and died at the stake in Oxford, October 16, 1555.

Under the reign of Mary, Latimer was committed to the Tower as a "seditious fellow". To the Tower Ridley and Cranmer were also sent, and in March of that year all three were brought before the Queen's commisisoners at Oxford, condemned for heresy, and sent back into confinement.

Eighteen months later Latimer and Ridley were brought down to Oxford to be burned. When stripped for execution Latimer had on a long shroud. There he stood, this withered old man — quite erect and perfectly happy, with a bag of powder tied around his neck. They embraced each other at the stake, knelt and prayed and then kissed the stake.

Just as the fire was lighted, Latimer addressed his fellow-sufferer in the memorable words, *"Be of good comfort, Brother Ridley, and play the man. We shall light such a candle in England today as will never go out!"*

As the flames leaped up he cried vehemently, "O Father of Heaven — receive my soul!" He seemed to embrace the flames. Having stroked his face, he bathed his hands in the fire and quickly died.

The amount paid by Queen Mary for lighting that fire was £1 5s. 2d. To Roman Catholicism that fire was the costliest ever kindled. To England — thank God — it was the light of religious liberty, the candle of the reformation.

—Adapted from *Life Stories of Remarkable Preachers*

Giles Tolleman A.D. 1544

A Martyr of Brussels

When an opportunity to escape prison offered itself he would not take advantage of it. "I would not do the keepers so much injury, as they would have to answer for my absence."

At the stake the executioner offered to strangle him before the fire was lighted, but he would not consent, saying that he did not fear the flames. There was a large pile of wood at the place of execution. He asked that the principal part of it be given to the poor, saying, "A small quantity will suffice to consume me."

He then died with much composure.

—*Dying Words* by A. H. Gottschall

Abandoned To Die Alone

P— K— was a talented and wealthy man, but he hated everything connected with God, the Lord Jesus Christ and the Holy Bible. He talked, lectured and published books and tracts against the Savior and the sacred Scriptures, circulating them freely wherever he could. His influence for evil was very great for many years.

From a near neighbor and from members of his household the following facts are learned concerning his death:

His death-bed beggared description. He clenched his teeth, and blood spurted from his nostrils while he cried *"Hell! Hell!! Hell!!!"* with a terror that no pen can describe. A neighbor declared that he heard him a quarter of a mile away.

His family could not endure the agony of that death-bed scene. They fled to an adjoining wood across the road and there remained among the trees until all became quiet at home. One by one they ventured back, to find the husband and father cold in death. He literally had been left to die *alone,* abandoned of God and of man.

—Milburn Merrill, Denver, Colorado,
Dying Testimonies by S. B. Shaw

"Why! Heaven Has Come Down To Earth"

"Precious in the sight of the Lord is the death of His saints." Co-worker with Dr. Redfield and the glorious little band of early Free Methodists was the Rev. William Kendall. He died February 1, 1858, and the closing scenes of his life were so blessed that we give them a place here:

He revived on the Sunday before his death and was very happy, his face radiant with glory. He said, "This is the most blessed Sunday I ever knew."

The next day he had a severe conflict with Satan, but gained a glorious victory. He said, "Jesus, the mighty Conqueror reigns!"

The next day he exclaimed, *"Why, Heaven has come down to earth! I see the angels. They are flying through the house!"*

After a little sleep, he awoke and exclaimed, "I have seen the King in His beauty — King of glory. I have slept in His palace!"

170

For a while he was delirious. Again he had a conflict with the powers of darkness, but quickly triumphed, exclaiming with a smile, "I can grapple with the grim monster, *death*."

On Sunday he was thought to be dying. His wife put her ear to his lips as he lay gazing upward and waving his arms, as though fluttering to be gone. She heard him breathe, "Hail! All hail!"

"What do you see?" she asked.

"I see light! light! light! I see—" He paused in silence for a while, then suddenly began to sing in a clear, though somewhat faltering tone:

Hallelujah to the Lamb who hath purchased our pardon.
We'll praise Him again when we pass over Jordan!

One asked, "Is all well?" He replied, with ineffable sweetness, three times, "*All is well!*"

The chill of death came and pointed to his speedy relief, but once more he revived and sang very sweetly, "O how happy are they, who their Savior obey."

Then followed with:

My soul's full of glory, inspiring my tongue;
Could I meet with the angels, I'd sing them a song.

A few more struggles of nature and the silver cord loosened — and the warrior fell to rise immortal.

—Adapted from an article in *Wayside Sketches*

Peter The Great, Czar Of Russia A.D. 1725

He was filled with remorse because of his cruelty to his son. In his dying hour he cried, "I believe, Lord, and confess — *help my unbelief!*"

—*Dying Words* by A. H. Gottschall

"Oh, I Can See The Angels All In The Room. Can't You See Them?"

My sainted mother's death was one of triumph and great victory. She was a woman of great faith and made the Bible her constant study. Some years before her death, realizing that she could be established in the faith, she went to God in earnest

171

prayer and made an entire consecration. By faith she was enabled to take Christ as a *complete* Savior and knew that the Blood of Jesus cleansed her from all sin. From that time she lived in an ocean of God's love and was kept from all sin by the power of God through faith.

One Sunday morning while preparing for church mother took a chill. From that time on until her death she knew she was going to die. She remarked to her eldest daughter, "I have been looking for something to happen for a long time to bring father back to Jesus, but I thought He was going to take Samuel" (their eldest boy).

She exhorted my father to give his heart to God, saying, "I am going to Heaven — meet me there." He had great faith in her prayers and begged her to pray that God would spare her life. "I cannot live without you and raise the children alone!"

With a heavenly smile upon her face and faith unwavering she said to him, "God will take care of you and the children. Weep not for me, I am going to glory!" Then she added, "Never touch liquor any more!" He promised her he would not. Then she exhorted us all to meet her in Heaven.

Suddenly she shouted aloud and praised God, saying, *"Oh, I can see the angels all in the room. Can't you see them?*

At her request, we sang, "I saw a wayworn traveler," and "Oh, come angel band". She joined with us, and while singing the last song her spirit went home to God.

From the time of mother's death our father kept his vow. He erected a family altar and taught us six children, both by example and precept, to trust in our mother's God and meet her in Heaven. Every night and morning he would take us to God in prayer around the family altar, and five years after mother's death he too died in the triumphs of faith and went to Heaven.

—Adapted from a letter by Mrs. Anna Crowson
of China Spring, Texas (about 1898)

"The Angels Say There Is Plenty Of Room Up There"

Kate H. Booth, of Buffalo, New York, offered the following account of her sister's happy death:

My sister was a devoted Christian, and to show the depth of her piety, I shall first quote from her diary:

"Friday, August 22, — I consecrated myself anew to follow God. The fire came down and consumed the sacrifice. All was put on the altar and remains there.

"Tuesday, August 26—I received such a baptism as I never received before, and today I say, 'Anyway, Jesus, only glorify Thyself.'

Give Joy or grief, give ease or pain,
Take life or friends away,
But let me find them all again,
In that eternal day.

"Sudden death would be sudden glory."

She was constantly praising the Lord for His mercy and grace and was thankful for every kindness shown. Some of her expressions were: "It's all right; it is all clear. Death has lost its sting—I am almost there."

One evening while the sun was setting and the autumn leaves were tinged with a golden hue, she said, *"Yea, though I walk through the valley of the shadow of death I will fear no evil, for Thou art with me. Thy rod and Thy staff, they comfort me."*

One day she had a vision of the unseen world. Her face became radiant with a divine glow, and it seemed as though she was about to leave us.

I called, "Oh, Jennie, What are your last words?"

She revived and said, "Be true. But what made you call me back?"

I said, "What did you see?"

"It's all right there," she replied and waved her hand in token of victory.

During her illness she often expressed the desire that she might retain consciousness to the last and requested all of us to pray that this wish might be fulfilled. Her desire was granted, and in full possession of her faculties she came to the river's brink.

As the end neared she would repeat the lines:

Labor is rest and pain is sweet,
If Thou, my God, art here.

Upon one occasion, she asked me to read the hymn commencing, "How blest the righteous when he dies." She thought it so beautiful that she requested it be sung at her funeral.

On Tuesday night she said, "It is a hard struggle tonight, but a glorious victory tomorrow."

Wednesday was her last day on earth—a bright and glorious

173

one too, for she felt she was soon to enter the presence of her Lord. It was the first of October and her father's birthday.

In the evening, just an hour or two before the end, the doctor came in. She looked up at him with a smile and said, "Doctor, how am I?" The tears were coursing down his cheeks, when she added, *"The angels say there is plenty of room up there!"*

—*Dying Testimonies* by S. B. Shaw

The Great Contrast — "Forever" or "Till Morning"

Edward Adams, the noted actor's last words were, "Goodby, Mary; good-by *forever!"* What a contrast to one of the martyrs who, while going to the stake, said to his wife, "Goodby, Mary, *till morning!"*

The next morning this Mary — the martyr's wife — while being put into a sack to be thrown into a pond, handed her babe to a kind neighbor and said, "Goodby, children! Good-by friends! I go to my husband. We will soon meet again — *Christ lights the way!"*

—L. B. Balliett, M.D., in *Dying Testimonies* by S. B. Shaw

"Then I Am Damned To All Eternity"

The following is adapted from an article by Rev. Thomas Graham, the well-known evangelist of the last century:

When I was holding a meeting in Middlesex, Pennsylvania, in 1843, a man named Edwards died.

He had killed a hog, and while preparing the sausages, he took some of the ground pepper and in fun attempted to make some friends sneeze. One of the company succeeded in doing so to him, causing him to sneeze twice. This broke a blood vessel.

The doctor was sent for, but to no avail. The rupture was so far up in the head that nothing could be done for him. When he was told that he must die, he shrieked so that he could be heard almost a mile away. He cried, *"Then I am damned for all eternity!"* and continued this fearful exclamation until he died.

—*Dying Testimonies* by S. B. Snaw

Albert E. Cliff

Well-known Canadian Writer

Albert E. Cliff, well-known Canadian writer, tells of the death of his father. The dying man had sunk into a coma, and it was thought he was gone. Then a momentary resurgence of life occurred. His eyes flickered open. On the wall was one of those old-time mottoes which said, "I Know That My Redeemer Liveth." The dying man opened his eyes, looked at that motto, and said, "I *do know* that my Redeemer liveth, for they are all here around me — mother, father, brothers, and sisters."

Long gone from this earth were they all, but evidently he saw them. Who is to gainsay?

—*Power of Positive Thinking* by Norman Vincent Peale
Prentice-Hall, Inc.

"Tell Alan I Still Have Faith In Him"

My mother professed Christianity, but was all her lifetime in bondage to the fear of death (Hebrews 2:15). Although a denominational church member, I was an alcoholic for many years, even estranged from all family contact for seven years. It was during this period that Mother died.

Before she died she became justified by faith in our Lord Jesus Christ and found peace with God, leaving this message for me, *"Tell Alan I still have faith in him."* Three years later, Jesus Christ, God's dear Son, set me free from alcohol, and I am "free indeed" (John 8:36).

As a child of God, for seven years now, I have been led by the Holy Spirit to be a witness to Jesus my Lord. Once God led me to send a postcard message to a 70-year-old man who had been a lifetime church member and was now on his death bed.

In the postcard I said, "Our weaknesses and inabilities are inconsequential, since Jesus Christ is our strength and peace. However, the joy of the Holy Ghost comes when we decide to dedicate our *all* to God's service."

The Spirit Himself then bore witness with this dying man's spirit that he was a child of God, and he was saved. Before he died he made this statement: *"Tell Alan it's all right now. I*

175

believe and understand it all." He then gave his first smile of true joy and was gone shortly thereafter.

—Alan Williams, Benton Harbor, Michigan, 1967

Dr. T. Dewitt Talmadge

The noted Dr. T. DeWitt Talmadge said, "We are speeding toward the last hour of our earthly residence. When I see the sunset I say: 'One day less to live.' When I bury a friend, I say, 'Another earthly attraction gone forever.'

"What nimble feet the years have! From decade to decade, they go at a bound. There is a place for us, whether marked or not, where you and I will sleep the last sleep, and the men are now living who will with solemn tread, carry us to our resting-place. Aye, it is known in Heaven whether our departure will be a coronation or a banishment.

"Once when I was in danger of going down at sea my own life suddenly seemed utterly unsatisfactory. I could only say, 'Here, Lord, take me as I am. I cannot mend matters now. Lord Jesus, Thou didst die for the chief of sinners. That's me! It seems, Lord, as though my work is done, and poorly done, and upon Thy infinite mercy I cast myself.

" 'In this hour of shipwreck and darkness I commit myself and her whom I hold by the hand to Thee, O Lord Jesus, praying that it may be a short struggle in the water and that at the same instant we may both arrive in glory!'

"Oh! I tell you a man prays straight to the mark when he has a cyclone above him, an ocean beneath him, and eternity close to him.

"And may God grant that, when all our days on earth are ended, we may find that, in the rich mercy of our Lord Jesus Christ, we all have weathered the gale!"

—*The Gold Star Family Album* (Summer 1967)

"Victory! Eternal Victory!"

The sainted Eunice Cobb, better known as "Mother Cobb", was born at Litchfield, Connecticut, February 13, 1793.

Mother Cobb was converted when twenty-four, and after

walking with God on earth for sixty years, He took her to Himself, to reign with Him forever in the courts above.

We select the following from an account of her life and death published in the *Marengo Republican*:

"During a pilgrimage of forty years with this people she ever exhibited an earnest zeal in the service of her Lord and Master. To her, religion was more than a name — a profession. It was a *reality*, a power revealed in the heart that led, controlled and adorned her whole life and being. She stopped at the Fountain, not only to drink but to wash and be made whiter than snow.

"Filled with holy enthusiasm for the salvation of souls, she devoted a large portion of her time to this work, visiting from house to house and talking and praying with all whom she came in contact. No work was so pressing as to take away time for prayer, and no public worship so imposing as to dissuade her from giving the most tender and thrilling appeals to the unconverted to accept Christ, and exhorting the believers to a higher, holier life. She was truly a godly woman, abundant in labors and in fruits.

"Mother Cobb loved everybody, regardless of name or sect. Though fallen asleep, she yet lives in the hearts of those who have been saved by her instrumentality or blessed by her counsel. We have no words that can do full justice to the eminently devoted Christian life and character of this mother in Israel. It has been fittingly said that her life is a grand commentary on the thirteenth chapter of First Corinthians, and this, to those who knew her, will be the most appropriate testimony for her Christian worth — the best epitaph that can be inscribed to her memory.

"Many friends called to see her, and to all she testified to her perfect faith in Christ and of His grace, not only to sustain but to cheer in a dying hour. *Heaven itself seemed open to her, and a holy ecstasy filled her soul.* Her last words were 'Victory! Victory! *Eternal victory!'* "

—Sixty Years' Walk With God

177

Sylvia Marie Torres

January 9, 1957 - December 12, 1966

"Yes, Lord Jesus . . . have Thine own way"

Our precious, talented and lovely little granddaughter fell asleep in Jesus just before Christmas. It was so hard to lay that little body of clay in the ground. But it will come forth in the morning, when the day breaks and the shadows flee away.

She spent many weeks in such intense suffering that an adult dose of morphine would not help. She said she knew how the Lord Jesus suffered for her.

"Only He suffered more," she would say.

When her knees and wrists were dreadfully swollen and painful, she said she knew how the Lord felt when they put the nails through His hands and feet.

The last time she went to the hospital she said, "If the Lord wants me to go back, I am not going to make a fuss any more, but just ask Him for grace to bear the pain."

One day she was so very miserable and her father was leaning over trying to stop her nose from bleeding while he sang softly to her. She suddenly said, "Daddy, don't sing, because you get my song all mixed up." When he said that he didn't know she was singing, she replied that she wasn't singing out loud. Earlier she had asked him to help her with the words to "Blessed Assurance, Jesus is Mine." No doubt she was singing that song.

Another time she asked her father if the pain would stop as soon as she got to Heaven.

Just a few hours before she died she murmured, *"Yes, Lord Jesus."* Then, a little later, again she spoke to Him the same words — *"Yes, Lord Jesus."* We were praying that the Lord would be very near and precious to her, and we know He was.

After she was gone, her mother found pinned to the wall behind a curtain in her room a little paper on which she had printed the words, *"Have Thine own way, Lord."*

Her doctor said she was truly a saint. Another said, "I have heard about the Lord, but now I have seen Him in a little girl." Someone else declared, "She has taught me more in a few short years than I have learned in the past forty."

—Mrs. Ralph F. Becker, Holland, New York

178

Jeanne D'Arc (A.D. 1431)

(Joan of Arc)

French heroine, "Maid of Orleans," is described as having been of a sweet, sympathetic nature, yet endowed with heroic patriotism.

She grew up strong and beautiful and imbued with the fervor of her religion. She said she saw visions and claimed to have revelations from angels, who pointed out her mission to be the rescuing of her people in a trying time. In this undertaking she was successful and became a world-renowned military leader.

Finally, through reverses — or rather through the ingratitude of the French — she fell into the hands of the English, who condemned her to be burned to death for sorcery. All the tortures that the age knew, all the cruel thrusts at the sensitive flesh, were tried!

"Say but that thy voices were false, fair maid. Pronounce thy spirit guides to have been delusions, and thou shalt escape the coming doom."

All persuasion was in vain, however, and her voice rang out amid the flames: "Yes, my voices *were* from God. My voices have not deceived me — *Jesus!*"

—Dying Testimonies by S. B. Shaw

Eternity Can Begin Now

By John L. Sherrill, Senior Editor, *Guideposts* magazine

I still remember that I whistled as I strode up New York's Park Avenue that spring morning three years ago. I stepped through the door of my doctor's office and nodded to his receptionist — an old friend by now. I'd been coming here every month since a cancer operation two years previous, and it was always the same: the doctor's skilled fingers running down my neck, a pat on the back, "See you in a month."

But not that day. This time the fingers prodded and worked a long time. When I left I had an appointment at Memorial Hospital for surgery two days later. What a difference in a spring morning!

I walked back down the same street in the same sunshine, but now a cold fear walked with me. All cancer patients know this fear. We try to stay on top of it in various ways. Now I

179

could no longer hold the fear down. It rose up, scattering reason before it: *this was the Fear of Death.*

I dived into the first church I came to, looking for darkness and privacy. It was St. Thomas Episcopal, on Fifth Avenue. Mechanically, I sat down. A few minutes later a young minister mounted the pulpit to give a noonday meditation. I didn't know it then, but this brief address was to provide the key which would rid me of this most basic of all fears.

At the time it seemed wretchedly irrelevant to my problem. His text was: *". . . Whosoever believeth in Him should not perish but have everlasting life."* I wasn't ready for everlasting life; it was life here and now I wanted!

The next morning, however, I was to hear these words again. My wife, Tib, and I were having coffee after a sleepless night when the phone rang. It was a neighbor, Catherine Marshall LeSourd.

"John," she said, "could you come over for a few minutes? I've heard the news, and there's something I've got to say to you."

Catherine met us at the door, wearing neither make-up nor a smile, which said more than words about the concern she felt. She led us into the family room and plunged in without polite talk.

"I know this is presumptuous of me. I'm going to talk to you about your religious life, and I have no right to assume that it lacks anything. After all, you've been writing for *Guideposts* for ten years. But often the people who are busiest with religion are farthest from the real, life-changing heart of it."

I looked at Tib. She sat still as a rock.

"John," said Catherine, "do you believe Jesus was God?"

It was the last question in the world I expected. I thought she would say something about God being able to heal — or prayer being effective — something to do with my crisis. But since she had put the question to me, I considered it. Tib and I were Christians in the sense that we wrote "Protestant" on application blanks, attended church with some regularity, sent our children to Sunday school. Still, I knew that these were habits. I never really had come to grips with the question, was Jesus of Nazareth, in fact, God?

"You might ask what difference it makes," said Catherine. "It spells the difference between life and death, John. The Bible tells us that when we believe in Christ, we no longer have to die, but are given everlasting life."

There it was again. But it was precisely at this point of

belief that I always had my difficulty. I knew what the Bible promised, and I admired and envied people who accepted it unquestioningly. For myself, there were roadblocks of logic which invariably halted me. I started to list them for Catherine, but she stopped me.

"You're trying to approach Christ through your mind, John," she said. "But it's one of the peculiarities of Christianity that you have to experience it *before* you can understand it. And that's just what I'm hoping for you today — that without understanding, without even knowing why, you make the leap of *faith* — right over all your doubts — *to Christ.*"

There was silence in the room. I had an eternity of reservations and, at the same time, a sudden desire to do exactly what she was suggesting. The biggest reservation, I admitted frankly: it didn't seem right to shy away all these years and then come running when I had cancer and was scared. "I'd feel like a hypocrite," I said.

"John," said Catherine, almost in a whisper, "That's pride. You want to come to God in *your* way. When you will. Where you will. Healthy. Maybe God wants you now, without a shred to recommend you."

When we left, I still had not brought myself to take that step. But halfway home, passing a certain telephone pole on Millwood Road in Chappaqua, a pole which I can point out today, I turned suddenly to Tib and said:

"I'm making that leap, Tib. *I believe in Christ.*"

That's all I said. Yet I believe now that in some mysterious way, in that instant, I died.

I didn't think of it in those terms at the time — but certainly it wrenched like death. It was a cold-blooded laying down of my sense of what was logical, quite without emotional conviction. And with it went something that was essentially "me." All the bundle of self-consciousness that we call our ego somehow seemed involved in this decision. I was amazed at how much it hurt, how desperately this thing fought for life, so that there was a real slaying required. But when it was dead and quiet finally, and I blurted out my simple statement, there was room in me for something new and altogether mysterious.

The first hint that there was something different about me came rather amusingly at the hospital. Shortly before the operation a snappy young nurse came in to give me an injection. Since Army days I have had a morbid horror of needles. Yet this time it was different.

181

"All right, over we go," said my nurse efficiently. But when she had finished, her tone changed. "My, you're a relaxed one! You act like you're taking your vacation here."

It wasn't until after she had left that I realized how true and how remarkable this was. I *was* relaxed. Before the operation, during it, and afterwards. As we waited out the report, my attitude was one of a man who had nothing to fear. How was it possible?

Then I had a strange thought: a man who already had died would certainly not be afraid of death. And that was just how I felt — as though death was behind me.

I wondered if there was any Biblical backing for this idea. Back home and still in doubt on the doctor's verdict, I got out a Bible and a concordance. And there it was in Christ's own words:

"In very truth," Christ told His disciples, *"anyone who gives heed to what I say, and puts his trust in Him who sent Me, has hold of eternal life and does not come up for judgment, but already has passed from death to life."*

How can I describe the excitement that leapt to me from that page? Was it possible that when I took that leap of faith a new life began for me, existing parallel to my earthly life but strangely independent of it? A life that was *born of the Spirit* and which would use my perishable body only temporarily?

If so, then I should see evidence of something new inside me that owed nothing to my earth-bound existence.

And I did.

The first evidence came when the doctor's report arrived. It was a hopeful one; but I found that this had ceased to be of primary importance to me. Something else seemed far more pressing: to discover what this new life was, where it came from, what it meant.

I had a strange new hunger to explore the New Testament, which I read with a sense of excitement and of recognition. Wasn't it likely that this was the new life, recognizing its natural environment of spirit, feeding on a new kind of food which it needed as my body needed food?

The same was true of church. Suddenly, I *wanted* to attend church: it was no longer a habit, but an experience which quenched a deep thirst.

And — perhaps the most important evidence of all — Christ, whom I had approached as a problem of logic, became for me a living Person. I feel now that it was Christ I sought and found in the Bible, in the sacraments, and in the company of Christians.

Three years have passed since the day Tib and I drove past that telephone pole on Millwood Road. They have been fabulous years, filled with meaning and excitement and wonder. I found, as the months passed and I came down from my mountain top, and slipped into old patterns I'd hoped I'd left behind, that the door always was open for my return. I always was drawn back. It was as if the new life which began that day was not dependent on my faithfulness, but on Christ's.

And it is this which gives me conviction that it is an undying life, a part of the eternity of God.

—Reprinted from *Guideposts* Magazine
Copyright 1963 *Guideposts Associates, Inc.,* Carmel, N.Y.

Ann Audeburt A.D. 1549

Ann Audebert was a French martyr. When the rope was put about her waist she called it her wedding-girdle wherewith she would be married to Christ. As she was burned on Saturday she said:

"Upon a Saturday I was first married, and upon a Saturday *I shall be married again!"*

—*Dying Words* by A. H. Gottschall

Maria, The Wife Of J. Hudson Taylor

*"For ten years past there has not been a cloud
between me and my Savior"*

The birth of their last child, Noel, was the occasion of the home-going of this precious saint of God, wife and fellow-laborer of that prince of missionary heroes, J. Hudson Taylor. We quote from the well-known biography of Mr. Hudson Taylor written by his son and daughter-in-law, who also themselves were devoted missionaries to China:

Born on the 7th of July, this little one was their fifth son and called forth all the pent-up love of his parents' hearts.

"How graciously the Lord has dealt with me and mine," Mr. Taylor wrote home afterwards. "How tenderly did He bring

183

my loved one through the hour of trial and gave us our last-born, our Noel. How I thanked Him as I stroked the soft, silky hair and nestled the little one in my bosom! And how she loved him, when with a father's joy and pride, I brought him to her for her first kiss, and together we gave him to the Lord."

But an attack of cholera had greatly prostrated the mother, and lack of natural nourishment told upon the child. When a Chinese nurse could be found, it was too late to save the little life. After one brief week on earth he went back to the Home above, in which his mother was so soon to join him.

"Though excessively prostrate in body," Mr. Taylor wrote in the same letter, "the deep peace of soul, the realization of the Lord's own presence, and the joy in His holy will with which she was filled, and in which I was permitted to share, I can find no words to describe."

She herself chose the hymns to be sung at the little grave, one of which, "O holy Saviour, Friend unseen," seemed especially to dwell in her mind.

Weak as she was, it had not yet occurred to them that for her too the end was near. The deep mutual love that bound their hearts in one seemed to preclude the thought of separation. And she was only thirty-three. There was no pain up to the very last, though she was weary, very weary.

A letter from Mrs. Berger in England had been received two days previously, telling of the safe arrival at Saint Hill of Miss Blatchley and the Taylor's children. Every detail of the welcome and arrangements for their well-being filled her heart with joy. She knew not how to be thankful enough, and seemed to have no desire or heart but just to praise the Lord for His goodness.

Many and many a time had Mrs. Berger's letters reached their destination at the needed moment; many and many a time had her loving heart anticipated the circumtsances in which they would be received — but never more so than with this letter.

"And now farewell, precious friend," she wrote. *"The Lord throw around you His everlasting arms!"*

It was in those arms she was resting.

At daybreak on Saturday, the 23rd of July, she was sleeping quietly, and Mr. Taylor left her a few moments to prepare some food. While he was doing so she awoke and serious symptoms called him to her side.

"By this time it was dawn," he wrote, "and the sunlight revealed what the candle had hidden — the deathlike hue of her countenance. Even my love could no longer deny, not her danger, but that she was actually dying. As soon as I was sufficiently composed, I said:

"'My darling, do you know that you are dying?'

"'Dying!' she replied. 'Do you think so? What makes you think so?'

"I said, 'I can see it, darling. Your strength is giving way.'

"'Can it be so? I feel no pain, only weariness.'

"'Yes, you are going Home. You will soon be with Jesus.'

"My precious wife thought of my being left alone at a time of so much trial, with no companion like herself with whom I had been wont to bring every difficulty to the Throne of Grace.

"'I am so sorry,' she said, and paused as if half correcting herself for the feeling.

"'You are sorry to go to be with Jesus?'

Never shall I forget the look with which she answered, 'Oh, no! It is not that. *You know, darling, that for ten years past there has not been a cloud between me and my Saviour.* I cannot be sorry to go to Him — but it does grieve me to leave you alone at such a time. Yet — *He will* be with you and meet all your need.' "

But little was said after that. A few loving messages to those at home, a few last words about the children and she seemed to fall asleep or drift into unconsciousness of earthly things. The summer sun rose higher and higher over the city, the hills and the river. The busy hum of life came up around them from many a court and street. But within one Chinese dwelling, in an upper room from which the blue of God's own heaven could be seen, there was the hush of a wonderful peace.

"I never witnessed such a scene," wrote Mrs. Duncan a few days later. "As dear Mrs. Taylor was breathing her last, Mr. Taylor knelt down — his heart so full — and committed her to the Lord — thanking Him for having given her, and for the twelve and a half years of happiness they had had together; thanking Him, too, for taking her to His own blessed presence, *and solemnly dedicating himself anew to His service.*"

It was just after 9 a.m. when the quiet breathing ceased, and they knew she was "with Christ, which is far better."

—*Hudson Taylor and the China Inland Mission*
by Dr. and Mrs. Howard Taylor

185

Samuel Rutherford

"I shall soon be where few of you shall enter"

This eminent Scotch Presbyterian was born in 1600 and died in 1661. He was commissioner to the Westminster General Assembly in 1643 and was for some time principal of St. Andrews College.

When on his deathbed, he was summoned to appear before Parliament to stand trial for having preached "Liberty and Religion." He sent word with the messenger, "Tell the Parliament that I have received a summons to a higher bar — I must needs answer that first. When the day you name comes *I shall be where few of you shall enter."*

—*Dying Testimonies,* by S. B. Shaw

Peter (About) A.D. 251

A young Martyr of Lampsacus

He was accused of Christianity before Optimus, who commanded him to sacrifice to Venus. To this he replied, "I am astonished that you should command me to worship a woman, who acocrding to your own history was a vile and licentious character and guilty of such crimes as your own laws now punish with death. *No, instead I shall offer to the one living and true God the sacrifice of prayer and praise!"*

For this statement his bones were torn apart upon a rack, his head cut off and his body given to the dogs.

—*Dying Words* by A. H. Gottschall

David Brainerd

This celebrated missionary to the American Indians was born at Haddam, Connecticut, April 20, 1718. His parents were noted for their piety and were closely related to high officials of the church and state.

In 1739 he entered Yale College, where he stood first in his class. He was greatly favored of God in being privileged to attend the great revival conducted by George Whitfield, Jonathan Edwards and Tenent.

President Edwards says in his memoir of Brainerd:

"His great work was the priceless example of his piety, zeal and self devotion. Why, since the days of the apostles none have surpassed him. His uncommon intellectual gifts, his fine personal qualities, his melancholy and his early death, as well as his remarkable holiness and evangelistic labors, have conspired to invest his memory with a book halo.

"The story of his life has been a potent force in the modern missionary era. It is even related that Henry Martyn, while perusing the life of David Brainerd, found his soul filled with a holy emulation of that extraordinary man, and after deep consideration and fervent prayer, he was at length fixed in a resolution to imitate his example."

Brainerd was a representative man, formed both by nature and grace to leave a lasting impression upon the piety of the church. Dying at Northampton, October 9, 1747, the last words of this eminent apostle were, "I am almost in eternity; I long to be there. My work is done. I have done with my friends — all the world is nothing to me. *Oh, to be in Heaven to praise and glorify God with His holy angels!*"

Little Hattie Buford's Last Prayer

(Daughter of Major-General John Buford)

This little girl, the daughter of Major-General John Buford, died in 1865 when only six years old. She had been taught to repeat the Lord's prayer, and as she lay dying, all of a sudden she opened her soft blue eyes and looking confidently into her mother's face, said, "Mamma, I forgot to say my prayers!"

Summoning what strength she had left, she clasped her little white hands together and, like a little angel, prayed thus:

> *"Now I lay me down to sleep,*
> *I pray Thee, Lord, my soul to keep;*
> *If I should die before I wake,*
> *I pray Thee, Lord, my soul to take."*

The prayer finished, she never spoke again.

—*Dying Testimonies,* by S. B. Shaw

Triumphant Death Of Margaretta Kloppstock

Kloppstock, the great German poet and author of the well-known epic poem, *The Messiah*, was born in 1724 and died in 1803. His wife, Margaretta, was a devoted Christian.

In her last moments, Margaretta, being told that God would help her, replied, "Yes — *into Heaven!*"

The last words she whispered were, " *'The blood of Jesus Christ cleanseth from all sin!'* Oh, sweet words of eternal life!"

—*Dying Testimonies* by S. B. Shaw

Dr. A. J. Gordon's Last Word Was, "Victory!"

One of the most well-known and devoted Baptist preachers of this country was Rev. Adoniram Judson Gordon, for many years pastor of Clarendon Street Baptist Church in Boston. He was a noted author as well as preacher, and his books are still in demand today.

Dr. Gordon went to Heaven February 2, 1895. "A short time before his death," says the memorial number of *The Watchword*, "he called his wife to his side and said, 'If anything should happen, I have selected four hymns I want to have sung. Write them down: "Abide With Me", "The Sands of Time Are Sinking", "Lord if He Sleep He Shall Do Well", and "My Jesus I Love Thee".' He was assured that his wishes would be regarded, and the subject was dropped.

"At 5:00 p.m. the doctor sat by him, and speaking with a cheery voice to rouse him said, 'Have you a good word for us tonight?' With a clear, full voice Dr. Gordon answered, '*Victory!*' This was his last audible utterance.

"Between nine and ten in the evening the nurse motioned to his wife that she was wanted. She bent to listen, as he whispered, 'Maria, *pray!*' As she led in prayer, he followed in a whisper, sentence by sentence, and at the close tried to utter petitions himself. However, his strength was not sufficient to articulate.

"Five minutes after midnight on the morning of February 2 he fell asleep in Jesus."

A Dying Welsh Soldier's Despair

I once went to visit a soldier who had brought himself from the army. He was dying, but did not know it. I sat down by his side and said, "I will read a bit of the Bible for you."

"Oh, you need not trouble; I am not so ill as all that," he replied.

Poor fellow. He thought that he must be very ill before anyone need offer to read a part of the Bible for him.

Next morning when I called I found him much worse. I learned that he was a Welshman and his mother was a Christian. Suddenly he threw himself back in bed. Wringing his hands, he cried, "Oh, what shall I do, what shall I do? I am as a dead man. The mark of death is upon me, and *I am not saved!*"

There is a time when God speaks and Christ may be found, *but there is also a time when He may not be found.* This young dying soldier sought and sought for Christ, but it was all in vain — Jesus had passed by. He finally became delirious and died in agony.

"Seek the Lord while He may be found; call ye upon Him while He is near." (Isaiah 55:6)

—From *Crown of Glory* (Author unknown)

A Little Girl's Glimpse Into Eternity

Mrs. William Barnes' wonderful conversion was brought about by the death of her little girl. The following is her own story of the child's passing:

"My little daughter, May, when but eight years old, was taken ill with scarlet fever and died four days later. During her short sickness, when asked if she was suffering, she would say that nothing hurt her, but that she did not want to stay with us any longer — *she wanted to go to Heaven.* She kept repeating this all through the long night.

"Toward the end she repeated the Lord's prayer and then sweetly thanked us for all that we had done for her, insisting that we should not worry about her. Suddenly she looked up and said, 'I thank Thee, dear Jesus. *Dear Jesus,* I thank Thee!' After that she sang some beautiful songs.

"Just before she died she raised her eyes toward Heaven and said, '*O Lord, my strength and my Redeemer.*' Then, with a peaceful look on her face, raised herself and with a glad expression said, *'Oh!'* and was gone. It was evident that she saw something which our eyes could not see.

"I think this message, dear reader, is for *you,* just as much as it is for me. The Bible says, *'A little child shall lead them.'* "

—Kate H. Booth, Buffalo, New York (1898)

"Oh, The Devil Is Coming To Drag My Soul Down To Hell!"

Miss A— was taken very sick and was informed that she could not live. Her parents had educated her to follow the ways and fashions of the world and had turned her away from the truth of God. Now she lay dying, surrounded by her young friends, with whom she had indulged in the pleasures of sin.

The wretched girl called her father to the bedside and in front of everybody said, *"Your heart is as black as Hell. If you had taught me to live for God, rather than spending your time quarreling with mother, I might have been saved."*

Turning to others, she pled with them, saying, "Do not follow my ungodly example. Do not do as I have done. Do not indulge in the hellish pleasures of the world! Oh, if I had only heeded the warnings. . . ."

Then she suddenly cried, "Oh, the devil is coming to drag my soul down to Hell! . . . I am lost, *lost forever!"*

Then she died.

—N. M. Nelms, Kopperl, Texas

Merritt Caldwell's Last Words —

"Jesus lives; I shall live also!"

This great and good man, principal of Wesleyan Academy in Maine and vice-president of Dickinson College in Pennsylvania, was a gifted writer. He was born in 1806 and died in 1848.

Shortly before his death he said to his wife, "You will not, I am sure, lie down upon your bed and weep when I am gone. You will not mourn for me when God has been so good to me.

"When you visit my grave, do not come in the shade of the

evening, nor in the dark of night — these are no times to visit the grave of a Christian — but come in the morning, in the bright sunshine when the birds are singing."

His last expressions were, "Glory to *Jesus!* He is my trust — He is my strength! Jesus lives; *I shall live also!*"

—From *Dying Testimonies* by S. B. Shaw

Count Zinzendorf Of The Moravians

To his family and friends the dying saint triumphantly said: "I am going to my Saviour. I am ready. There is nothing to hinder me now. I cannot say how much I love you all. Who would have believed that the prayer of Christ, 'that they all may be *one,*' could have been so strikingly fulfilled among us! I only asked for first-fruits among the heathen, and thousands have been given me. Are we not as in Heaven! Do we not live together like the angels! The Lord and His servants understand each other. *I am ready.*"

A few hours later as his son-in-law pronounced the old Testament benediction.—*"The Lord bless thee and keep thee, the Lord make His face shine upon thee and be gracious unto thee, the Lord lift up His countenance upon thee and give thee peace"*— this dear man of God fell asleep in Jesus and was absent from the body and at home with his Lord

"I See Two Angels Coming For Me"

In regard to your book, *Voices from the Edge of Eternity,* I have in my possession a letter from my grandmother, written in 1873. She writes about the wife of the pastor Bernard who was the pastor of the French Church in Bern, Switzerland.

This Pastor Bernard was the pastor who instructed my mother. He was a true believer, and at that time many were converted to Christianity through him.

I quote from this letter: "Mme. Bernard died after very much suffering from neuralgia-asthma and at last dropsy. What a sad time for the poor girls, to say nothing of the Pastor himself. The end was very peaceful and nearly her last words were, *'I see two angels coming for me.'*"

—Mr. Y. Courvoisier, Suisse, Switzerland

"I Cannot Be Pardoned; It Is Too Late! Too Late!"

"Because I have called, and ye refused; I have stretched out my hand, and no man regarded; . . . I also will laugh at your calamity; I will mock when your fear cometh. . . . Then shall they call upon Me, but I will not answer; they shall seek Me early, but they shall not find Me. For that they hated knowledge, and did not choose the fear of the Lord."

—Proverbs 1:24, 26, 28, 29

Miss— was an amiable young girl who died at the age of sixteen. She was the daughter of respectable and pious parents in one of the New England states. Considerable attention had been bestowed on the cultivation of her mind, but to what extent she had been imbued with Christian truth in childhood, I have not been able fully to learn. It is certain that from her earliest years she had regarded religion with respect and expected to become a Christian before she died.

One morning in particular, the first impression she had when she awoke was that she must receive Christ *then* — that her soul was in imminent danger of being lost if she delayed. She deliberated and reasoned. Finally, she prayed and made a deliberate resolution that she would repent and accept God's offer of salvation before the close of that day. However, the day had its cares and pleasures. Activity and company filled its hours, and the night found her almost as thoughtless as she had been for months.

The next morning this spiritual impression was renewed and deepened. The violated vows of the previous morning gave her some uneasiness, but she now formed her resolution firmly, and was so fixed in her purpose that she felt sure everything would be all right. The agony of her soul gave way to the soothing reflection that she should *soon* be a Christian. She had now taken — as she imagined — "one step". She had formed a solemn purpose and had given a pledge to repent *that day*. She felt, as she expressed it, "committed," and hardly had a doubt as to the accomplishment of her purpose.

But this day also passed as before. She did, indeed, several times during the day think of her resolution, but not with that overwhelming interest she had felt in the morning — and nothing *decisive* was done.

The next morning God again spoke to her heart, and she again renewed her resolution, only to have it dissipated as before. Thus she went on resolving and breaking her resolutions, until at length her anxiety entirely subsided and she lapsed into her former state of unconcern.

It was not that she became completely indifferent. She still expected and resolved to be a Christian; but her resolutions now looked to a more distant period for their accomplishment, and she returned to the cares and pleasures of the world with the same interest as before.

About this time she went to reside in a neighboring village, and I did not see her for about three months. Suddenly I was called at an early hour one morning to visit her on the bed of death.

About daybreak, on the morning of the day she died, she was informed that her symptoms had become alarming and that her sickness would probably be fatal. Her intelligence was surprising, and though she sought desperately to "find God", her distress became so intense and her energies so exhausted that she finally was forced to conclude that her soul was lost and that nothing could now be done. For a moment she seemed as if in a horrid struggle to adjust her mind to her anticipated doom. Oh, that word *"lost"*. Her whole frame shuddered at the thought.

It was nearly noon. Most of the morning had been employed either in prayer at her bedside or in attempting to guide her to the Savior. But all seemed ineffectual. Her strength was now nearly gone. Vital action was no longer perceptible at the extremities, the cold death-sweat was gathering on her brow and dread despair seemed ready to possess her soul.

She saw, and we all saw, that the fatal moment was at hand — and her future prospect one of unmingled horror. She shrank from it. Turning her eyes to me, she called on all who stood around her to beseech once more the God of mercy in her behalf.

We all knelt again at her bedside, and having once more commended her to God, I tried again to direct her to the Savior. I was beginning to repeat some promises which I thought appropriate, when she interrupted me, saying with emphasis, *"I cannot be pardoned; it is too late — too late!"*

Alluding to her vain and fatal resolutions, she begged me to charge all the youth of my congregation not to neglect salvation as she had done — not to stifle their conviction by a mere resolution to repent.

"Warn them, *warn them* by my case," she said.

After that she again attempted to pray, but only fainted. She continued thus alternately to struggle and faint, every succeeding effort becoming feebler, until the last convulsive struggle closed the scene, and her spirit took its everlasting flight.

The Bible says that "man looketh upon the outward appearance," but that "God looketh upon *the heart.*" *"Keep* thy *heart* with all diligence; *for out of it flow the issues of life."*

"Seek ye the Lord while He may be found, call ye upon Him while He is near."

—Rev. E. Phelps, D.D., from *Dying Testimonies*

To Live Each Day

Parents never are prepared for the day that their children become young men and women. But inevitably, faces that once wore smiles of egg yolk and jam come to us washed and serious, bearing news that is startlingly mature.

With our son Bob it was his decision to pay his own way through college. He said his schooling would mean more if he earned his own money. When he told me this, I suddenly realized I wasn't talking to a boy in knee pants any longer.

A similar awareness occurred this spring when my only daughter, Billie Kay, a 15-year-old sophomore at Mississinewa High School, surprised my husband and me with her spiritual perceptiveness. This first came through some themes she prepared as English assignments. One was entitled "The Last Week of My Life." Billie Kay wrote:

"Today I live; a week from today I die. If a situation came to me such as this, I would probably weep. As soon as I realized that there were many things to be done, though, I would try to regain my composure.

"The first day of my suddenly shortened life, I would see all my loved ones and assure them that I loved them. I wouldn't hint that anything was wrong because I wouldn't want to remember them sorrowing but as being happy. I would ask God to give me strength to bear the rest of my precious few days and give me His hand to walk with Him.

"On the second day I would awake to see the rising sun in all its beauty that I had so often cast aside for a few extra moments of coveted sleep. I would gather all my possessions and give them to the needy, trying to console them as much as possible and urge them to consult God for courage.

194

"The third day, I would spend alone in a woods with the presence of God's creation and goodness around me. In the sweetness of nature I would sit and reminisce of my fondest memories.

"On my fourth day I would prepare my will. The small sentimental things I would leave to my family and friends. This being done, I would go to my mother and spend the day with her. We have always been close and I would want to reassure my love to her especially.

"Friday would be spent with my minister; I would speak to him of my spiritual life. I would like to go with him to see those who were ill and silently be thankful that I knew no pain.

"Saturday I would spend seeing the shut-ins I had so often put off until another day. On this night before my death, I would probably remain awake fearing my impending death, and yet also preparing for it, knowing that God was by my side.

"Upon awakening Sunday I would make all of my last preparations. Taking my Bible, I would go to my church to spend my last hours in prayer. I would ask Him for the courage to face the remaining hours that I might die gracefully. I would hope that my life had bearing on someone and had glorified His holy name. My last hours would be spent in perfect harmony with my God . . ."

This is the end of Billie Kay's theme, "The Last Week of My Life," but it is not the end of the story. Billie Kay's English paper which was dated Friday, March 15, 1963, was finished just *seven days* before her life was snuffed out in an automobile accident.

On March 22, about 11 o'clock, the car in which Billie Kay was a passenger was struck from the rear and rolled over two or three times. Then it caught fire.

My daughter's three friends were pulled out of the wreckage with injuries from which they have since recovered. Billie Kay, who died instantly, was pinned inside.

The last time I saw Billie Kay was earlier that evening when my husband and I dropped her off at a church meeting. She joined friends, laughing and talking.

The events which followed in the next few hours still bring on a vertigo. My husband, Joe, was at work. I was lying down reading when I heard the doorbell ring. When I opened the door, I looked into the face of a police officer.

I don't remember much of anything for the next few hours. I never had known a pain so piercing. Over and over we asked ourselves the question which accompanies all tragedy: why? Why?

At the moment we could not understand how her death could figure in God's plan. Such a waste it seemed: taking a life in its bud — a life which promised to be as productive as Billie Kay's. She was an excellent student, planning to go to college like her brother; a wonderful Christian, active in our church. How could a loving God permit such a thing to happen?

If I told you that now I accept this tragedy with complete resignation, I would not be telling the whole truth. It is so difficult to accept. Yet, now, a few months after our loss I am able to praise God for His abiding love; praise Him for understanding when we were ready to desert Him for "failing" us; thank Him for loaning us an angel for the short time He did.

You see, I now know that our children are not ours, but God's. He sends them for us to shepherd, but they do not belong to us.

Too often, I think, we count up our material accumulations and boast about what is ours when really not even the next breath we take is ours without God's grace. Since Billie Kay has gone, I have had time to think a great deal. I have come to realize the importance of listening for God's calling and responding immediately. Time is so precious. None of us know exactly when our personal judgment day will come. Each fleeting moment wasted is one less minute we have to do Christ's bidding.

Joe and I know that Billie Kay's life was not a waste, but a great inspiration — to us and to many others. It was a life which fulfilled His purposes. By our standards 15 years does not connote completeness, but our finite minds can't understand God's yardstick. He does not measure life by length alone, I am sure.

Though I doubt that Billie Kay had any premonition of her death as some have suggested, I feel — without reservation — that she was prepared for it, for she wrote another essay in January, entitled "A Visitation." This also reassures me that Billie Kay was in the center of God's will. Here, in part, is what she wrote:

"I am walking in a forest to escape the noise of the city when suddenly the path all about me grows dim, until at last a heavy fog surrounds me. And finally nothing but deep, lasting darkness fills my entire being; yet it is strangely peaceful and I feel as though I am in the presence of Someone powerful and great. . . .

"Peace, wonderful peace is now flooding my entire person and I feel no want or pain . . . Then approaching me on the path are two glowing yet very gentle eyes, drawing closer and closer. . . .

"Within these gentle eyes I find peace beyond understanding. I am no longer driven with wants and duties. I feel content, secure. I fall on my knees and pray — for what I do not know. The eyes tell me to rise. Though he did not speak, suddenly I realized this was death. He seemed to tell me not to be afraid for it was an eternal, lasting place, a part of everything . . .

"As I walked home I thought of that one phrase over and over in my mind: 'It is a part of everything,' and when one thinks about it, death really is a part of everything. I fear death no longer and I feel I have a purpose in life. The great power I felt and saw must have been the Almighty Himself. I shall not speak of this until the right time, as it was much too wonderful. Yes, I will keep it in my heart until the right time, maybe even until death."

As I re-read Billie Kay's essays, I find a guide for my life. I see clearly that I must live each day, not as if I had seven days remaining, but as if today I die. Whatever comes, I take great solace in Jesus' promise, *"Let not your heart be troubled: ye believe in God, believe also in Me. In my Father's house are many mansions; if it were not so, I would have told you. I go to prepare a place for you, and if I go and prepare a place for you, I will come again, and receive you unto Myself; that where I am, there ye may be also."*

I rest assured that Billie Kay has already taken residence in my Father's house.

—Betty Bothwell, Marion, Indiana

—Reprinted from *Guideposts* Magazine
Copyright 1963 *Guideposts Associates, Inc.*, Carmel, N.Y.

The Awful End Of A Scoffer

In the year 1880 several of us held a little street meeting off Brightside Lane, Sheffield, England, our object being to extend an invitation to passersby to come to the services at the little Primitive Methodist Chapel which was close by.

We stopped on the street, close to the home of the subject of this sketch (whose name I do not remember) and commenced to sing and talk to the people. Suddenly this man came out of his house in a great rage, saying that we were disturbing the peace and ought to be prosecuted. He caught the attention of some of the people and told them that the Bible was a humbug, Christianity a fraud and churches and ministers an imposition on the people. He declared that society should be rid of them all. We endeavored to reason with him, but it was in vain.

The following week some of the Christians called at his home and offered to pray with him and give him some literature, but he scornfully refused all their offers. Abusing their good intentions, he criticized the narrowness of Christianity and boasted of the great freedom of infidelity.

Several times after that he made a point of meeting us on the street, endeavoring to confuse the people and break up our meeting. His presence was such an annoyance to us and so detrimental to the meetings that we could scarcely hold them.

The last time he tried to interfere was on a Sunday morning. He came walking down the street with a large stick in one hand and an axe in the other. We were singing and as soon as he got close he began to chop the wood. Of course, he wanted to draw the attention of the people away from us. The chips began to fly around, and we thought it best to move on.

From that time we all began to offer special prayer for his conversion. However, God did not answer our prayers in the way we thought He would. The next Sunday we went to our street meeting, feeling that in some way God would give us a victory over the man, but to our surprise he did not turn up. I inquired about him and found that he had suddenly become very ill.

The following week I was called to his room and found him in a very dangerous condition. He was much changed in his mind and very mild, tender and teachable. But he could not repent. Many Christians visited him and tried to lead him to Jesus, but their efforts were all in vain. He said that *he knew he was lost and doomed forever.*

In a few days I called again and found him very close to the crossing. I told him of God's boundless mercy and how it had reached even Nebuchadnezzar and Mannasseh,* and that God had given His Son for him also. His answer was simply to insist that it was too late now, since he had sinned against light and knowledge when he knew better. The fact of having disturbed our meetings weighed upon his mind, and he told me to faithfully warn all such scoffers of their danger. He wept bitterly as we talked to him of his lost condition and said that if he could only live his life over again he would live for God. But it was a vain hope — life was now past and his *last* chance gone. The distress of his mind became worse and worse as the end approached, and he finally died in great agony of soul.

To live without Christ is only to exist, *missing the whole point of life.* To be without Christ on a deathbed is terrible. To go into eternity without Christ is midnight darkness forever. Oh, the thought of an *eternity* without Christ!

—Rev. Fredrick Scott, from *Dying Testimonies* by S. B. Shaw

* See Daniel 4 and II Chronicles 33

Rev. Hiram Case

*"Hear that music! They don't have such music
as that on earth."*

A few weeks before his death my husband, Rev. Hiram Case, said, "It seemed as if I were stepping into a very cold stream, which sent a shiver through my entire being. In the twinkling of an eye, however, the place was lit up with a glory that far out-shone the noonday sun. What I saw and felt was unutterable. Words are too lame to express what I saw and felt of the presence of the Lord with me."

My husband had some relatives who were Adventists. He said he wished they could know how he felt when he thought he was dying. They would never again think that their spirits sleep in the grave until the resurrection, but would know beyond a doubt that immediately after the spirit leaves the body it is with the redeemed host in a conscious existence in the presence of the Great Redeemer of men.

He talked freely about dying, saying that while it was hard to part with us, the family, the Lord knew what was best. At another time he heard the heavenly music. He said, "Hear that music! *They don't have such music as that on earth.*"

The presence of the Lord was with him during all these trying days, and when the power of speech and sight was gone,

199

by the pressure of the hand and the farewell kiss he gave us the token that "All is well!"

—By his wife, Mrs. Gertrude M. Case of Clyde, New York

From *Dying Testimonies* by S. B. Shaw

Edward Gibbon, The Noted Infidel

"All is dark and doubtful"

Edward Gibbon, the noted historian and infidel writer, was born at Putney, England, 1737.

Bishop J. F. Hurst, in his *History of Rationalism,* says: ". . . By a sudden caprice he became a Roman Catholic, and afterwards as unceremoniously denied his adopted creed. . . . In due time he found himself in Paris publishing a book in the French language. He there fell in with the fashionable infidelity and so yielded to the flattery of Helvetius and all the frequenters of Holbach's house that he jested at Christianity and assailed its divine character.

"He has left less on record against Christianity than Hume, but they must be ranked together as the last of the family of English Deists."

Rev. E. P. Goodwin, in *Christianity and Infidelity,* summarizes Gibbon's life as one of the fairest, as well as one of the ablest, of infidels. He points out that Gibbon has given us an autobiographical account, in which, amid all the polish and splendor of the rhetoric of which he is such a master, there is not a line or a word that suggests reverence for God; not a word of regard for the welfare of the human race; nothing but the most sordid selfishness, vain glory, desire for admiration, adulation of the great and wealthy, contempt for the poor and supreme devotedness to his own gratification.

He died in London in 1794. His last words were, *"All is now lost—finally, irrecoverably lost. All is dark and doubtful."*

—*Dying Testimonies* by S. B. Shaw

200

"O Glory! O Glory!! O Glory!!!"

"Precious in the sight of the Lord is the death of His saints"

At a very early age Mrs. Susan C. Kirtland gave her heart to God. Though her life seemed full of privation and disappointment, she was a cheerful, devoted Christian, well described by the motto she so often expressed in words, *"It is better to suffer wrong than to do wrong."*

While visiting at our home in Burr Oak, Michigan, she suddenly became ill and after one painful week went to be with the Lord on April 3, 1864.

At the time I was less than four years old, but I distinctly remember how, while lying there in great suffering, she taught me the beautiful verse, *"I love them that love Me; and they that seek Me early shall find Me,"* carefully explaining the meaning of the words and lovingly pressing home the lesson to my heart.

As soon as it was known that she was dangerously ill, her brother, who was an able physician, was summoned. But it was too late.

A few hours before her death she sensed from mother's manner that something was wrong and inquired. With much feeling, mother answered, "Susan, we fear your stay with us is very short."

Calmly she replied, "Well, if it be so, I don't know when I could have had a better time to leave this stage of action!"

Two of her four children were with her. While they stood weeping by her bedside, she tenderly and earnestly exhorted them to live for God and meet her in Heaven, also sending loving messages to the other two who were absent. Then she bade good-by to all the friends who were present. No other preparation was needed; she was ready to go.

As the circle of those who loved her so dearly watched around her bed, her face suddenly lighted up with indescribable joy as she evidently caught sight of things hidden from others' eyes. Eagerly raising both hands, while still looking upward, she exclaimed in a voice of holy triumph which no words can describe, *"O glory! O glory!! O glory!!!"* — and was gone.

To her there was no dark valley — no gloom. Christ was sufficient as she entered into that *"inheritance incorruptible, undefiled, and that fadeth not away!"*

—Adapted from an article by Mrs. Etta E. Sadler Shaw

—*Dying Testimonies* by S. B. Shaw

201

"Come On, I Am Ready To Go!"

During a wonderful revival meeting, my sister, Filura Clark, then nineteen years of age, and myself, two years younger, were saved and found great peace with God. Oh, what happy times we had together after that, living for the Lord while other young people went after the things of the world!

But then my dear sister was taken ill and only lived a few days. How very hard it was to part with her! It seemed as if my heart would break, the blow was so great. Yet, what a blessed, happy death. Actually, it was not death to her. *She did not think of death, for Heaven and eternal life with Jesus completely filled her thoughts as the moments sped along.*

She called us one by one to her bedside, took our hands, bade us good-by and begged each of us to meet her in Heaven. After she had bidden the family farewell, she said to her physician, "Now, doctor, *you come.*" — and she bade him good-by, requesting that he too meet her in Heaven. He was overcome by the affecting scene.

As we stood there weeping she said to us, "Don't weep for me. *Jesus is with me, I will not have to go alone!*" As soon as she said that, she suddenly looked up as though she saw someone waiting for her, and said, *"Come on, I am ready to go!"*

She actually wanted to go; her work on earth was done.

Her death had a wonderful influence in the community, especially upon the young people. Many turned to the Lord, saying, "Let me die such a death as hers." Nor can I describe the blessing this experience has meant to me personally over the years. It has strengthened me and helped me to live according to the blessed truths of the Bible! When trials and temptations have arisen, her dying testimony has been the means of bringing my soul nearer to the Lord than it ever had been before. *Praise the Lord!*

—Mrs. Wealthy L. Harter, Fort Wayne, Indiana

"Oh, It Is Too Late Now! There Is No Help For Me!"

During some meetings several years ago we experienced a blessed visitation of the Holy Spirit. Among many who were touched by God was a young girl of about seventeen years. All through the meetings the Holy Spirit strove with her, and I talked with her at different times — but she always resisted.

The last evening of the services I went to her side. Again she stood weeping and trembling. I urged her to seek God. She said, "Oh, I cannot, I cannot!"

I replied, "Yes, leave your young friends and come." But she still said, "Oh, I cannot, I cannot!" Afterward she said that the young people would have laughed at her had she gone.

She left the church and went to her boarding place (she was boarding and attending school). Upon entering she made the remark that she did not come there to get religion, but rather to get an education, adding that she could attend to religion afterward *at any time.*

That very night she was taken violently ill and continued to grow worse for one week, then passed into eternity.

She said to those of her young associates who came to see her, "Oh! I ought to have sought the Lord in that meeting!"

I was with her the last day, and before she died I tried to point her to the Lamb of God. But her agonizing reply again and again was, *"It is too late now. Oh, it is too late now! There is no help for me!"* In this deplorable condition she passed into eternity.

—Julia E. Strail, Portlandville, New York
Dying Testimonies by S. B. Shaw

Cardinal Jules Mazarin. A.D. 1661

Julius Mazarin, a famous cardinal and prime minister of France, was born in the kingdom of Naples in the year 1602. The greatness of his abilities was conspicuous even in his early years, as he studied the interests of the various states in Italy and the kingdoms of France and Spain. Becoming profoundly skilled in politics, he was introduced into the French cabinet through the influence of Cardinal Richelieu.

That cardinal made him one of the executors of his will, and during the minority of Louis XIV he had the charge of public affairs. His station and great abilities, however, excited the envy of the nobility of France, which occasioned a civil war that continued several years. Mazarin was at last forced to flee. A price was set on his head and his fine library was sold.

However, this disgrace did not long continue, and he returned to the court with even more honor than he had previously enjoyed. His conduct of the affairs of the kingdom was executed with so much ability and success that he obtained the French king's most unreserved confidence.

Although Mazarin was a man of great ambition and pursued with ardor the chase of worldly honors, a short time before his death he perceived the vanity of this pursuit and lamented the misapplication of his time and talents. He became greatly affected at the prospect of death and the uncertainty of his future condition. Upon one occasion he cried out, *"Oh, my poor soul! What will become of thee? Whither wilt thou go?"*

To the queen dowager of France, who came to visit him in his illness, and who had been his friend at court, he said, "Madame, your favors have undone me. *Were I to live again I would be a humble monk rather than a courtier."*

—Adapted from an article in *Power of Religion*

The Death Angel Stood Before Her

This testimony comes from Bob Bucher, a personal friend of the editor. Bob is active in the industrial and professional photography field:

When I was only a few months old, my mother, who was a very godly woman, was awakened one night to see an angel standing at the foot of her bed. The angel said he was going to take me, but mother said, "No, you are not!"

The next morning she went over to my crib and found me very weak and frail. When she lifted my little hand it just fell back where she had picked it up. She was very frightened.

At that time my father was working for the American Express in a little town named Bucyrus, Ohio. He had been called to the ministry but had held back. When he came home for lunch that noon Mom told him what had happened and that I was dying.

Dad at once got down on his knees beside the crib and asked God to forgive him, promising that he would obey the call to serve Christ. God heard that prayer and *Mom actually felt the death angel leave the house.* She went over to see what change had come over her baby boy. Imagine her joy when she saw that life had already returned and my face was flushed with living blood. I began to cry for food.

From that day my father preached the Gospel and served the Lord with a glad heart till the day of his death. As a layman, I also am serving Christ.

I am thankful that my father said yes. Not only did that "yes" mean a life of ministry on his part, but also the mantle fell on me, and now also upon my sons. They too know Christ, and one is now serving Christ in the United States 'Army.

Yes, I know that Christ has the keys of life and death!

—Bob Bucher, Reseda, California (1968)

The Glorious Translation Of Helen Carpenter

"She speaks as if she were going on a delightful journey"

Helen A. Carpenter was born in Hamlin, New York. Although sensible to God and deeply conscientious, even as a child, she didn't completely give her heart to God until she was seventeen. Her entire life after that, however, was characterized by unswerving devotion to His cause.

When nineteen, while engaged in teaching school, she took a severe cold which developed into tuberculosis and terminated her earthly life at the age of twenty.

During Helen's illness she rapidly ripened for Heaven, and her young friends who called upon her would afterwards say, "One would not think Helen was going to die. *She speaks as if she were going on a most delightful journey!*"

About a week before the end her mother, sitting by her couch, became suddenly conscious of a most heavenly influence pervading the entire room. It was so powerful that she could scarcely refrain from shouting aloud. She wondered if Helen, on whose countenance rested a pleased expression, felt it too.

The next day Helen said, "Ma, you thought I was asleep yesterday while you were sitting by me. I wasn't, and two angels came into the room. The walls did not hinder their coming. It was just like the words to that song:

> *My spirit loudly sings,*
> *The holy ones — behold they come,*
> *I hear the noise of wings. . . .*

It was all true, only I did not hear any noise."

A few evenings later her mother, observing her to be unusually restless, placed her hand upon her brow and found it damp with the dew of death. She said to her daughter, "Helen, I think you are very near home. Have you any fear?"

"Not a bit," Helen replied; "call the family, so that I may say good-by to them."

As they gathered about her she bade each one a loving farewell, telling them she was going to Heaven, because of the blood of the Lamb and enjoining them to meet her there.

She then said, "I have been thinking of the verse, *'He that spared not His own Son . . . '"* Her voice began to falter when she got this far, so her mother repeated the rest of it for her. They asked if she would like to have them sing, and she replied, 'Sing until I die — *sing my soul away!"*

For some time one of her sisters sang the sweet songs of Zion. Then, as the dying girl's eyes closed in death, her sister, Mary, bent over to catch the last expression. Suddenly Helen gave a start of delightful surprise, as though she saw something glorious beyond conception — and her happy spirit went to be forever with the Lord. But the look of inexpressible delight remained on her lovely countenance.

She was by nature so gentle and retiring that her friends feared she might have some fear when she came to the "swellings of Jordan," but the grace of her Heavenly Father enabled her to pass joyously in holy triumph to the skies.

Her sister, Mary Carpenter, afterward went to Monrovia, Africa, as a missionary and died there. While dying, she said, "Living or dying, *it's all right."* Thus, she too submitted her will to the will of her Heavenly Father, whose wisdom saw it better for her to come to Heaven than to labor in Africa.

—L. M. F. Baird, Alabama, New York
From *Dying Testimonies* by S. B. Shaw

Testimony Of Rufus Jones

The late Rufus Jones, one of the most famous spiritual leaders of our time, tells about his son Lowell who died at twelve years of age. He was the apple of his father's eye.

The boy took sick when Dr. Jones was on the ocean bound for Europe. The night before entering Liverpool, while lying in his bunk, he experienced an indefinable, inexplainable feeling of sadness. Then he said that he seemed to be enveloped in the arms of God. A great feeling of peace and a sense of a profound possession of his son came to him.

Upon landing in Liverpool he was advised that his son had died, his death occurring at the precise hour when Dr. Jones had felt a sense of God's presence and the everlasting nearness of his son.

—*Power of Positive Thinking* by Norman Vincent Peale

God Is Mightier Than Man

When I was a child I remember my father taking me to a church in Herfordshire where an infidel was buried. This man ordered his tomb sealed with large stone slabs and high railings put around it. All this was to make it impregnable.

However, as time passed a tiny bird dropped a seed in a crevice of the stones. That little seed had taken root, and the big stone slabs were rent asunder by the tree that had grown there. *God was mightier than man!*

How it deepened my faith as I stood there and contemplated that sight.

—Vera L. Staley, North Bristol, England (1967)

He Beheld Heaven

I went out as a missionary to Brazil in 1924. During the first nine months in that land I studied the Portuguese language in Rio de Janeiro, my teacher being a Presbyterian minister named Senor Menezes who died during those first months of study.

His wife told me that at the hour of death he called her to him and said, "My dear, I have preached many times on Heaven, but I never dreamed of a Heaven as beautiful as the one I *now behold!*"

—Rosalee M. Appleby, Canton, Mississippi
Retired Southern Baptist Missionary

Sophia Rubeti A.D. 1861

Sophia was a young lady who lived in Highland, Kansas. After her death, the following verses were found written in her own hand on the inner lid of her Bible.

Worlds could not bribe me back to tread
Again life's weary waste;
To see again my days o'er spread
With all the gloomy past.
My home from henceforth is in Heaven;
Earth, sea and sun, adieu!
All Heaven is unfolded to my eyes,
I have no sight for you.

Just before passing away she exclaimed, "I hear delightful music. *Oh, it is delightful!* Listen and I think you can hear it. *Jesus* is coming — they are coming — raise me up!"

—*Dying Words* by A. H. Gottschall

"Jesus, Have Mercy Upon Father"

In a shanty on First Avenue in New York City, little Mary lay dying. Suddenly she turned toward her mother and said, "Mother, I am dying, *but I am not afraid.*"

"Not afraid to die?" said her non-Christian mother.

Little Mary replied, "Not when you have Jesus with you, mother. *Oh, mother, you must love my Savior!*"

Soon at the bedside, on bended knees, was the drunken father. The little daughter rested her hand on his head as she repeated three times, at intervals, *"Jesus, have mercy on father!"*

Shortly afterwards she was numbered with the angel choir in Heaven, and three months after her death both of her parents were converted and from that time led Christian lives.

—Rev. L. B. Balliett, M.D., of Allentown, Pennsylvania

Dying Testimonies by S. B. Shaw

Cardinal Borgia

"I am to die, although entirely unprepared."

Caesar Borgia, a natural son of Pope Alexander VI, was a man of such conduct and character that Machiavelli in his famous book, *The Prince,* referred to him as a pattern to all princes who would act the part of wise and political tyrants.

He was made a cardinal, but since this office imposed some restraints upon him he soon determined to resign in order to have greater scope for practicing the excesses to which his natural ambition and cruelty prompted him. After this he was made Duke of Valentinois by Louis XII of France.

He was a man of consummate dexterity and finesse and always seemed prepared for every event. However, the reflections he made a short time before his death, in 1507, reveal that his wit was confined to the concerns of earth. He obviously had not acted upon that wise and enlarged view of things which becomes a being destined for immortality.

"I have provided," said he, "in the course of my life, for everything *except death.* Now, alas! I am to die, although entirely unprepared!"

—Power of Religion

"O Jesus! Come And Take Me Now — I Am Ready!"

Nannie Belle Gilkey died of tuberculosis at the age of twenty. During the intense suffering that came toward the close of her illness she manifested a sweet spirit of patience and proved the truthfulness of God's promise, "As thy days, so shalt thy strength be."

When Jesus came for Nannie, He found her waiting and willing to go with Him. For three days before her death she knew that her time was short, and on the day that she died she was very happy, singing several times in the afternoon, "Anywhere with Jesus I can safely go," and "I am so happy in Jesus — From sin and from sorrow set free."

Once she said, "Jesus is *so near.* Do you not feel that He is near, Mamma?"

At times her suffering was intense. Once she cried, *"Oh, what shall I do?"* When told to look to Jesus — that He was the only one who could help her — she looked up and said, "Yes, Lord!"

Jesus then came so near that she exclaimed, *"Oh, He is coming, He is coming! Oh Jesus! Come and take me now — I am ready!"*

A few minutes before she left us she waved her hand and said simply, "Good-by all." Then she went to be forever with the Lord.

—Sadie A. Cryer of Rockford, Illinois

Carnaval

Carnaval lost his reason through the death of the young woman who was the object of his devoted affection. He then spent his life wandering about the streets of Paris in a vain search for her, not fully comprehending that she was dead.

When about to die he suddenly started, as from a long reverie, his countenance illuminated with sudden joy. Reaching out his arms, as if clasping some object before him, he uttered the name of his long-lost love, and with his last breath exclaimed, *"Ah, there thou art at last!"*

—Dying Testimonies by S. B. Shaw

Victorious Death Of Jane, The Protestant Queen Of Navarre

This excellent queen was the daughter of Henry II, King of Navarre, and Margaret Orleans, sister of Francis I, King of France. She was born in the year 1528.

From her childhood she was carefully educated in the Christian faith, to which she steadfastly adhered all her days. Bishop Burnet says of her: "That she both received the Reformation and brought her subjects to it; that she not only reformed her court, but the whole principality to such a degree that the Golden Age seemed to have returned under her — i.e., Christianity appeared again with its primitive purity and lustre."

210

Being invited to attend the marriage of her son to the King of France's sister, this illustrious queen fell victim to the cruel plots of the French court against the Protestant religion. Her fortitude and genuine piety did not, however, desert her in this great conflict, and at the approach of death.

To some who were about her near the end, she said, "I receive all this as from the hand of God, my most merciful Father —nor have I, during my extremity, feared to die, much less murmured against God for inflicting this chastisement upon me. I knew that whatsoever He does with me, He so orders it that, in the end, it shall turn to my everlasting good."

She expressed some concern for her children, as they would be deprived of her in their tender years, but added, "I doubt not that God Himself will be their father and protector, as He has ever been mine in my greatest afflictions. I therefore commit them wholly to His government and fatherly care."

When she saw her ladies and women weeping about her bed, she calmed them, saying, "Weep not for me, I pray you. God, by this sickness, calls me hence to enjoy a better life. I believe that Christ is my only Mediator and Savior, and I look for salvation from no other. I shall now enter into the desired haven, towards which this frail vessel has been a long time steering."

Then she prayed, "O my God! In thy good time, deliver me from the troubles of this present life, that I may attain to the felicity which thou hast promised to bestow upon me."

—Adapted from an article in the *Power of Religion*

A Young Girl Overcomes Pain and The Fear of Death

"Good-bye! I am going to rest."

In the latter part of the nineteenth century, in Milan, Tennessee, Ella Bledsoe, young daughter of Dr. Bledsoe, lay dying. Being near neighbors and both Christians, Ella and my sister had been together much of the time and had learned to love each other very tenderly.

Ella had been ill for about nine days. Her Christian father had heretofore kept her under the influence of opiates to ease her pain, but not willing that she should pass out of this world stupified by these drugs, he had ceased to administer them.

When my sister Dorrie and I heard that Ella was dying, we at once prayed to God that she might not pass away without leaving a dying testimony. We hastened to her bedside and found her tossing from side to side in the painful agonies of the "last enemy", death.

My sister approached her, and sitting on the side of the bed, she took one of her hands in her own and said, "Ella, are you afraid to die?" For a moment all that life offers to a young girl seemed to rush in before her youthful gaze, and she replied, "I hate to die." Then turning, like Hezekiah, with her face to the wall for a few moments, doubtless in communion with her Heavenly Father, she turned back and said to Dorrie, "Good-bye — *I am going to rest,*" and extending her hand to me, she said, "Good-bye. Meet me *at rest.*"

She then called her family to her bedside, one by one, and kissed them and bade them "good-bye", requesting and exhorting them to meet her "Where the weary are at rest".

This was an affecting scene which impressed all that were present with the reality of the joy of the Christian experience. When all things around us fade away, Christ enables us to rejoice even in the face of death. Thank God!

—Adapted from an article by T. L. Adams
of Magdalena, New Mexico

"Who Were Those Two Shining Ones?"

Many years ago a missionary went to the South Sea Islands to work among a cannibal tribe. After many months he converted the chief to Christianity. One day this old chief said to the missionary, "Remember the time you first came among us?"

"Indeed I do," replied the missionary. "As I went through the forest I became aware of hostile forces all around me."

"They did indeed surround you," said the chief, "for we were following you to kill you, but something prevented us from doing it"

"And what was that?" asked the missionary.

"Now that we are friends, tell me," coaxed the chief, "who were those two shining ones walking on either side of you?"

—*Power of Positive Thinking,* by Norman Vincent Peale
Prentice-Hall, Inc.

They Died At Dawn

A true story of how seven soldiers of the Red Army went to Heaven during the Finnish-Russian War. It was written by an eminent engineer in Finland by the name of Nordenberg.

I offered my services to the government, and was appointed an officer in General Mannerheim's Army. It was a terrible time. We beseiged a town which had been taken by the Red Army and retook it. A number of Red prisoners were under my guard, and seven of them were to be shot at dawn on Monday. I will never forget the preceding Sunday.

The seven men were kept in the basement of the Town Hall, and in the passage my men stood at attention with their rifles. The atmosphere was filled with hatred. My soldiers were drunk with success and taunted their prisoners. Some swore and beat on the walls with their bleeding fists; others called for their wives and children who were far away. At dawn they were all to die.

We had the victory; that was true enough. But the value of this seemed to diminish as the night advanced. Then something happened. One of the men doomed to death began to sing.

"He is mad," was everybody's first thought. But I had noticed that this man, Koskinen, had not raved and cursed. Quietly he sat on his bench, a picture of utter despair. Nobody had said anything to him; each was carrying his burden in his own way.

Koskinen sang rather waveringly at first, then his voice grew stronger and became natural and free. All the prisoners turned and looked at him as he sang . . .

Safe in the arms of Jesus, Safe on His gentle breast,
There by His love o'er shaded, Sweetly my soul shall rest.
Hark it's the voice of angels, Borne in a song to me,
Over the fields of jasper, Over the crystal sea.

Over and over again he sang that verse, and when he finished, everyone was quiet for a few minutes. Then a wild looking man broke out with, "Where did you get that, you fool? Are you trying to make us religious?"

Koskinen looked at his comrades with tear-filled eyes as he quietly said, "Comrades, will you listen to me for a minute? You ask me where I got this song. It was from the Salvation Army — I heard it three weeks ago. My mother sang about Jesus and prayed to Him."

He stopped a little while as if to gather strength. Then he

213

rose to his feet, being the soldier that he was, and looked straight in front of him.

"It is cowardly to hide your beliefs," he continued, "The God my mother believed in is now *my* God. I cannot tell how it happened, but last night as I lay awake I suddenly saw mother's face before me. It reminded me of the song that I had heard. I felt I had to find the Savior and hide in Him. I prayed that Christ would forgive me and cleanse my sinful soul and make me ready to stand before Him Whom I should meet soon. It was a strange night — there were times when everything seemed to shine around me. Verses from the Bible and the song book came to my mind and brought messages of the crucified Savior and the blood that cleanses from sin — and the Home He has prepared for us. I thanked Him, and since then this verse has been sounding inside me. *It is God's answer to my prayer.* I could no longer keep it to myself; within a few hours I shall be with the Lord — *saved by grace.*"

Koskinen's face shone as if by an inward light. His comrades sat there quietly. He himself stood there transfixed. My soldiers were also listening to what this Red revolutionary had to say.

"You are right Koskinen," said one of his comrades at last, "If only I knew there was mercy for me too, but these hands of mine have shed blood — and I have reviled God and trampled on all that is holy. Now I realize that there is a Hell, and that it is the proper place for me." He sank to the ground with despair on his face.

"Pray for me Koskinen," he groaned, "Tomorrow I shall die, and my soul will be in the hands of the devil."

These two Red soldiers went down on their knees and prayed for each other. It was no long prayer — but it reached Heaven — and we who listened to it forgot our hatred. It melted in the light of Heaven, for here were two men who were soon to die seeking reconciliation with their God.

A door leading into the Invisible stood ajar, and we were all entranced by the sight. Let me tell you shortly that by the time it was four o'clock, all Koskinen's comrades had followed his example and began to pray. The change in the atmosphere was indescribable. Some of them sat on the floor, some on the benches, some wept quietly, others talked of spiritual things. None of us had a Bible, but the Spirit of God spoke to us all. Then someone remembered those at home, and there followed an hour of intense letter writing. Confessions and tears were in those letters.

214

The night had almost gone, and day was dawning, but no one had slept a moment. "Sing the song once more for us, Koskinen," said one of them. And you should have heard them sing — not only that song but verses and choruses long forgotten. The soldiers on guard united with them, for the power of God had touched all. Everything had changed, and the venerable Town Hall's basement resounded in that early morning hour with the songs of the Blood of the Lamb.

The clock struck six. How I wished I could beg grace for these men, but I knew that it was impossible. Between two rows of soldiers they marched out to the place of execution. One of them asked to be allowed to sing Koskinen's song once again, and permission was granted. Then they asked to be allowed to die with uncovered faces. So with hands lifted to Heaven, they sang with might and main, *"Safe in the arms of Jesus."*

When the last line had died out, the lieutenant gave the word, "Fire!" We inclined our heads in silent prayer.

What happened in the hearts of the others I do not know, but as far as I was concerned, I was a new man from that hour. I had met Christ in one of His lowliest and youngest disciples, and I had seen enough to realize that I too could be His."

—From *Youth's Living Ideals* (August 1967)

Legrant D' Alleray

This aged Frenchman and his wife were arraigned before the tribunal during the Reign of Terror. The judge hinted at an evasive reply to the charge, which the brave old man declined.

"I thank you for the efforts you make to save me, but it would be necessary to purchase our lives by a lie. My wife and myself prefer rather to die. We have grown old together without ever having lied, and we will not do it now to save a remnant of life."

—*Dying Words* by A. H. Gottschall

Theodore Parker. A.D. 1667.

A distinguished American rationalistic lecturer — "Oh, that I had known the art of life, or found some book or some one had taught me how to live!"

—*Dying Words* by A. H. Gottschall

215

"How Beautiful Everything Appears"

When I was a soldier in Memphis, Missouri, a comrade said to me, "I wish you would go over to that house yonder and stay with them tonight. They are in terrible condition there."

About dark I went over and did indeed find things in a dreadful state. The house was dilapidated, almost ready to fall down, and the cellar was full of muddy water. I ascended an old pair of stairs on the outside of the house and entered a small room. It contained no furniture, not even chairs or bedsteads, nothing but an old trunk.

On this trunk sat an elderly lady with a little child in her arms. The child was almost dead, and on the floor lay another child that had died only a few minutes before. A third was very low.

The lady pointed to an old pile of dirty bed quilts on the floor in one corner of the room, saying, "There lies the mother, and we don't think she will live until morning. What is worse," — I thought, What *can* be worse? — "we are looking for the father to come home tonight drunk."

About midnight he came; but that awful scene of the dead and dying did not affect the poor drunkard's heart. He drew out his bottle of whiskey and begged me to drink with him!

But there was one of that family who was deeply penitent, earnestly desiring to "flee from the wrath to come" — it was the broken-hearted mother. At her request I often visited her after that night and would talk to her of the Savior and sing to her of Heaven.

One day, while calling to see her, I found her cold and sinking fast. Death was folding her in its cold embrace, but just as those dark billows began rolling over her, they were turned to bright dashing waves of glory. She suddenly looked up and said, *"How beautiful everything appears!"*

A lady, who was present, said to her, "I do not see anything beautiful."

"No," replied the dying woman, "there is nothing in this house but dirt and rags, *but I see things beautiful and lovely."*

Her face then lit up with a happy look, and as her countenance broke into a smile, her spirit took its flight to bright mansions of bliss. I stood and looked upon her lifeless form, with the peaceful expression on her face, and thought about the fact that death to the child of God is but the gate of Heaven.

—Samuel G. Bingaman, Williams, Oregon
Dying Testimonies by S. B. Shaw

"My Peace Is Made With God! I Am Filled With Love!"

"Mark the perfect man, and behold the upright: for the end of that man is peace."   —PSALM 37:37

My dear father, William H. Whitford, was suddenly seized with a severe hemorrhage of the lungs and died a few days later. He was a devoted Christian, and as long as he was able to speak, he would greet us with a cheery, "Praise the Lord!"

He had suffered from a complication of disorders which often caused him severe pain. When suffering, he would often go to God in prayer and secure relief and get richly blessed in his soul.

One morning his face was lit up with a holy light as he shouted, "Hallelujah! Glory to God!" A sister, who was in the next room, said that she too felt the power of the Holy Spirit and began rejoicing in God. Oh, how the Spirit would come upon us during those last days. Indeed it was a heavenly place — the gloom was all taken away. It did not seem like dying.

Although father was eighty-two when he died, his mind was very clear all the time, and he would think of everything needful to be done. His only desire to live was to help me, as we lived alone. But he also gave that to the Lord.

He talked about his funeral very calmly and selected the text, Psalm 37:37, and desired that the old hymns be sung. I asked him if he wanted flowers, to which he replied, "Oh, no. I want it very plain — clothed in *righteousness*."

He sang with us a short time before he went, and it was marvelous how his face glowed with joy while singing. "Hallelujah! Glory to God!" he shouted. Then he clapped his hands and said, "If I could only get up, I feel I could leap and shout for joy. *Peace, peace — my peace is made with God! I am filled with His love!* Jesus alone heaves into sight!"

It seemed as though he could actually see Heaven. His last

words were, "Oh, bless the Lord! Praise the Lord!" and thus he went sweetly to sleep, safe in the arms of Jesus.

—Written by his daughter, Mrs. S. A. Slade, of
Portland, New York, 1898

"I Am As Much Lost As Though I Were In Hell Already!"

Another lady and I were asked to visit a neighbor who was sick and in terrible distress of soul. We went to his home and found the poor man pacing the floor and groaning. I said to him, "Mr. C—, we have come to help you, if that is your desire."

"I know it," he replied, "You are all right; but it is too late. I attended your meetings two years ago. The Spirit said to me, '*Hurry! Go to the altar! Plead with God for mercy!*' I could scarcely sit on the seat. But I didn't. Then I came to Marengo and was under deep conviction, but I would not yield. *Finally, the Spirit left me, and I am as much lost as though I were in Hell already!*" He struck his breast, "I feel the fire is kindled here already. It is too late; I am going to Hell — and my sons with me!"

He lived two weeks. It was a place of darkness and devils until he died.

—Mrs. H. A. Coon; *Dying Testimonies* by S. B. Shaw

"Children, Is This Death? How Beautiful; How Beautiful."

I thought it might be to the glory of God to give you an account of my mother's death. She died July 28, 1888, in the township of Winnebago City, Faribault County, Minnesota. About six months before her death I left home to enter the work of the Lord. At that time, and also for years before, mother had what we often call an up-and-down experience. On July 1, I got word to return home to see her die.

On my arrival I found mother very low, but having a strong faith in God. I said, "Mother, you have a better experience than you have ever had!"

218

"Yes, Johnnie," she said, "about three months ago I got what I have longed for for years."

Mother's disease was of a dropsical character. With limbs swollen, she would suffer intensely; but her faith in Jesus never wavered. She would often speak of the glorious prospects in view. The morning she died, about four a.m., a sister and I were sitting by her bed fanning her, when she suddenly opened her eyes and said, "Children, is *this* death? How beautiful — *how beautiful!*"

I said, "Mother, you will soon be at rest. It won't be long before you shall have crossed over and are at home."

Mother never could sing to amount to anything, but on this occasion she sang as if inspired from Heaven,

> *I long to be there*
> *And His glories to share*
> *And to lean on my Savior's breast.*

About four hours later we were around her bed having family worship, when, without a struggle, she passed away to be forever with the Lord.

— Rev J. T. Leise

Charles V, Emperor Of Germany, King Of Spain And Lord Of The Netherlands

"I have tasted more satisfaction in my solitude in one day than in all the triumphs of my former reign."

Born at Ghent in the year 1500, Charles V is said to have fought sixty battles, most of which were victorious. He obtained six triumphs, conquered four kingdoms and added eight principalities to his dominions — an almost unparalleled instance of worldly prosperity and greatness of human glory.

But all this fruit of his ambition and all the honors that attended him could not yield true and solid satisfaction. While reflecting on the evils and miseries which he had occasioned, and being convinced of the emptiness of earthly magnificence, this great man became disgusted with all the splendor that surrounded him. He felt it both his duty and privilege to withdraw from it and desired to spend the rest of his days in spiritual retirement.

Accordingly, he set about to resign all his dominions to his

219

brother and son, and after an affectionate farewell to these and the retinue of princes and nobility who had respectfully attended him, he departed to a retreat in Spain, a vale of no great extent, watered by a small brook and surrounded with rising grounds covered with lofty trees.

As soon as he landed in Spain, he fell prostrate on the ground and kissed the earth, saying, "Naked came I out of my mother's womb, and naked I now return to thee, thou common mother of mankind."

In his humble retreat the once great king now spent his time in spiritual communion with God and in innocent employments. In solitude and silence he buried there his grandeur and ambition, together with all those vast projects, which for nearly half a century had alarmed and agitated Europe and filled every kingdom in it, by turns, with the terror of his arms and the dread of being subjected to his power.

Far from taking any part in the political transactions of the world, he restrained his curiosity even from any inquiry concerning them. He seemed to view the busy scene he had abandoned with an elevation and indifference of mind born of a thorough experience of its vanity, as well as the pleasing reflection of having disengaged himself from its cares and temptations.

The full proof of the happiness of those last years is seen in the short but comprehensive testimony this extraordinary man left to posterity — *"I have tasted more satisfaction in my solitude in one day than in all the triumphs of my former reign. The sincere study, profession and practice of the Christian religion have in them such joys and sweetness as are seldom found in courts and grandeur."*

—From an article in the *Power of Religion*

The Window Of Heaven

Thirty years have passed since the experience I am about to describe, 30 years of active life as a minister's wife and as a mother. But it remains, to this day, the most vivid and extraordinary happening in my whole existence.

When our first son, "Phipsy," was four years old, I became ill with a glandular condition and was told that I must have a thyroid operation to save my life. Accustomed to trusting all my cares to God, I did not fear the operation. It was far harder to come to terms with the future of our child, should I not be there. After a heart-wrenching night, peace came when I knew that his Creator loved Phipsy more than I possibly could, and would guide his future. I knew also that he would be happy with his earthly father, so I could let go of him and pack my bag for the hospital.

My husband, Harold, took me to Crile's Clinic. Dr. Crile himself was to operate. As only a local anesthetic was used during the surgery, the doctors kept me talking and singing in order to more readily locate the vocal cords.

I was feeling rather pleased about my ability to think of things to say and sing in spite of the unpleasantness when suddenly, to my amazement, I seemed to be looking down at myself and the group around the operating table from a short distance just over their heads. The nurse was saying with a startled expression, "Doctor, her pulse is going." Then I started through what seemed to be a long, dark passageway, and as I went along I thought calmly, "This must be what they call dying."

This journey continued uneventfully for some time, and I was beginning to wonder how long it would last when I emerged into an overwhelmingly wide space of light—a pulsing, living light which cannot be described in words. Here my body felt light and free, and for a little while I drifted about with no apparent destination. Finally, it was with great relief and pleasure that I found myself sitting on what seemed to be a cloud, or some kind of heavenly island, looking into an enormous convex window which resembled one-half of a huge crystal ball. I knew that it was not glass, for I could easily have stepped through to the other side; at the same time the thought came to me that I must be looking through a "window" into one bright spot of heaven.

What I saw there made all earthly joys pale into insignificance. I longed to join the merry throng of children singing and frolicking in an apple orchard. The air had a brilliant clarity that made small details stand out in a new light: the orchard in translucent white and pink, startling shades of green, reds, yellows and russets—for there were both fragrant blossoms and ripe red fruits on the trees.

As I sat there drinking in the beauty, gradually I became aware of a Presence: a Presence of joy, harmony and compassion. My heart yearned to become a part of this beauty. But somehow, I could not bring myself to go through the

221

window. An invisible, tenacious restraint pulled me back each time I leaned forward with that intention. I remember thinking that I had lost consciousness of my identity, and that my name no longer mattered. All I needed to do was to keep my eyes wide open and step through the window to be a part of what I saw. I frowned at my inability to move, and gradually, unable to bear the light and vibrant life of this small corner of heaven, my eyes closed tight. As I squeezed them tighter I seemed to recede farther and farther away from that convex window.

After another long journey through the passageway, I returned to the bed upon which a body was lying, motionless and limp, while nurses and doctors were working over it. Reluctantly I entered it through what seemed to be the natural door, the former soft spot at the top of my head, at the same time asking myself, "Why must I return? Do I have to come back? Could I ever get that weak frame back into action again?" Experimentally, I moved one finger, wondering at the same time who "I" was.

One of the nurses exclaimed, "Glory be! She's coming to. It's been 15 minutes." I tried again to remember my name with no success, but another name did come to me — "Harold", and then "Phipsy." They were the ties that had pulled me back, and I needed them now if I was to stay. With great effort I whispered my husband's name.

Then suddenly I knew — I was Julia.

"Am I Julia? Can *this* be Julia? This flattened out figure with the bandaged neck?" I did not want it to be Julia, and yet I did—if there were a Harold and a Phipsy waiting. But to have left all that glory, for this painful return, was almost unacceptable. Then a dearly loved voice spoke—a hand held mine — I *did* want to stay.

The rest of that day and the next, that other world was far more real to me than the one to which I had returned. I insisted that my husband hold my hand day and night; when he had to leave from sheer exhaustion, my sister came. I sensed that there was some mysterious link between my soul and the palm of my hand, and felt that my staying in this life depended upon the pressure of love through the hand of another holding mine. The lure of that heavenly place that I had glimpsed was very strong. But their firm grasp, even though they did not entirely understand, kept me from escaping again to its freedom.

During the next 24 hours, while I was hovering between two dimensions of life, all the meanings of life and death seemed to pass before my inner eyes. Awareness came strong that the dying of the earthly body was not a calamity. Death was a natural transformation into another phase of living, where one could go right on joyfully progressing, if ready. One graduated from this room of learning into another, just as real and important.

I believe there is a comparison to be drawn between birth of the spirit and childbirth. We know that if the infant has ready the equipment for breathing—nostrils, lungs and air-passages, then he is able to live in a world of air. However, if the fetal development is incomplete or faulty, he is unprepared for a world where breathing is a necessity.

In like manner, in this life, if one's soul or spirit remains undernourished, underdeveloped and unrelated, then it cannot enter into or function freely in the highest form of life to which it is capable of attaining. It came to me with certainty, then, that one *began* there in the next world, where he *leaves off* here in this life.

This seemed to give a deeper meaning to suffering, to all experience and to one's everyday relationships. Not to grow spiritually, seemed to me then, and still does, the *real* death of the individual.

Thus, I believe that my brief glimpse through the window of heaven was a flash of revelation about the meaning of life itself.

Now I watch eagerly as each new day brings its lesson and its blessings, and I am at peace in the belief — no, the conviction — that in the sight of God the world we live in and the world of my vision are really one.

—Julia Phillips Ruopp, Minneapolis, Minn.
Reprinted from *Guideposts* Magazine
Copyright 1963 *Guideposts Associates, Inc.,* Carmel, N.Y.

"Oh! Do You Hear The Music?"

May Wilcox of Marengo, Illinois, died when only twenty-one years of age. She was a self-sacrificing, devoted Christian. Shortly after conversion she felt called of God to work for

223

souls and began to give her life "for others' sake". She proved faithful in her ministry and in every way was a worthy example of a child of God.

> While fighting in ardor in mid-day of life,
>   The Master in mercy ended earth's strife;
> She said, in much wonder, "I've only begun;"
>   He smiled back in answer, "Come, faithful one — well done!"
> She looked at the white harvest, the sheaves yet unbound;
>   She reached forth to gather — He gave her the crown.

At the close of a series of meetings in Bradford, Illinois, May went to her home to recruit for the next battle, but instead was stricken with typhoid fever. She lingered in its heat and suffering a little over a month; then Jesus came and took her to Himself.

Once during her sickness her mother came in; but the dying girl was unconscious of all around and failed to recognize her. Her mother then said, "May, do you know Jesus?"

"Jesus? Oh, *yes,* I know Jesus!"

The mentioning of His name brought consciousness to her. She well knew that name.

Shortly before she passed away the loved ones who were then outside of the ark of safety were called to her bedside. She tried to exhort them to prepare to meet God, but her tongue was too swollen and they could not understand. However, the Lord did enable May to tell — in a more elegant way than words — of the glories that filled her soul in that wonderful hour, for she suddenly threw up her arms and exclaimed, clearly, *"Oh! Do you hear the music?"*

The unsaved ones standing around her bed saw the light that came from Heaven into that little room, and they *felt* its divine influence. God had spoken!

Her soul then took its flight, and the career of one triumphant in life, and now also in death, was ended.

—Sadie A. Cryer, Rockford, Illinois

"Madge Is Dead, And David Is Crazy"

It was the spring of 1891 and Rev. C. B. Ebey was holding special services at Colgrove, California. Among others, two young ladies and their brother were awakened to their need of

Christ. However, they held back from making the decision.

The younger of the two girls was a bright, healthy girl of fourteen named Madge. One day Reverend Ebey said to her, "Madge, I believe this meeting is being held for *you*."

The girl sensed these words were from God and after thinking it over decided she must surely give her heart to God. Her brother, David, then intervened. He dearly loved her, and knowing that if she became a Christian their worldly pleasures together would end, he persuaded her to wait a few years. "Then," he said, "we'll *both* get saved." Thus they agreed and said to the Holy Spirit, "Wait until a more convenient season."

A few weeks later Reverend Ebey received the startling message that Madge was dead and that he should come to her home immediately. He went as quickly as he could and was met at the door by the distraught mother.

"Oh, Brother Ebey," she sobbed, "You have come to a *sad* home. *Madge is dead, and David is crazy!*"

Gradually he unraveled the story from the weeping woman. When the doctor had said that Madge could not possibly live, David went wild and rushed to her bedside. There he knelt and prayed, as only a sinner could, that God might save his sister's soul. He then urged Madge to pray, but she was too sick to make any effort and died without leaving any evidence of salvation.

The strain of realizing that his beloved sister was dying without Christ, and that *he* was the cause of it, was too much for the young man. His reason gave way.

—Rev. F. A. Ames from *Dying Testimonies* by S. B. Shaw

The Artist And The Gypsy Girl

Many years ago in the old city of Dusseldorf, in northwest Germany, there lived an artist by the name of Stenburg. A Roman Catholic, he had been taught doctrine and ceremony, but knew nothing of Christ as his own Savior from the guilt and power of sin.

He had been engaged to paint a great picture of the crucifixion, and this he was doing, not from any real love of Christ or faith in Him, but simply for money and fame.

One beautiful spring morning Stenburg was seeking recreation in the forest near Dusseldorf when he came upon a gipsy girl named Pepita plaiting straw baskets. She was unusually beautiful, and Stenburg determined to engage her as his model for a picture of a Spanish dancing girl. After some bargaining, she at last agreed to come three times a week to his studio.

At the appointed hour Pepita arrived. As her great eyes roved around the studio she was full of wonder; then the large picture of the crucifixion caught her eye. Gazing at it intently and pointing to the Figure on the cross in the center, she asked in an awed voice, "Who is that?"

"The Christ," answered Stenburg carelessly.

"What is being done to Him?"

"They are crucifying Him."

"Who are those about Him with the bad faces?"

"Now, look here," said the artist. "I cannot talk. You have nothing to do but stand as I tell you." The girl dared not speak again, but she continued to gaze.

Every time she came to the studio, the fascination of the picture grew upon her. Finally she ventured to ask another question.

"Why did they crucify Him? Was He bad — *very bad?*"

"No, very good."

That was all she learned at that interview, but it added a little to her knowledge of that wonderful scene.

At last, seeing she was so anxious to know the meaning of the picture, Stenburg one day said, "Listen, I will tell you once and for all. Then ask no more questions!" So he told her the story of the Cross — new to Pepita, though so old to the artist that it had ceased to touch him. He could paint that dying agony without the quiver of a nerve — *but the thought of it wrung her heart.* Tears filled her eyes.

Pepita's last visit to the studio had come. She stood before the great picture, loath to leave it. "Come," said the artist, "here is your money, and a gold piece over."

"Thanks, Master," she murmured. Then, again turning to the picture, she said: "You must love Him *very* much since He has done all that for you — do you not?"

Stenburg could not answer.

Pepita went back to her people, but God's Spirit sent the gipsy girl's words home to the artist's heart. He could not forget them. *"All that for you,"* rang in his ears. He became restless and sad. He knew he did not love the crucified One.

Some time later Stenburg was impressed to follow a few poor people who gathered to hear the Bible read. There, for the first time, he met those who had a living faith. Hearing the simple Gospel message, he was made to realize *why* Christ hung on the cross for sinners. He saw that *he* was a sinner, and therefore Christ was there for *him,* bearing his sins.

He began to know the love of Christ and soon could say, "He loved *me,* and gave himself for *me."*

At once he longed to make that wondrous love known to others. But how could he do it? Suddenly it flashed upon him —he could paint. His brush could spell out the love of Christ! Praying for God's help, he resumed his work on the crucifixion picture and painted as never before. When finished, the picture was placed among other paintings in the famous gallery of Dusseldorf. Underneath the artist had placed the words:

"All this I did for thee; what hast thou done for Me?"

Eternity alone will tell how many were led to Christ by those words and that picture.

One day Stenburg saw a poorly-dressed girl weeping bitterly as she stood by the picture. It was Pepita.

"Oh, Master, if He had but loved *me* so," she cried.

Then the artist told her how He *did* die for her, poor gipsy girl though she was, as much as for the rich and great. He did not weary now of answering all her eager questions. He was as anxious to tell as she to hear of the love of Christ.

As Pepita listened, she received, and the age-old miracle of spiritual new birth took place. She went from that room a "new creature" in God's wonderful love. Thus the Lord used Pepita's words to bring the artist to Himself, and then used the artist's words to reveal Himself to her.

Months afterward Stenburg was suddenly called by a dark-looking stranger to visit a dying person. Following his guide through the streets into the country, and then beyond into the deep forest, at last they came to a few poor tents in a sheltered spot. In one of these he found Pepita. She was dying in poverty, but she was happy in the precious love of Christ.

He watched her die, while she praised her Savior for His love, *knowing* His love, *knowing* that He had taken all her sins away and that she was going into His blessed presence to be forever with Him.

Long after this, when the artist, too, had gone to be with the Lord, a wealthy young nobleman found his way into that picture gallery in Dusseldorf. As he gazed upon the picture and the words underneath it, God there and then spoke to his heart. Hours later, when the guard came to close the gallery for the day, the young man was still on his knees in tears before that scene.

That young man was the famous Count Zinzendorf, who

from that day became an earnest Christian and later became the father of the renowned Moravian missions, by means of which God led thousands of men and women in many lands to Himself.

—*Selected*

"I Am Halfway Between Two Worlds"

When my mother, Eleanor Herrick, died of cancer in December, 1964, it was a time of joy and triumph instead of sadness and defeat. Mother was a "born-again" Christian of deep faith.

In her final illness she spent about two weeks in the hospital. My brother, Don, and I were with her every day. The last three days she started slipping into a coma and spoke little to us.

Next to the last words she spoke to me were, "Oh, Arline, I feel as though I am cradled in love — from this side and the next."

The next day she spoke her last words. When I entered her room the patient in the bed next to hers called me over and asked, "Who is Margaret? Your mother has been talking to Margaret all morning." I told her that Margaret was my mother's sister who had died years ago.

Then I went to Mother's side, took her hand, and told her who I was. She spoke her last words in this world.

"Oh, Arline, it's so strange here. I'm in a 'never-never' land. I'm halfway between two worlds. Ma and Pa are here and I can see them, but I can't see you any more."

—Arline Sexauer, Northridge, California

Grandma Kirk

The story of the founding of the famous Prairie Bible Institute in Three Hills, Alberta, Canada.

Mother and Father Kirk laboured for the Lord in Western Canada until their retirement from active missionary service in 1920. The family then built them a little home at Bethel, a point east of Three Hills in Alberta.

228

Meanwhile, God's day of visitation was near at hand. As Mother prayed for us children over the years, she learned to wait patiently for God's time. He has an appointed time for everything, even though, according to our limited understanding, He sometimes works slowly.

How long God worked with Abraham! Abraham went through many breakdowns and failures as God was training him. Moses, though one of the greatest men who ever lived, had to have preparation. It took him an extra forty years to learn not to do things in his own way. *It seems that the Lord has to work with us a long time until we are not so critical of other people and not so proud of ourselves.*

It wasn't long before a spirit of prayer and intercession began to settle upon some of the local people. None of the families understood what they were praying for. "Lord, reveal Your will," they prayed, "Make known Your plan."

When one or more persons really get down to do business with God, things are bound to happen. Within a year from the time the prayer meetings began, Mr. L. E. Maxwell came to help out with the growing Bible classes, and this was the beginning of Prairie Bible Institute, which is now perhaps the largest school of its kind in the world.

At first, Mother and Father Kirk were not very interested in seeing a Bible school started. But as time went on they recognized the sovereign call of God and the anointing of the Lord upon the Bible ministry of Mr. Maxwell.

As Mother and Father observed that the new Bible school was being founded upon the same Bible principles that had governed their lives — surrender to God, separation from the world, sacrificial giving and missionary outreach — they doubtless must have praised God for the higher plan He was beginning to unfold.

When the time came for Father and Mother to leave their little farm home because of failing strength, their son Roger moved the building from Bethel to Three Hills, Alberta. He made it his home for many years. At one time, he decided that he would build a beautiful new home. He could afford it at last. As he was thinking about the new home, the words of a song flashed into his mind:

A tent or a cottage, why should I care?
They're building a palace for me over there!

"That settles it!" Roger exclaimed. "Mother and Father's home is good enough for me. I love it!"

The Lord had provided for Mother and Father all along

the way. Now, He was providing to the end of the journey. Most of the family were around them in their old age.

To the end of their days, they lived very simply, giving all that they could do without to foreign missions. In Mother's last years, she lost her eyesight, and appeared to be very tired So she spent most of her time sitting in her rocking chair by the window praying.

At one time she became seriously ill and thought it was her last illness.

"Roger, I'm going Home!" she exclaimed joyfully to Roger who was standing by. "I'm under His wings! *I just feel He is covering me with His feathers!*"

To Roger, it sounded like "He is cuddling me!" At any rate, the presence of the Lord was very near as Mother entered the dark valley.

But Mother recovered for a time, and she was disappointed. To her, Heaven was the real Homeland, and all her earthly life was just a pilgrimage leading her to the Father's house.

At last, in 1936, at the age of eighty-three, Mother went Home. Father followed her in 1940. He was in his eighty-seventh year. Both insisted on simple, homemade coffins for their last earthly resting place.

Surely *"they . . rest from their labours; and their works do follow them."*

—From *Raise Up The Foundations* by Juanita C. Snyder

The Death Of Sir Francis Newport

Sir Francis Newport was taught in early life the great truths of the Gospel; and when yet a young man it was hoped that he would become a tribute and a blessing to his family and the nation. However, the result was far otherwise. He fell into company that corrupted his principles and morals, and became an avowed infidel. The life of dissipation which followed soon brought on a disease that was incurable.

When he realized that he must die, he threw himself on the bed, and after a brief pause, exclaimed, "Whence this war in my heart? What argument is there now to assist me against matters of fact? Do I assert that there is no Hell, while I feel one in my own bosom? Am I certain there is no retribution after death, when I feel present judgment? Do I affirm my soul to be as mortal as my body, when this languishes, and the soul is vigorous as ever? Oh, that someone would restore to me that ancient gourd of piety and innocence! Wretch that I am, where shall I flee from this breast? What will become of me?"

An infidel companion tried to dispel his thoughts, but he only answered, "That there is a God, I know, because I continually feel the effects of His wrath. That there is a Hell I am equally certain, having received an earnest of my inheritance there already in my breast. That there is a natural conscience I now feel with horror and amazement, being continually upbraided by it with my impieties and all my iniquities brought to my remembrance."

To the dismay of his former friend, he continued, "Why God has marked me out for an example of His vengeance, rather than you, or anyone of my acquaintance, I presume, is because I have been more religiously educated and thus have done greater despite to the Spirit of Grace. Oh, that I were to lie upon the fire that never is quenched a thousand years to purchase the favor of God. But it is a fruitless wish. Millions of millions of years will bring me no nearer to the end of my torments than one poor hour. Oh, eternity, eternity! Who can discover the abyss of eternity? Who can paraphrase upon these words — *'forever and ever'*?"

When some of his friends thought him insane, he said, "You imagine me to be melancholy or distracted. I wish I were either; but it is part of my awful judgment that I am not. No, my apprehension of persons and things is more quick and vigorous than it was when I was in perfect health — and it is my curse, because I am thus more sensible of my condition.

"Would you be informed why I am become a skeleton in three or four days? It is because I have despised my Maker and denied my Redeemer. I joined myself to the atheist and profane and continued this course, in spite of many convictions, till my iniquity was ripe for vengeance. *The just judgment of God overtook me when my security was the greatest and the checks of my conscience were the least.*"

As his mental distress and bodily disease were hurrying him into eternity, he was asked if he wanted prayer offered on his behalf. Turning his face away, he exclaimed, "Tigers and monsters! Are you also become devils to torment me? Would you give me prospect of Heaven to make my Hell more intolerable?"

Soon after this his voice failed, and uttering a groan of inexpressible horror, he cried out, *"Oh, the insufferable pangs of Hell!"* — and was gone.

—Adapted from an article in *The Contrast*

I Saw The Spiritual World

Have you ever given thought to the subject of death? What transpires when we lose sight of the known and enter the unknown? I never gave this subject much thought until 1948, when a serious event in my life jolted me into some serious thinking.

Before I relate my unusual experience, may I say I thought I was living an interesting and sensational life. *But real living began after this event.*

In mid-winter a natural gas explosion and fire wrecked our home. The gas line broke and the inside of the house became an inferno, like a "ball of fire" under pressure. At the time I was in the basement. To get outside I had to run through the flames. In the frozen snow stood my wife with one of the children she had rescued. "Maureen is in the bedroom," she cried.

The heat was insufferable, but I went back in. Searing flame licked at me. I felt my way through the fire with our six-week-old baby in my arms. I was rushed to the hospital with third degree burns covering 65 percent of my body. At that time medical statistics showed that the human body could not survive with more than 40 percent burns.

So far as man's philosophy knows, the end of life's journey is an end in blackest night. What happened next may appear to be more fantasy than reality. But I traveled into that land beyond death and returned. I will relate some things to you just as I saw them.

One of the first things the soul is conscious of in the resurrection world is the sense of weightlessness when the soul leaves the physical body. It is the earthly body that gives the soul that heavy gravity feeling. It is quite an experience to look back at your physical body lying on a hospital bed. When I got over the shock of separation from the earthly body, and realized that I was now in the spiritual world, I was amazed at the vast difference between the two worlds.

First, is the clear separation of light and darkness. The light is soft, gentle, and constant, whereas the darkness has depth, weight

232

and is very depressing. There seems to be no time factor in the spiritual world; also, no sense of distance or space as we know it here. But there are rules and regulations with areas which are reserved for classified beings. A popular concept of the world after death is that people imagine they flit around like butterflies, going wherever they want to and doing just as they please. Nothing could be further from the truth. There is a system of order in the resurrection world.

There are two distinct places of abode with a great gulf of separation between them. There is a Power there that prohibits the individual soul from travelling from one place to another. I stood amazed when I noticed that all classes of people were going to both places — the rich and poor, good and bad, including the vilest of humanity. Some entered the place of marvelous peace and contentment, while others went into utter darkness, where the agony is something that has never been experienced here on earth.

I pondered, why did the stream of humanity divide and some go to the place of safety and peace but the rest went to the place of agony? What was the qualification that gave some permission to enter the place of contentment?

After I returned and again took up abode in this earthly body, the Spirit of God led me to the Bible, which showed me Christ is the only entrance into the area of eternal pleasure after the death of your mortal body. Only since I have accepted Christ as my own personal Savior do I have the assurance of peace and contentment with eternal life.

—Geo. Godkin, of *Geo. Godkin and Sons Contractors, Ltd.*
Turner Valley, Alberta, Canada

Sir John Mason

"Were I to live again, I would change the whole life I have lived in the palace for an hour's enjoyment of God in the chapel."

A strong testimony to the importance of spiritual life is given by Sir John Mason, who, though but sixty-three at his death, had flourished in the reigns of four sovereigns (Henry VIII, Edward VI, Mary and Elizabeth), had been privy-counselor to them all and an attentive observer of the various revolutions and vicissitudes of those times.

Toward his latter end, being on his death-bed, he spoke thus to those about him: "I have lived to see five sovereigns, and have been privy-counselor to four of them. I have seen the most remarkable things in foreign parts and have been present at most state transactions for the last thirty years. I have learned from this experience of so many years that *seriousness is the greatest wisdom, temperance the best physic, and a good conscience the best estate.* And were I to live again, I would change the court for a cloister, my privy-counselor's bustle for a hermit's retirement, and the whole life I have lived in the palace for an hour's enjoyment of God in the chapel. *All things now forsake me, except my God, my duty and my prayers."*

From the regret expressed by Sir John Mason, it appears that his error consisted not in having served his king and country in the eminent stations in which he had been placed, but in having suffered his mind to be so much occupied with business as to make him neglect, in some degree, the proper seasons of spiritual retirement and the prime duties which he owed to his Creator.

—Adapted from an article in *Power of Religion*

"It Is Jesus, Father, Who Has Come To Take Me"

A little girl, Naglie, was a resident of Jerusalem. Her mother too was a Christian and had learned to love Jesus in Miss Arnott's school in Jaffa.

Just before Naglie died she said, "It is *Jesus,* Father, Who has come to take me. There He is at the foot of my bed; He calls me to come."

—*Dying Words* by A. H. Gottschall

Tonight Or Never!

At the close of a meeting held in a mining district, a stalwart miner, in deep anxiety of soul, walked up to the preacher to inquire what he had to do to be saved from the guilt of his sins.

The servant of Christ told him how God, in infinite love and pity, had given His Son to be the sinner's Substitute and bear the judgment of sin in the sinner's stead. He showed him, from Scripture, that the Lord Jesus came into the world *"to seek and to save that which was lost!"*

All this seemed dark to the miner. The burden of unforgiven sin pressed heavily upon him, and as the hours passed, the preacher urged him to turn from self and sin, and look to *"the Lamb of God which taketh away the sin of the world."*

When eleven o'clock came, the preacher told the miner it was time to go home. He suggested that he should return to the chapel on the following evening.

With an agonized look, the poor fellow replied: "No, I *won't* leave — it must be settled tonight or never!"

They remained together, talking and praying. Hours passed, and still the miner could not grasp the soul-saving truth. The preacher began to despair, but as the clock struck three, the light of the glorious Gospel suddenly burst upon the seeking man. He saw and believed that the work of Christ on the cross had satisfied the justice of God on account of his sins. Joy and peace filled his heart. Rising from his seat, and clasping his hands together, he exclaimed, "It's settled now. *Christ is mine!"*

Together the two men thanked God, and soon afterward the miner was on his way to work in the coal-pit, happy and rejoicing.

In the course of the day a sudden crash was heard by those in the neighborhood of the pit. Quickly the news spread that part of the roofing of the mine had fallen in, burying a number of miners beneath it. Immediately men were set to work digging towards those who were known to be underneath.

After working for some time they heard a faint sound. Digging with renewed energy in that direction they soon reached the newly converted miner. Life was not quite gone, for he was speaking. Eagerly they listened, and the words they caught were these: *"Thank God, it was settled last night."*

These were the last words he uttered. When his body reached the surface, life was extinct. The happy, redeemed spirit had *"departed to be with Christ, which is far better."*

Little did the miner think how solemnly true the memorable words which he had uttered the preceding night were to prove in his own case — "It must be settled tonight or never."

—*Bible Truth Publishers,* Oak Park, Illinois

Sent Back From Heaven For Seven Years

If Jewel Rose could lean down over the battlements of Heaven and call back a message to his fellow workers here on earth, surely he would lift his hand, turn on that beaming smile

235

of his that made one feel the sun was shining and all was right with the world, and shout: *"Have faith! Never fear! My God can do anything!"*

And standing happily beside him, his beloved wife, Florence, would smile her complete agreement — for God in his loving kindness called them both home on February 16, 1968.

During the years since Jewel's miraculous healing, these two people have ministered side by side in the Gospel field, and it was so fitting that they should pass through the gates together.

In 1953 Mr. Rose was elected to the International Board of Directors of the Full Gospel Business Men's Fellowship International, and from 1958 to 1967 also served as International Secretary-Treasurer. For two years, 1965 to 1967, he also served as Business Manager at the International Headquarters in Los Angeles. However, in 1967, he felt it necessary to resign all official positions and give his full time to preaching the Gospel. In fact, Mr. Rose and Florence were on their way to another Gospel meeting when God called them home.

A few months ago Jewel had remarked that he felt that he would be "going home soon." His wife said quickly, "Then I want to go too." He replied, "Well, Mama, the Lord can take care of that."

"I visited the beautiful gate," Mr. Rose testified. "I wanted to go in then, but the Lord sent me back to preach the Gospel and testify to His glory." He was referring to seven years ago when in answer to prayers of several men from his church, God brought him back to life when given up as dead by his doctors.

After this miraculous healing, he felt that the Lord impressed upon him that he would have seven more years and thus began to anticipate the end as the seven years drew to a close.

One week before the end, with no outward reason whatever, he told Mr. Cecil Poole, District Superintendent of the Pentecostal Church of God, that he felt his time was now up. His wife Florence then said that she had always wanted them to go together and that she thought the reason God brought him back to life was partly for this reason, as well as to continue his ministry.

On February 16, these two precious lovers were together, arm in arm, as they drove to meet a preaching engagement. Mr. Rose must have mistakenly turned off the highway at the wrong road and decided to back up in order to get back on the main road. Suddenly a car appeared and struck them from the rear.

When the highway patrolman arrived, he said he found them both dead, still sitting arm in arm, looking straight ahead. Neither of them had a scratch, though the car was totally demolished.

This time there will be no returning, at least not until Jesus comes; for Jewel and Florence Rose have gone home, so abundantly ready and with their arms filled with sheaves.

An empty chair at the council table — the voice of a mighty prayer warrior silenced — the absence of his never flagging spiritual strength in helping to carry the burden of the Lord's work — all these things the Fellowship feels keenly and with a sense of great loss. Yet the loss is compensated by our last memory of Jewel, standing on a convention platform, his head thrown back as though looking upward toward Heaven, his voice booming out in the song: *"Oh, that will be glory for me . . . when by His grace I shall look on His face, that will be glory — be glory for me!"*

—Adapted by the editor from an article
in the *F.G.B.M.F.I. Voice*, March, 1968

The Scottish Martyr, Patrick Hamilton

On the first of March, 1528, some eight years before Tyndale was betrayed and executed, Archbishop Beaton condemned Patrick Hamilton to be burned because he advocated the doctrines of the Reformation.

The principal accusations were that he taught it was proper for the poor people to read God's Word and that it was useless to offer masses for the souls of the dead. Hamilton admitted the truth of these charges and boldly defended his doctrines. He was, therefore, quickly condemned, and to avoid any possibility of his rescue by influential friends, in but a few hours the stake was prepared before the gate of St. Salvador College.

When the martyr was brought forth, he removed his outer garments and gave them to his servant, with the words. "These will not profit me in the fire, but they will profit thee. Hereafter thou canst have no profit from me except the example of my death, which I pray thee keep in memory; for, though bitter to the flesh and fearful before man, it is the door of eternal life, which none will attain who denies Christ Jesus before this ungodly generation."

His agony was prolonged by a slow fire, so that his execution lasted some six hours; but through it all he manifested true heroism and unshaken faith. His last words were, *"How long, O Lord, shall darkness brood over this realm? How long wilt Thou suffer this tyranny of man? Lord Jesus, receive my spirit!"*

Thus, in the bloom of early manhood died Scotland's first Reformation martyr, and his death was not in vain. A Romanist afterwards said, "The smoke of Patrick Hamilton infected all it blew upon." That was true, for though his mouth was closed, the story of his death was repeated by a thousand tongues. It emboldened others to seek a martyr's crown and stirred up many more to defend the truths for which he died and to repudiate the hierarchy which found it necessary to defend itself by such means.

"Humanly speaking," says the author of *The Champions of the Reformation,* to whom we are chiefly indebted for the facts of this sketch, "could there have been found a fitter apostle for ignorant, benighted Scotland than this eloquent, fervent, pious man? Endowed with all those gifts that sway the heads of the masses — a zealous and pious laborer, in season and out of season — what herculeaen labors might he have accomplished! What signal triumphs might he have achieved! So men may reason, *but God judged otherwise.* A short trial, a brief essay on the work he loved and longed for was permitted to him, and then the goodly vessel, still in sight of land, was broken in pieces."

—Heroes and Heroines

"Praise Him, All Of You!"

Ethel was a bright, beautiful young girl with whom we were acquainted. Her mother was a Christian and endeavored to impress upon her daughter's mind the importance of being "born again" — not of water, *but of the Holy Spirit* — but through the influence of roommates and associates while attending boarding school, Ethel had been influenced to believe that simply making a public confession of faith in Christ and receiving baptism by immersion were all that was needed.

Ethel's mother knew from past experience that God was faithful, so by persistent faith and daily prayer she called upon Him to show Ethel the error of resting upon church ordinances for spiritual safety. She patiently pointed out that only the Blood of Christ and a saving faith in its atoning merits could secure to her soul eternal life and a home in Heaven.

One day, after much prayer, the mother was greatly comforted by receiving the assurance of the Holy Spirit that God would eventually turn Ethel from the error of building her hopes on a foundation of sand.

Not long after this, although only twenty-two, Ethel knew that she stood with the billows of death rolling very near her feet. She then began to realize that water baptism would not avail to rescue her soul from the perils of sin and the coming judgment. "Man's extremity is ever God's opportunity," and the Holy Spirit began to convince her of her need of Jesus as a *personal* Savior.

The conflict of her soul with doubts and fears was short but severe. Faith at length triumphed. Only five days before her death, after lying speechless for hours, her mother, who was near her couch, heard Ethel say with great effort, "Whosoever — will — *may come.*"

Just then the saving power of the Holy Spirit fell upon her heart, and as a bright smile overspread her beautiful young face, she exclaimed, "Praise Him — all of you *praise Him!*" Those were Ethel's last words on earth.

—Mrs. V. E. Markin, Litchfield, Ky.

Lady Hope's Visit With Charles Darwin

It may surprise many students of evolution to learn that in the closing days of his life, Charles Darwin returned to his faith in the Bible. The following account is told by Lady Hope, of Northfield, England, a wonderful Christian woman who was often at his bedside before he died:

It was one of those glorious autumn afternoons that we sometimes enjoy in England when I was asked to go in and sit with Charles Darwin. I used to feel when I saw him that his fine presence would make a grand picture for our Royal Academy, but never did I think so more strongly than on this particular occasion.

He was sitting up in bed, propped up by pillows, gazing out on a far stretching scene of woods and corn fields which glowed in the light of a marvelous sunset.

His features lit up with pleasure as I entered the room. He waved his hand toward the window as he pointed out the beautiful sunset scene beyond. In his other hand he held an open Bible, which he was always studying.

"What are you readng now?" I asked.

"Hebrews," he answered. " 'The Royal Book' I call it." Then as he placed his fingers on certain passages, he commented on them.

I made some allusion to the strong opinions expressed by many on the history of the Creation, and then their treatment of the earlier chapters of the book of Genesis. He seemed distressed, his fingers twiched nervously and a look of agony came over his face as he said, "I was a young man with unformed ideas. I threw out queries, suggestions, wondering all the time about everything. To my astonishment the ideas took like wildfire. People made a religion of them."

Then he paused, and after a few more sentences on the holiness of God and "the grandeur of this Book," looking tenderly at the Bible which he was holding all the time, he said: "I have a summer house in the garden which holds about thirty people. It is over there (pointing through the open window). I want you very much to speak here. I know you read the Bible in the villages. Tomorrow afternoon I should like the servants on the place, some tenants, and a few neighbors to gather there. Will you speak to them?"

"What shall I speak about?" I asked.

"*Christ Jesus,*" he replied in a clear, emphatic voice — adding in a lower tone, *"and His Salvation.* Is not that the best theme? Then I want you to sing some hymns with them. You lead on your small instrument, do you not?"

The look of brightness on his face, as he said this, I shall never forget; for he added: "If you make the meeting at three o'clock, this window will be open, and you will know that I am joining in with the singing."

* * * *

Was there ever a more dramatic scene? The very soul of tragedy is here exposed to us! Darwin, enthusiast for the Bible, speaking about "The grandeur of this Book," reminded of that modern evolutionary movement in theology which, linked with skeptical criticism, has destroyed Biblical faith in multitudes. Darwin, with a look of agony, deploring it all and declaring, "I was a young man with unformed ideas." What an overwhelming criticism! The "unformed ideas" of the young man Darwin are the basis of modern theology!

—Oswald J. Smith, Litt.D., from an article in *Prayer Crusade,* published by The Little Church by the Sea, Inc.

"Ma, I Shall Be The First Of Our Family Over Yonder"

Asa Hart Alling, eldest son of Rev. J. H. and Jennie Alling, died at the age of 14 in Chicago, April 19, 1881. He was converted and united with the church when eleven. While most boys were devoting their spare time to fun and sport, he applied himself to works of love. Numerous aged and infirm people living near Simpson church will bear record to the good deeds by his youthful hands. In the public school he took high rank and led his classmates. For his years he was well advanced.

On Friday, April 15, he complained of being ill, but insisted upon going to school. He soon returned in distress, however, and went to bed never to leave it. He was smitten with cerebro-spinal meningitis.

At times he suffered great agony, but through it all he proved himself a hero and a Christian conqueror. He realized that his sickness was fatal and talked about death with composure. He put his arms about his mother's neck and gently drawing her face close to his own, said, "Ma, I shall be the first of our family over yonder, but I will stand on the shore and wait for you all to come."

He then requested his mother to sing for him, "Pull for the shore." She, being completely overcome with grief, could not sing. He said, "Never mind, ma; you will sing it after I am gone, won't you?"

To a Christian lady who came to see him, he said, "Will you sing for me? Sing, 'Hold the fort!' " She sang it. "Now sing, 'Hallelujah! 'tis done.' " He fully realized that the work of his salvation was done, and he was "holding the fort" till he should be called up higher.

He bestowed his treasures upon his brother and sisters. He gave his Bible to his brother Treat and, as he did so, said to his father, "Pa, tell aunty (who had given him the Bible) that I died a Christian."

His last hours of consciousness were rapidly closing. He remarked, "Ma, I shall not live till morning; I am so tired and want to go to sleep. If I do not wake up, good-by — *good-by all!*" A short time afterward he fell asleep in Jesus. "He was not, for God took him" (Genesis 5:24).

He had reached the shores of eternal life for which he had pulled so earnestly and with success. His funeral was attended by a large concourse of people who thronged the church. We all felt as if we had lost a treasure and Heaven had gained a jewel.

—G. R. Vanhorne

The Last Words Of John Wesley

This great servant of Christ went to Heaven March 2, 1791, in the eighty-eighth year of his life, after preaching the Gospel for sixty-five years.

Shortly before his death, Mr. Wesley said, "I will get up." While they arranged his clothes, he broke out singing in a manner which astonished all about him:

"I'll praise my Maker while I've breath,
And when my voice is lost in death,
Praise shall employ my nobler powers:
My days of praise shall ne'er be past,
While life, and thought, and being last,
Or immortality endures.
Happy the man whose hopes rely
On Israel's God; He made the sky,
....And earth and seas, with all their train:
His truth forever stands secure,
He saves the oppressed, He feeds the poor
And none shall find His promise vain."

Once more seated in his chair, he said in a weak voice, "Speak, Lord, to all our hearts, and let them know Thou loosest tongues." Then he again sang a couple of lines:

To Father, Son and Holy Ghost,
Who sweetly all agree. . .

Here his voice failed, but after resting a little, he called to those who were with him to "pray and praise." He took each by the hand, and after affectionately saluting them, bade them farewell.

After attempting to say something which they could not understand, he paused a little, and then, with all his remaining strength, said, "The best of all is, God is with us!"

And again, lifting his hand, he repeated the same words in holy triumph, *"The best of all is, God is with us!"*

Most of the following night he repeatedly tried to repeat the hymn he had sung, but could only say, "I'll praise, I'll praise."

242

On Wednesday morning the end was near. Joseph Bradford prayed with him about ten o'clock in the morning, while eleven friends knelt around the bed.

"*Farewell*," said the dying man—and it was the last word he spoke. Immediately after, without a groan or a sigh, he passed away. His friends quietly rose and, while standing around his bed, sang:

> "*Waiting to receive thy spirit,*
> *Lo! the Savior stands above;*
> *Shows the purchase of His merit,*
> *Reaches out the crown of love!*"

—Adapted from Kenyon's *Life of John Wesley*.

Miracle Words On A Vietnamese Battlefield

. . . and Sgt. John McElhannon's quest for God begins.

George was different. Some of the other marines professed Christianity, but George lived it. His sergeant, John McElhannon, a Navajo Indian, did not claim to believe anything. However, he saw in George a man to be respected and admired, and they soon became good friends.

One day their company was attacked during a battle with the Viet Cong and George was critically wounded. John rushed to where the stricken George lay and encouraged him, "You're going to be all right; take it easy and save your strength."

In his very weakened condition, George could only say a few words—"John, you need God." *But he said them in the Navajo language!* *

Sgt. McElhannon was astounded. He had often tried to teach George words and phrases in his native tongue, but to no avail. Now, in flawless Navajo came these startling words — which proved to be the last George would ever speak in this life.

Soon afterwards John also was struck down in battle and had to return to the States to recuperate. As he lay in the hospital the dying words of his fallen comrade went through his mind and he couldn't forget them,—"*John, you need God.*" He determined that he must find "George's God."

After a futile visit to at least one church in San Francisco, John went to Fresno, California, to visit his mother. There he again took up his quest to find the God Whom George had known and loved so ardently. He tried one church but found nothing to satisfy the longing in his heart. Then, just as he was planning to leave the city, he decided to try once more. As he picked up the phone-book to scan its pages, the name "Bethel Temple" attracted his attention. A call to the pastor finally led to a Saturday night young peoples' meeting in a home.

It took only a few moments in the warmth and love of that home meeting to convince John that these young people knew George's God. He became so excited that at first the group became alarmed. However, as he unburdened his heart and told them about George, suspicion turned to joy. With their eager prayers and help the young soldier soon put his faith in Jesus Christ and found George's God to be *his own* God. The quest was ended, and today 1st. Lieut. John McElhannon of the U. S. Marines has his own inspiring testimony.

—Adapted from original sources by the editor.

*The young marine — enabled by the Holy Spirit — was employing the gift of "tongues" in the more unusual expression of the gift which enables the believer to speak in a known language unknown to him (see Mark 16:17, 18; I Corinthians 12:7-11; Acts 2:4-6).

Jesus Christ

"I, if I be lifted up from the earth, will draw all men unto me."

The following testimony is composed of selected passages from the Gospels of Matthew and John in the New Testament (King James Version).

The story commences at the close of Jesus' three years of ministry when he was about thirty-three years of age:

"Jesus, going up to Jerusalem, took the twelve disciples apart in the way and said unto them, 'Behold, we go up to Jerusalem; and the Son of man shall be betrayed unto the chief priests. . . . and they shall condemn him to death, and shall deliver him to the Gentiles to mock and to scourge and to crucify — and the third day he shall rise again.' "

"Jesus knew that his hour was come that he should depart out of this world unto the Father. . ." Therefore, after reaching Jerusalem, and while eating the *Passover Supper* with the disciples, "he took the cup and gave thanks. . . 'Drink ye all of it, for this is my blood of the new testament (covenant), which is shed for many for the remission of sins.' "

Anxiety filled the hearts of the disciples. Jesus knew this and said to them, " 'I go to prepare a place for you, and if I go and prepare a place for you I will come again and receive you unto myself, that where I am there ye may be also . . . .Peace I leave with you. *My* peace I give unto you. . . .Let not your heart be troubled, neither let it be afraid.' "

" These words spake Jesus and lifted up his eyes to heaven and said, 'Father, the hour is come; glorify thy Son, that thy Son also may glorify thee. . . . I have glorified thee on the earth; I have finished the works which thou gavest me to do. And now, O Father, glorify thou me with thine own self, with the glory which I had with thee before the world was.

" 'O righteous Father, the world hath not known thee; but I have known thee, and these (my disciples) have known that thou hast sent me. I have declared unto them thy name, and will declare it, that the love wherewith thou hast loved me may be in them. . . .' "

When he was betrayed and the soldiers took him, one of the disciples drew a sword and started to defend him. Jesus at once restrained the young man. " 'Put up again thy sword. . . . for all they that take the sword shall perish with the sword. Thinkest thou that I cannot now pray to my Father and he shall presently give me more than twelve legions of angels? But how, then, shall the Scriptures (Old Testament prophecies) be fulfilled?' "

He was arraigned before Pilate, the Roman governor. Pilate asked him, " 'Art thou the King of the Jews?'

"Jesus answered, 'My kingdom is not of this world. If my kingdom were of this world, then would my servants fight, that I should not be delivered. . . . but now is my kingdom not from hence.'

"Pilate therefore said unto him, 'Art thou a king then?'

"Jesus answered, 'Thou sayest that I am a king. To this end was I born and for this cause came I into the world, that I should bear witness unto the truth. Every one that is of the truth heareth my voice.' "

Pilate then attempted to dismiss the charges against Jesus, saying, " 'I find no fault in him.' " The Jews, however, were insistent — " 'By our law he ought to die, because he made himself the *Son of God!*' "

When the governor heard this charge he was disturbed and at once returned to the judgment hall and asked Jesus, " 'Whence art thou?' "

Jesus did not answer. " 'Speakest thou not unto me?' " exclaimed the frustrated ruler. " 'Knowest thou not that I have power to crucify thee, and have power to release thee?'

"Jesus answered, 'Thou couldest have no power at all against me except it were given thee from above.' "

After this Pilate determined to release Jesus, but the Jews brought political pressure to bear, and Pilate was finally forced to order his execution.

As Jesus hung on the cross little was said aside from committing his mother to one of the disciples for personal care and forgiving one of the dying thieves who was crucified with him. However, after several hours, he suddenly cried with a loud voice, " 'My God, my God—why hast thou forsaken me?' "

Then, "Knowing that all things were now accomplished . . . he said, *It is finished!*' " And with that amazing victor's cry, "bowed his head and dismissed his spirit." *

*The declaration that Jesus "dismissed His spirit" sets His death off from that of other men — He died of His own volition when He could say of His sufferings as a sacrifice for sin in our stead, "It is finished." This is in accordance with what He said several months before the crucifixion: "I lay down my life that I might take it again. No man taketh it from me, but I lay it down of myself. I have power to lay it down and I have power to take it again" (John 10:17, 18).

I SHALL NOT DOUBT...
Immortality

To every created thing, God has given a tongue that proclaims a resurrection. If the Father deigns to touch with Divine power the cold and pulseless heart of the buried acorn and make it burst forth from its prison walls, will He leave neglected in the earth the soul of man, made in the image of his Creator? If He stoops to give the rose bush, whose withered blossoms float upon the autumn breeze, the sweet assurance of another springtime, will He refuse the word of hope to the sons of men when the frost of another winter comes? If matter, mute and inanimate, though changed by the force of nature into a multitude of forms can never die, will the spirit of man suffer annihilation when it has paid a brief visit, like a royal guest, to the tenement of clay? No. I am as sure that there is another life as I am that I live today.

In Cairo, I secured a few grains of wheat that had slumbered for more than three thousand years in an Egyptian tomb. As I looked at them, this thought came into my mind: if one of those grains had been planted upon the banks of the Nile the year after it grew, and all its lineal descendants planted and replanted from that time until now, its progeny would today be sufficiently numerous to feed the seething millions of the world.

A grain of wheat has the power to discard its body and from earth and air fashion a new body so much like the old one that we cannot tell one from the other. If this invisible germ of life in the grain of wheat can thus pass unimpaired through three thousand resurrections, I shall not doubt that my soul has the power to clothe itself with a new body, suited to its new existence, when this earthly frame has crumbled into dust.

WILLIAM JENNINGS BRYAN
[1860-1925] Orator, editor and famed American statesman.